Julie was brought up in Wakefield, West Yorkshire and left grammar school with 8 'O' levels and a sense of humour. Much to her mum's disappointment, she 'worked' as a disc-jockey and entertainer for twelve years and used the endless opportunities of dressing up to disguise her big bum!

At 29 she met Brian and finally grew up. The next sixteen years she worked for a large mail order company, during which time she embraced the introduction of the "Call Centre" culture before retiring at 45 to enjoy travelling and spending time with Brian and their two dogs, Jack and Jill.

OUR SPANISH WINTERS - A DIARY

Julie Wilson

Our Spanish Winters - A Diary

Vanguard Press

VANGUARD PAPERBACK

© Copyright 2006
Julie Wilson

A CIP catalogue record for this title is
available from the British Library

ISBN 1 84386 234 4

*Vanguard Press is an imprint of
Pegasus Elliot MacKenzie Publishers Ltd.*
www.pegasuspublishers.com

First Published in 2006

**Vanguard Press
Sheraton House Castle Park
Cambridge England**

Printed & Bound in Great Britain

Dedication

Dedicated to the memory of
Joan Wilson – wonderful Mum-in-law and friend.

Acknowledgments

I wish to thank my family, friends and everyone I have ever met, as each encounter, however brief has been an experience, which has become part of who I am today.

My mum and dad continue to be wonderful supportive parents – I have inherited my dad's nose and lack of teeth, and my mother's big bum and under-active thyroid. What a start in life – Cheers!

Janet, my sister, has become my best mate and we look back fondly on the time in our twenties when it dawned on us life was like a pantomime and we would have to press on, without Cinderella!

Thanks to Simon and Ian who have always made me feel like a very special mum – even though I have been through the joy of childbirth.

But mostly I owe my utter joy of life to the most unexpected but welcome encounter, when my life was at its lowest ebb. Brian bounced in and took me for a drink on December 8th 1987 and let me pay half towards the Indian take-away on the way home! He's made me laugh every day since, and he's gorgeous.

Part One

Monday 24th November 2003.

I woke up this morning at half past four, unable to contain my excitement. It reminded me of being five years old on Christmas day – but in reality I am forty-five and this is the first day of our adventure to Spain for a short winter! At least it isn't raining today so we can do any final chores without getting wet.

Brian woke up–or did I accidentally wake him? And after several cups of tea we got showered and dressed before closing our home up for the next eleven weeks. Yesterday we had packed the car up so we could have a reasonably early start. We had a drive today of three hundred and sixty miles from Ingleton where we live down to Folkestone ready for the ferry crossing from Dover to Calais at 7am on Thursday. Last thing before getting in the car was to make sure Jack and Jill our two dogs had been to the loo.

Our caravan, a "dealer special," was in essence a Coachman Amara four berth. We stored it at Derrick's farm in Cowan Bridge – only about four miles from home and had been to the farm yesterday to ensure it was well packed and the weight evenly balanced. It was left in the yard ready for us to hook up and get straight off today.

It was 9.45 when we left the farm with what seemed like all our possessions some in the caravan, some on the back seat of the car and the rest in the top box on the car roof! Down the M6 seemed to be the "quickest" route and we estimated that with a good run and a couple of stops at the services we would arrive in Folkestone around half four. Who were we kidding! Road works at the Thelwall Viaduct (just for a change) and various traffic jams meant that we actually arrived in the dark at twenty to seven!

First mistake, one of many, was that having put our last caravan in part exchange for this brand new one in September when we retired to Ingleton, we had collected it from the suppliers and taken it to Derrick's to store until we went to Spain and until yesterday we hadn't even been in it let alone familiarised ourselves with the layout or set-up. So now we found ourselves fumbling about in the dark with one inadequate torch and no idea where the electric plugged in! The inside of the caravan was unbelievably hot as the heater appeared to be set on full. I think we must have packed something against the dial for the heating without realising where it was! Once we had found the electric point, I turned the heating off and threw some bedding onto the fixed bed so we could go to the pub for a few drinks and then get a good night's sleep. Brian walked and fed the dogs and filled one of the water barrels, then off we went to the pub The Royal Oak.

We were warmly welcomed by our friends Janice and Malcolm whom we had first met on holiday in Goa in 2000. They had sold their pub and moved into a static caravan on a site at the back of The Royal Oak. Janice had gone back into nursing and Malcolm was running a delivery business. When we first told them we were thinking of taking the caravan to Spain for the first time, they suggested we stay at the small site at the pub as it was only a five minute drive to the port at Dover. We decided to stay for a couple of days so we could catch up with their news and spend some time together. After a few rounds of drinks we decided to ask for the menu as we thought we could have a meal at the pub to save anyone having to drive. Unfortunately, the landlord informed us that the chef had walked out yesterday so there was no food!

By this time none of us were in a position to drive so we all went back to Janice's to see what she could throw together! We had chicken Kiev with oven chips and peas and after the long day we'd had it was a feast! It had just started to rain when we made our way back to our home for the next eleven weeks and we were in bed and asleep for midnight.

Tuesday 25th November 2003.

Most of the morning we spent organising the caravan. We were not unpacking fully until we got to our final destination at La Manga in Spain on Sunday but we needed to get to our toiletries, food and clothes for the journey. It had rained all night so the field we were in was very muddy and we couldn't help trail mud into the caravan and Jack and Jill still hadn't learnt to wipe their own paws. Luckily the carpet was still covered with a plastic adhesive cover from the factory so we decided to leave this down until we got to Spain.

At two o'clock we drove into Folkestone and took the dogs for a run on the shingle beach. Back at the site we spent the rest of the afternoon with Janice and when Malcolm finished work we had a few drinks and a lovely curry that Janice had made for us. As they spend around three months a year in Goa, they have no excuse for not making an authentic curry.

An early night was called for but this was not to be. The rain began as we got into bed around ten o'clock and then the winds picked up. Set on a hillside I would imagine the site would be very picturesque on a nice day as you can see across the sea to France – but when the weather is bad, the site is very open and exposed as we found out! By midnight the rain was pelting down and the winds were picking up speed, neither of us could sleep as the caravan was being blown every few minutes. Thank goodness we had decided not to put the awning up!

Wednesday 26th November 2003.

We were still awake at six o'clock and were having yet another cup of tea Janice rang us at seven on my mobile to see if we were OK and to tell us the winds had reached sixty miles an hour in the night but would be calming down shortly. After breakfast she would come into Dover with us so we could see how easy the route was to the ferry port. And she was right no problem.

By mid-afternoon the winds had virtually gone so we both managed to get a few hours' sleep. Teatime fish and chips in Folkestone were very nice, washed down by a few drinks at the pub – to help us sleep! In the pub we met a couple from Lancashire who were retired and they were on this site for a night before catching the nine o'clock ferry to Calais. They had done the trip to Spain for five years and stayed in the Benidorm region for the winter. It was nice to meet people who had already done the journey we were planning through France to Spain and who had enjoyed it. We had an early start tomorrow as we had to check in at six, an hour before we set sail. Alarm set for 5. 00am an hour should be plenty of time to pack up, hook up and set off. Or so we thought!

Thursday 27th November 2003.

Yes, we slept well and woke up just before the alarm. Why does that happen? Anyway I put the kettle on – must have my first cup of tea as soon as I wake up – and we got washed and dressed ready to pack up. Outside, it was blowing a gale and was very dark – why were we surprised how dark five o'clock was? Still using the poor torch, we packed everything up and were well on time as we started to hook the caravan onto the car. Ten minutes later we were no further forward. For some inexplicable reason we just couldn't seem to line the tow bar up to the caravan and the more we tried the more we argued! I think we were both frustrated that it was dark and the fact that we were now running a bit late made Brian quite agitated.

As you come on our adventure with us through this book, you will get to know Brian and he's certainly better for knowing! He likes to be on time for everything and when we fly abroad he insists we get to the airport an hour before check in time so he can try for extra legroom. (This proved vital a few years ago when we were flying to Lefkas. Unknown to us, this was the last Danair flight and there were only three of us on the flight, so we could almost choose which half of the plane we wanted!).

So Brian was getting flustered thinking we would be late for the ferry and they wouldn't let us on. However, we finally got hooked up and left the site at six thirty, only half an hour before sailing.

This was a new experience for us – we had never taken the caravan on a ferry and were quite nervous about what to do and of course Brian was worried that we would be in big trouble for being so late. But the procedure was very straightforward and we were soon parked in the bowels of the ferry. We were surprised that no one had checked the dogs or told us off!

Five minutes later the ferry departed and we soon found our way to the restaurant and had the special full English breakfast including coffee and toast for £4. 99.

We were travelling with Seafrance as they had the best deal when I made enquiries a few weeks before – £314 return including the dogs. It always pays to shop around and I found it was best to have all information to hand before ringing different companies e.g. travel dates, preferred sailing times, car dimensions and engine size, caravan length, height and width.

Ninety minutes later we docked in Calais. A very pleasant and calm crossing and we were relieved to see that Jack and Jill had been asleep in the car for the journey.

A few weeks before, we had been to France with our friend Neville who has a cottage there. We travelled from Plymouth to Roscoff and took the dogs to make sure they would travel OK on the ferry. That crossing was about seven hours and an hour after setting off I asked a member of staff if I could go down below to check on the dogs, as I was worried they wouldn't settle. When I approached the car, I could see they were both fast asleep, so that put my mind at rest.

We were the first off the ferry today and I think we were the only caravan on that crossing. France was an hour in front so it was 9. 30 and the roads were quiet but it was foggy. I was worried that Brian would forget to drive on the right hand side of the road but he had no problem! Because it was foggy, we needed the car lights on then we suddenly remembered that we hadn't fitted the headlamp beam adapters! We had them with us in the car but knowing that it would be mid-morning when we arrived in France we wrongly assumed it would be bright daylight. So we pulled off at the next services.

One book that I bought and was already using was "Le Guide Selected AutoRoute's France" by Karol Libura. Weeks before we set off I had planned our route using a good map book and our Routemaster on the computer. Because this was our first time towing the caravan through France and Spain we decided we would use the motorways even though we knew we would have to pay tolls on them. This book shows you the main motorway routes through France and includes every stopping area, with details of which facilities you will find at each one, the distances between them, where the tolls will be and how much you will be charged, together with some really useful travel information for your journey. Don't leave home without it!

At the services, I opened the packet containing the headlamp adapters – only to find the most confusing instructions I have ever seen! There was a huge list of makes and models of cars but ours wasn't mentioned. After eighteen months of test drives and research Brian had finally decided which car he was going to buy when he retired and so we bought a Kia Sorento. Being a relatively new model it didn't get a look in on the instruction sheet so it took me about half an hour to work out where to stick the adapters. By the time we had sorted the dogs out, had a coffee and stuck the headlamp converters on – guess what? It was daylight and we didn't need the car lights on.

Before setting out on our adventure, some friends Tony and Ann, who had taken their motor home to France, told us about the excellent motorway service stations. They explained that they were ideal places for a short break or even an overnight stay as they had places specially designated for caravans.

Although I had read a couple of scary stories about caravans and motor homes being broken into during the night at these places, I thought we would be reasonably safe if we chose one of the bigger and busier service areas, and we had after all got the added security of our trusty dogs. So we were going to stay tonight at the services at Macon St Albain which was just over 400 miles from Calais.

At our next stop around lunchtime I decided to see exactly what the facilities were like for caravans at the services. Maybe I live in a fantasy world (it has been said!) but I had a visual picture of an area set aside for caravans, with electric hook-ups, water points and shower blocks and maybe a few flower beds? The reality was a parking area for the night-that's it! Of course you could usually get a meal or a sandwich depending which services you chose but to say I was disappointed was the understatement of the day. Brian on the other hand thought I was mad and said the services were exactly as he imagined. Bully for him!

It began to get dark around four o'clock and we reached our stopover at eight o'clock French time. We parked in a fairly busy area with a few lorries around us and we went into the services and had a meal which contained chicken and cabbage and was quite nice, together with a bottle of wine to toast our first day in France. Getting into bed at nine we wondered if we would sleep due to the noise of the traffic on this very busy road. Before we had time to wonder – we were asleep! Good night.

Friday 28th November 2003.

Waking at six thirty after a reasonable night's sleep we got dressed, locked the caravan, put the dogs in the car and were off just before seven. We arrived at Lyon at 7. 30am not a good idea! This appeared to be rush hour and there were lanes and lanes of cars, lorries, motor homes and caravans, and Brian was moving into "panic mode"! Although he has become more confident pulling the caravan since we first started about eight years ago, he is a very cautious driver and is very aware that behind our 4x4 car we have a further seven and a bit metres of caravan to consider during every manoeuvre. On top of this, he also thinks that every time a driver pips his horn this translates as "Brian, you are doing something wrong"!

The road signs are quite clear but the sheer volume of traffic and the size of Lyon is very daunting. We had paid a toll of 38 euros as we entered Lyon and at this moment in time I would have paid any amount to have been "beamed" safely to the other side of this city.

I do enjoy the map reading and navigating – despite various surveys which say women are no good at it – what do they know? However, the mistake I made today was to look ahead on the map to see what seemed like the next big town or city was likely to be, so I could follow the anticipated signs. The next big place appeared to be Orange but as we were struggling through the maze that was Lyon there was not one sign for Orange!

Somehow through good luck rather than good management we emerged at the other side of Lyon on the correct road going in the right direction. Hooray! This great achievement was rewarded shortly as we stopped for coffee and croissants at the next service area.

Parlez vous francais? No we don't. However; I took French at school and even passed my o'Level – but now I am here I can't remember any of it! I don't know why but the only phrase I can recall is "Voici la plume de ma tante" which I think translates as "Here is my auntie's pen"! I am now struggling to imagine in which dire circumstances this sentence may be of any help to anyone. Everyone seemed to speak a little English so we didn't really have a problem. We British are generally very lazy with other people's languages and think if we repeat what we want in a much louder and slower voice we will be understood!

We were back on the road after a short stop and were well prepared for the tollbooths as I followed the route with my book "Le Guide". Not previously having seen how toll roads worked we were quite apprehensive until we got the hang of it. There are around a dozen different lanes that you can drive into towards the booths. Each one is clearly marked above the lane with the different choices i. e. lorries, caravans, cars, cash and credit card, and a green illuminated arrow shows you which lanes are currently open. Be prepared and have your money ready.

The booths are at our passenger side of course as they are made for the French drivers who sit at the left-hand side, so this was just another task for me to do!

Once you've paid and the barrier has been lifted, it's a bit like "Wacky Races" with everyone getting back into a reduced number of lanes but the procedure seemed very well organised and we drove straight through each one without any delay or problems.

The motorway was very easy driving for Brian because there was not a lot of traffic and he was able to set the cruise control most of the time. He was also delighted with his choice of car and said towing the caravan was no problem with this Kia. The weather was clear and dry and I was giving him a running commentary about the facilities at each service area even if he didn't want to know just to pass the time.

Diesel and petrol was cheaper than England and we stopped a few times to fill up and usually gave the dogs a bit of a walk and a drink before setting off again.

By mid afternoon we were approaching the Spanish border. Well before we got there I was getting all prepared – I had our passports to hand, and all the documents for Jack and Jill were in a file I had prepared.

Earlier this year when we had made the decision to spend a few weeks in Spain over the winter, we had several trips to the vets to get the dogs ready to go. This involved having them both chipped, then having them vaccinated against rabies with a blood test several weeks later. The paperwork involved was very confusing – They each needed several bits of paper called Pets1, Pets 2 and Pets 5, also their rabies certificates.

Weeks before we set off I had contacted DEFRA, which is the Department for Environment, Food and Rural Affairs. They were very helpful and sent me a list of registered vets in France for our return journey. Although we hadn't yet planned our route home in February, we knew that we would have to visit a registered vet between twenty-four and forty-eight hours before we arrived back in England. At this stage I didn't want to think about the logistics of this procedure – I was sure we would meet other people when we got to Spain who could recommend a stopover near a vet's. Hopefully!

So, I was Mrs Organised with all the documents relating to the dogs in a file which of course has photos of them all over the front. I know what you are thinking – get a life! But I like to be prepared usually.

There were signs indicating we were approaching the Spanish border – then nothing – we drove through and no one stopped us. There wasn't anyone on duty or checking anything, which I found quite surprising. I suppose I was a bit disappointed that nobody wanted to look at my beautifully presented file!

Tonight we were going to stop in a small fishing village called L'Ametlla de Mar which is near to Tarragona. When planning our route and stops, I used a book which my eldest stepson Simon had

22

bought me – Alan Rogers' "Europe". One of the things I wanted was a site not too far from the motorway so that we had less chance of getting lost.

I had rung this site a few weeks ago as Brian thought they would probably be full and wouldn't have room for us! He always looks on the down side of everything – his philosophy is "Always expect the worse – then anything better than that will be a nice surprise!" When I rang them they said "No need to book"– they were very quiet so we could just come and stay as long as we wanted.

We would be covering 553 miles today which, on reflection, was a bit too far. But at 7.00pm as it was getting very dark, we turned off the motorway, paid a toll and followed the signs for the village. There were signs for the campsite but we were struggling to see them as it was so late. We turned at the junction in the village and the Alan Rogers book explained that the site was about two miles away from the village centre.

Almost there we thought. We were on a deserted road which was more like a mountain track than a road, when we heard quite a loud banging. Brian pulled into the side of the road and said he thought he knew what the noise was – he had clipped the kerb coming through the village and would bet me any money we had a puncture on the caravan! I wasn't interested in the odds of this happening – I just wanted to get there and to be honest we weren't really sure we were on the right road!

It had been a long day so we needed to stay calm and try not to fall out – even if a puncture at this stage was my worst nightmare. Brian got out of the car and yes he was right – a flat tyre on the caravan on the driver's side. Thinking caps on first thing to do is put up the red warning triangle, which you must carry at all times. We positioned this several metres behind the caravan so we could be seen though not easily as we were in almost total darkness.

The spare tyre was under the caravan and, after some effort it was released. Then Brian got the jack out and assured me he would have this tyre changed in no time – if I could just keep the torch shining in the right place instead of talking rubbish and worrying! Five minutes later Brian declared that this bottle jack was too tall and wouldn't go under the bottom of the caravan so he got another jack from the boot of the car. Jack and Jill were wondering what was going on – and so was I!

Guess what? The car jack wouldn't fit either. Brian explained that the tyre was so flat that the caravan was very near the road surface and what we now needed was a scissor jack but where from? I suggested that we unhooked the caravan and I drive to the site which should only be a mile or so away, whilst Brian stayed with the caravan.

Not only was I worrying that Brian would be all right although he describes himself as "six foot two of throbbing gristle" I was also now having to drive for the first time ever, on the wrong side of the road, in the dark not knowing where I was going to end up. Various Stephen King books sprung to mind but I tried not to get upset or emotional and stay positive.

About a mile and a half down this dirt track a sign appeared – "Welcome to Camping L'Ametlla". What a relief. As I drove up to the reception desk I noticed that the site seemed very quiet, but there was a light on in the main building. I introduced myself to the girl behind reception but she could only speak a little English. I tried my best to explain that we had had a puncture and was there any other caravanners on the site who spoke English; she indicated that she didn't know what I was talking about! I picked up a magazine that was on the counter and pointed to a picture of a caravan tyre and finally she seemed to understand.

She then proceeded to make a telephone call – the gist of which I gathered was a call to a local garage, but they could only suggest we sleep at the side of the road tonight as they could not come out before tomorrow lunchtime!

I explained this was not really a good solution and she then said I could go and talk to the other caravanners- but there were only two others here and they were both German!

Whilst in the reception area, my eyes were drawn towards the cigarette machine. I stopped smoking on July 20th when I gave up work to retire. Although it has been hard at times I knew it was a habit I could not afford if we were to enjoy early retirement and survive on Brian's police pension. But just at that moment, I could have eaten a packet of Regal King Size!

A walk onto the site took my mind off cigarettes for a moment and I went to the first caravan to speak to the lady and her husband who were sat in their awning having a glass of wine. They spoke a bit of English and after I explained our predicament, they picked up their jack and both got into the car with me to return to Brian and our lopsided caravan!

I could tell that Brian was relieved to see us and after about twenty minutes the spare wheel was fitted, we hooked back up and returned to the site. What a relief.

We thanked the German couple and as soon as we had parked up for the night, we opened a bottle of wine that Neville had given us back in England and we had brought with us to save for Christmas Day! Although Brian had stopped smoking three years ago, he said he could really have fancied a cigarette so I confessed to being attracted to the machine in reception but we both resisted the urge!

After all the excitement (?) of the day, we ended up eating cheese and biscuits and bacon sandwiches as we were too tired to go out or make a meal. At least we were staying here two nights so we could get the spare tyre sorted out without rushing about the next day. Neither of the dogs nor we took much rocking to sleep.

Saturday 29th November 2003.

What a difference a day makes! After the trauma of the previous day we woke up around eight o'clock to a lovely sunny morning. I think the weather can really influence our moods and today's blue skies certainly made me feel brighter. As we opened the blinds and the sun came in Brian asked me "What's everybody wearing?" Now just for a moment I wondered if he had been a fashion model in a previous life or if he was going through a midlife crisis at fifty-five and needed to dress in this season's designs! What he meant to say was "Is it warm enough for shorts or will I look silly?" Of course there was no one else around at that time in the morning so I said I thought it was warm enough for shorts, and it was.

I got showered in the new and exceptionally clean facilities on site and then went to reception to collect the croissants I had ordered the previous evening - yes, in the middle of my dilemma last night the receptionist asked if I wanted to order croissants! I think I would have ordered a dozen Eccles cakes if she had asked me!

Whilst we sat in the sun eating our croissants and drinking coffee we thanked our neighbours again for helping us with the tyre. We decided to drive into the village to see where we could get the tyre fixed and we pulled in at the garage to fill up with diesel and to ask where we could get a new tyre. As luck would have it, the bloke in front of us was the local policeman filling his car with petrol. After we explained what our problem was, he indicated for us to follow him and he took us to the tyre-fitting garage about half a mile away. It was on a small one-way industrial estate and we would never have found it without him.

In less than an hour we had a new spare tyre which cost us 62 euros and the peace of mind that we were now legal again. We drove back to the village and walked into the harbour where we had a coffee and treated ourselves to an English newspaper. At 2 euros it was quite expensive but Brian likes to keep up with the sport and I like to read a paper now and again. We bought a bottle of red wine to give to the German couple to say thanks for being there last night.

Back at the site I checked out the laundry facilities. After travelling since Monday I had quite a pile of washing. There were two washing machines and one dryer and you bought tokens and powder from reception. I went back to the caravan to get the washing and Brian decided he'd got a few more "bits" if I was washing! What's all that about with blokes? "Well, these jeans are in the wardrobe but if you're washing they could do with a clean". So I ended up with a full white wash, a full colour wash and decided I might as well change the bedding and wash that too. I wasn't sure what the facilities would be like at La Manga so at least we'd be all clean when we got there.

Early afternoon was glorious so we took Jack and Jill down to the beach. Now I haven't really introduced you to them yet so here goes Jill was found wandering the streets in Wakefield where we used to live. She was handed in at the local police station where Brian happened to be on duty. Our last dog, an alsatian called Frankie, had died several years before and like most dog owners we said we would not have another dog. However, on this day in March 1999 Brian couldn't resist this black puppy which we later found out was a Patterdale terrier, so he brought her home. We couldn't decide on a name for her so Brian jokingly suggested calling her Jill – because almost all of my close friends well at least eight of them are called Gill or Jill, honest!

This gets very confusing when a Jill rings or sends me a text and I have to explain which Jill it is! So the name stuck and of course eighteen months later when a friend appeared on her way to the police station (allegedly) with a white Jack Russell cross puppy that she had just saved from being drowned (allegedly), we had to take him in! It made sense to call him Jack so now we have the pair of them.

They are very different temperaments, though – Jill has a mind of her own and isn't frightened of anything but Jack is very nervous and shy and wants to be cuddled and stroked all day! He is afraid of all dogs except Jill and if cornered will nip another dog through fear. But they are great together and bring us a lot of pleasure, even though they are tying.

The beach at L'Ametlla was deserted so we could let the dogs have a good run. They travel really well in the car and it does make them tired but since leaving home last Monday we had travelled over thirteen hundred miles and they were ready for a swim and a play. We walked along the beach for about a mile and the dogs were in and out of the sea, chasing sticks and each other.

After two hours we made our way back and the dogs sat in the sun to dry. We had a glass of wine whilst deciding what to do for a meal.

Around six o'clock we went back into the village, had a drink in the local square then went into one of the restaurants in the harbour. Quite a few of the bars and restaurants were closed as this was out of season. We chose the house special paella and a bottle of house wine. I am not a lover of fish but Brian eats anything and everything except turnip (but he will eat it mashed up with carrots). But as this was our first proper meal in Spain I thought we should eat traditionally and I could pick out any bits I didn't like.

We were nibbling at the bread the waitress had brought, when she placed on our table a dish of something fried. Brian recognised it as squid and although we hadn't ordered it we thought it must be a free starter. I didn't eat any but Brian was tucking in nicely when the waitress reappeared and took the half-eaten dish away! We gathered that she had taken it to the wrong table and the chef was not very pleased with her but Brian enjoyed his free starter and thought she was a lovely lass!

The paella was excellent and after coffees and wine we paid the bill of 30 Euros and went back to Jack and Jill who were still asleep in their beds. As the saying goes let sleeping dogs lie.

Sunday 30ᵗʰ November 2003.

The final part of our journey to La Manga in the Costa Calida was finally here. Another nice sunny day, we were up and off by eight-thirty. The scenery on this last leg of the journey was gorgeous orange groves at the sides of the road, the sun beating down and the prospect of missing a cold December in England was wonderful. I was inspired to text nearly everyone I knew just to let them know what they were missing! Some of the replies were unprintable and were green with envy, how lucky we were to have the chance to experience an adventure like this.

By lunchtime the temperature was 22 degrees and we had stopped a few times for toilets, drinks or diesel. The tolls were much cheaper in Spain but the services were much less frequent and the facilities were sometimes quite basic. Not quite as bad though as the first toilet I came across in France that was just a hole in the floor, no hand rail or crocheted poodle to cover the toilet roll! I was quite gobsmacked and returned to the car on that occasion with my knees together and quickly reviewed my "Le Guide" book to find the next available "proper" toilet.

As we got to Alicante we drove up to the tollbooth and as usual I went to open my electric window, money in hand. Unfortunately, the window wouldn't open and after a minute or so trying every button I could see to no avail, I had to get out of the car, pay the man then get back in. How embarrassing. Neither of us knew why this fault had developed so we stopped at the next services to read the manual. It would appear that the "child safety" button on the driver's side had been activated to stop all windows except the drivers being opened. Brian was absolutely certain he hadn't touched the button but he was absolutely certain about his previous two wives and look where that got him! Anyway, we were once again on the road with all windows working.

It was three o'clock when we arrived at La Manga and we felt excited but nervous as we wondered whether we would like what we found and if we could live here for eleven weeks. We pulled up to the barrier at the side of reception and I went in with my printed receipt for the deposit I had paid via the Internet. The receptionist spoke good English and she asked me to tell Brian to reverse, go round the small roundabout and drive into the car park. When I told him he was horrified at the prospect of all this manoeuvring in front of people but he did it very well.

We couldn't remember why we had chosen this particular site except that several years ago we talked about perhaps having a static caravan abroad when we retired and this was one of the sites which sent us details through the post. Brian could remember being quite impressed by what they had to offer and, in particular, their value for money. I wouldn't say he's tight but he doesn't like being ripped off and likes good value.

Anyway, we were here now and I had requested on my email

one of the larger plots. This site has two sizes of pitch and we thought a bigger one would be better for our awning etc. She gave me a security card to get in and out of the barriers, an information sheet about the site and a map of how to get to our allocated plot – O93.

I went back to the car park where Brian was walking the dogs and showed him the map. The site was larger than we imagined and it was over half a mile from reception down to the furthest plots near the beach. The site was arranged in rows and blocks and the one way system on the map looked relatively easy to follow.

Following the directions given, we drove towards the sea, turned left after waiting for people to move their abandoned cars near the beach, then first turning right into O block. I got out of the car and walked to where our plot was, only to find there were two cars parked in it! A minute later a Spanish chap came and moved both cars up the road and out of our way.

Brian turned into our "aisle" which was a very tight squeeze, and as he did so I could hear a crunch on the right hand side of the caravan. It was caught on some trees on the corner and I could see quite a big dent already. From nowhere, about six people arrived to inform us that it was impossible to get a caravan in this way and really we should have ignored the instruction given and come in from the other side! Cheers.

I was pleased to meet Rod, an English chap who calmed us down and suggested we unhook the car, drive it up to the plot which I did whilst the men pushed the caravan the rest of the way so as not to cause any further damage. It was lovely to see a friendly face that spoke English and could help us. I could have kissed him.

Both Brian and I were quite tetchy by now and through clenched teeth were trying to be civil! I was trying not to blame him for the damage as I was supposed to be seeing him safely round the corner. But deep down I thought it was his bloody fault. He was trying not to get annoyed at me as I was getting upset and a bit tearful and it was the last thing he needed!

So, as soon as the car and caravan were parked up, he instructed me to take the dogs and walk to the beach or somewhere for ten minutes out of his way. I snatched the dogs' leads and set off purposefully with no real idea where I was going! I reminded myself of my Mum she often went off in a huff with the "monk-on", as we say in Yorkshire.

How could things change so much in a day? A few hours ago we were thanking our lucky stars that we were here and now I could cry! I walked down to the beach and was shocked to see a sign saying "No Dogs on the Beach". There were kids and dogs running about and cars parked anywhere and when I walked back to our plot I realised we were opposite the toilets and the rubbish bins, which were overflowing!

Brian was in the process of setting the caravan up and he had calmed down. So he listened to me rambling on about there being nowhere to walk the dogs and hating this plot and it's too busy and where's all the rubbish come from and then he poured me a sherry and gave me a cuddle!

We agreed it was disappointing that "we" (now it's a joint accident) had damaged the side of our brand new caravan, but it was just one of those things and it could have happened to anyone except it didn't, it happened to us.

"Let's make the best of things" was the attitude which got us through the tedious job of setting up and the rest of the day. In the evening we went down to the beach bar and restaurant and tried the menu of the day-three courses including a drink for 9 euros and after a pint of sangria life didn't seem that bad.

When we got back to the caravan I rang my Mum on the mobile phone, to let her know we had arrived safely. I tried not to sound disappointed and said things like "Oh, we'll get used to it" and "I think it will look better in the morning as we're both tired" – but my Mum told me later she knew I hated it that day!

Before going to bed I decided to use the toilet and shower block opposite. It was old fashioned but clean – and as I sat on the loo thinking of the eventful day, I reached for the toilet paper but there wasn't any! Shock horror! Luckily I had my handbag and things with me – don't ask! When I emerged from the loo I realised that the paper was on the wall outside the cubicles and you were free to take as much in with you as you required! I must remember that tomorrow, otherwise I can see me hobbling out of the cubicle with my knickers round my ankles – not a pretty site.

Monday 1st December 2003

White rabbits, white rabbits, white rabbits. And it's raining cats and dogs! After yesterday's poor start I thought today's would be a new chapter but rain was the last thing I was expecting. We were woken at eight o'clock by what turned out to be the refuse collection lorries.

Not a good idea to put the awning up in the rain so we decided that task could wait. We got in the car and drove up to the supermarket on site, as we needed to stock up with a few things. Having spent 67 euros we had some fresh water, fruit and veg, bread, wine and brandy, dog food and some liver for tea. The prices didn't seem too bad but we thought the site supermarket would probably be more expensive than elsewhere due to the captive audience. But for convenience today we didn't mind.

Around three o'clock it stopped raining and became a bit brighter so we took Jack and Jill for a walk. As we got down to the beach that I had been to yesterday, we noticed people walking dogs further along to the left. We stopped to talk to an English couple with their dog who explained that dogs were not allowed on the area of beach belonging to the site, but to the left and right of this area you could walk as far as you wanted with your dogs. This was a great relief and we walked along the "public" beach for about a mile and as no other dogs were in sight, Jack and Jill had a great run around and then went swimming in the sea.

La Manga del Mar Menor is a strip of land with white sand beaches. It is 13 miles long and separates the Mediterranean Sea from the Mar Menor (the Minor Sea), which is a lagoon that is considered to be the world's largest swimming pool, due to its calm and warm waters which never drop below 18 degrees. The dogs were very reluctant to come out of the water but eventually we all walked back to our caravan.

Please accept my apologies in advance if I keep changing from the Centigrade scale to the Fahrenheit! I'm sure there is some very complicated way of calculating one to the other but I think you'll get the idea!

I made liver and onions for tea, washed down with some very palatable red wine. After tea I played Scrabble on my own – how sad is that? Brian won't play any games unless he's a good chance of winning or he can cheat. He will play Trivial Pursuit as he does have an excellent general knowledge but he will only play other games like cards for as long as he can get away with cheating. So I play Scrabble on my own and play both hands and I do enjoy it because one half of me always wins!

I rang my sister Janet at 9 o'clock, and at half past we were all asleep.

Tuesday 2nd December 2003.

Today certainly looked more promising – the sun was trying to get out and we decided this was the day to put the awning up!

When we first started caravanning in 1996, someone told me that the test of a good marriage was putting an awning up together and still being friends! As soon as we bought and erected our first one, I knew what she meant. The process needs co-operation, patience, teamwork and a sense of humour together with a really good diagram.

At the time of ordering our new caravan we also selected a brand new awning. We told the salesman we wanted a good quality awning but our most important requirement was ease of erection. He selected the Isabella Ambassador Crown which he explained wasn't cheap but it was excellent quality with the most up to date fibre glass poles and about the simplest to put together. When we told him about the arguments we went through with our last porch awning, he said that porch awnings, despite being small, are the hardest to put up. I don't know whether he just made this up to make us feel better but it worked.

So now we had the job of unpacking our brand new awning and ground sheet. We had a bottle of red wine and some brandy at hand for those moments when you want to scream- should we need them. We also agreed before we started, that neither of us were good at this so we would be patient and not shout or swear at each other and that we had all day to do the task if necessary so no need to rush.

With the poles and instructions in front of us we began. I wondered whether we should perhaps have had a trial run in case any bits were missing or we really couldn't put it up correctly but what was the point in wondering – we were here now so let's give it our best effort.

After an hour we seemed to be making slow progress but one of our Dutch neighbours came across to help. He seemed to know what he was doing so we gratefully accepted his guidance. His name was Joop and he spoke very good English and was soon knocking us into shape. Whilst he was helping, another Dutchman, who had just left the shower block in his dressing gown, came to offer his assistance! Again he spoke English well so the three men were doing a fine job.

The day was getting quite warm and after the basic frame was up, we thanked our friends and stopped for a cold drink and a very nice pizza that we'd bought at the shop. It was half past two when we finally completed it and it looked great. At last I could start putting things in the awning and get the inside of the caravan looking more homely and clutter free.

At 3 o'clock we took the dogs down to the beach for a good run and a swim and when we got back I made a lasagne for tea.

In the evening we again met Rod with his wife Wendy as they were passing our caravan. They said if we needed any help with anything we'd only to ask and they were only about four pitches away from us so I felt better already.

By six o'clock, the temperature had dropped and it was quite cool "cardigan weather" as my Mum would call it. So we put the heating on in the caravan, read for a while then were in bed for 8.30! Well it had been quite a tiring day for us, and we had got the awning up and were still speaking. Brian brought me an aspirin and a drink of water. I explained I didn't need it as I hadn't got a headache and that was that. Bedtime!

Wednesday 3rd December 2003.

A cloudy morning and quite cool, and I was still feeling a bit down maybe a bit homesick. It seemed like a long time to be away from family and friends and then there was Christmas coming up.

Our family has always made a fuss at Christmas and like most women I would spend months looking for something a bit different for everyone.

When we decided we were coming to Spain for Christmas I had originally thought about buying everyone's presents before we came and bringing theirs to us with us but good old sensible, tight (!) Brian thought we should agree with our family and friends not to buy presents as it was getting out of hand.

I hate to admit it but he was right again. It was getting more and more difficult every year knowing what to get everyone and when I had talked about it with close family they agreed we should stop being so silly. However, I was still going to buy for my nieces and nephews whilst they were young enough to enjoy Santa coming.

My sister Janet and husband Jimmy have two boys. Jake will be 13 at Christmas and Connor will be 10, and my brother Chris has three children with his former partner- Katie (5), India (4) and

Joshua just one year old. Brian's sister Pam (my favourite sister-in-law!) and her husband Gary have Hannah who will be 17 but still loves Christmas. So their presents were wrapped before we left England and sent to Santa.

As I was feeling a bit mardy, Brian decided to have a walk round the site and find the advertised gym to see what it was like. He would also call at the supermarket and buy some gas for our new barbecue

Almost an hour and a half later he returned I was getting a bit worried that he'd got lost as the site is huge and quite confusing. He had found the gym at the top of the site and had a quick look round it He said it would be closed down in England due to health and safety issues! It was very small with an exercise bike that was just functioning, some weights that had most of their safety catches missing, a sauna big enough for anyone under five foot and an indoor pool which looked very nice.

At home he does his best to keep himself fit He still plays cricket all summer and goes to the gym when he gets time, so he thought it would be worth joining whilst we were here as he would probably go two or three times a week He looks well for 55 but that's just my opinion and I'm biased! I said I would go to reception another day to get his membership.

He had no luck with the gas for the barbecue as the shop said the fitting we had wouldn't fit any gas canister they sold. We were disappointed as we bought the barbecue to bring to Spain and were hoping to do a lot of cooking on it weather permitting. So we decided to go to the local hardware shop in the next village of Los Belones. The hardware shops are called "ferreterias" and once we got in there I thought I was never going to get Brian out again! It was like an Aladdin's cave of everything you could think of for the home, garden, D. I. Y, camping everything! We took the gas fitting but they shook their heads and didn't have anything resembling this at all. We did however spend 36 euros on a colander, a cheese grater, a frying pan, a bowl, some cups and some wineglasses!

Brunch was a fry-up when we got back, then Brian took the dogs for a two-hour walk whilst I sorted out the inside of the caravan and gave it a really good clean.

Later, I made a sausage and onion casserole, but when I came to mash the potatoes we didn't have a potato masher so I made a mental note that we needed to buy one, and made do with a fork. Brian tried fiddling with the radio and found a station called

Spectrum, which was all-English, and so we now had something to listen to other than a few CDs.

It was nearly 9. 30 when we went to bed – aren't we cheeky!

Thursday 4th December 2003.

It had rained most of the night and the day was cloudy and didn't look too promising. I decided to walk up to reception to get Brian's gym membership, but didn't realise how far it was – nearly half a mile. I was almost ready to collapse when I got there!

The reception staff were very helpful and spoke good English. I explained I wanted membership for the gym. It was 55 euros for 30 sessions and I was given a green membership card.

Before we had set off to Spain, my Mum and Dad had said they would like to come over for a couple of weeks after Christmas and stay in some wooden chalets that were shown in the information pack the site had sent to us before we arrived. I promised my Mum I would have a look at them and see what they were like and get the prices for her. I had passed them on the way up to reception and I asked if I could have a look at one. The girl indicated that one of the security men would take me to them and I was to follow him. When we got outside, he hopped onto a motorised golf buggy-type machine and I was walking behind him. However, he soon picked up quite a speed and I was jogging after him as fast as my meaty fat thighs could carry me!

I was out of breath when we got there and I was hoping he didn't mistake my deep breaths for heavy excited breathing, as he was the double of the old TV detective Frank Cannon! He showed me round one of the chalets which was very basic – a room with a plastic table and four chairs, together with a couple of cooking rings and a tiny cupboard, a bedroom with a double bed and a bathroom with toilet and shower. Clean but sparse and the price was 40 euros a night and you could also rent clean sheets. I really couldn't see my Mum in here for a fortnight. She's not Hyacinth Bucket but she's not used to camping either! So I thanked him for his time and set off back home.

Brian was pleased with his membership and said he would start at the gym the next day. I decided I needed to do some washing so whilst I was doing that, he went up to the supermarket on site to get some prawns to make a curry for tea.

A few months before we set off I had bought a pressure washer from a camping shop. It was lightweight and ideal for small loads so I unpacked it and set it up on the table in the awning. It needed filling with warm water and I was thankful that we were opposite the sinks where I could get as much as I needed. My first wash was a few pairs of knickers and a T-shirt and I turned the handle as shown until the pressure built up and continued turning for several minutes. The water had to be drained off and then replaced with clean water to rinse and then drained again. So I was left with clean clothes but they needed to be wrung out well before I placed them on a clothes airer that we had brought with us.

I wondered if Brian could put up a washing line at some stage but for today the clothes would hopefully dry in the awning. We had a small fan heater, which I put on a high setting and aimed towards the washing. There was a laundrette on site, which was 6 euros for a wash and dry, and I thought I would just use that to wash the bedding every so often.

At three o'clock we took Jack and Jill onto the beach and we had a really good long walk to tire them out.

Gorgeous prawn curry and rice for tea which Brian made and he also washed up! I think he knew I was still a bit homesick and he was doing his best to make me enjoy it. I had a few glasses of Muscatel which he'd brought from the shop as a treat. I like the odd glass of sweet sherry at home and this drink was just as sweet and went down really well. The dogs must have swallowed some seawater, as they were also very thirsty.

Friday 5th December 2003.

The sun was here again hooray! Brian went to the gym at 9. 30 whilst I put the washing on the airer outside as it still wasn't dry.

When he got back, he said he'd got a surprise Christmas present for me. Apparently the gym was free it's the swimming that you have to pay for, so he gave me the membership card which entitled me to 30 swimming sessions! Now when we both retired I promised to stop smoking and as a result have put on almost two and a half stone, honest! I know I should try and get more exercise but swimming has never been one of my favourite things. Along with a lot of women I am put off because it means washing my hair when I've been for a swim but Brian explained this wouldn't be a problem as you had to wear a hat! So I now had to look for a swimming cap to buy, so that I can get my money's worth from the gym membership which turned out to be a pass for the pool which I didn't really want!

With the sun finally shining, it seemed a shame not to be using the barbecue. So we got in the car and headed towards Alicante where someone had told us there was a camping shop just off the motorway, where we thought we could probably buy the adapter that we needed. Why do we set off with only half the information and expect these obscure places to appear from nowhere?

Map in hand, we reached Alicante no problem, but there was no sign of a camping shop. The day was getting warmer and as we drove round in circles Brian was becoming increasingly agitated. We had to keep stopping to let the dogs have a walk and some water. We thought we were only going to be out an hour or so, otherwise we would have let the dogs relax in the caravan in the shade back at home.

We did find a "Camping" shop but when we got there it was more like a huge garage with a few bits for sale like a chair and a watering can and a windbreak. We showed the assistant our gas fitting and he shook his head but suggested we try the "Ferreteria" so we drove to the next town, parked up and found the hardware shop.

Again, this shop had every item you could imagine but they had nothing to fit our barbecue. I looked around for a potato masher but it seemed to be the one kitchen utensil that they didn't stock. How strange.

Six and a half hours later we arrived back at the site with nothing to show for our efforts but a receipt for filling up with diesel! It was seven o'clock so the supermarket was closed but Brian managed to rustle up spaghetti bolognaise for supper.

When we had returned we had noticed a few public phone boxes around the site so after supper I took the euro coins I had in my purse and went to phone my Mum to cheer myself up. Still trying to sound positive I told her what a lovely sunny day it had been and how we had wasted it driving round aimlessly! But I assured her I was feeling a bit better as the days went by. Everyone was fine at home and she was disappointed when I described the chalets to her. But I said not to worry as I had noticed a few caravans and bungalows on the site which were for rent and I would make enquiries over the next week or so. When all my euros had gone I went back home and went to bed.

Saturday 6th December 2003.

Our sunniest day yet it was a lovely day and very warm from the moment we woke up at 8.30. After yesterday's driving marathon we decided not to venture far and so we set off on a drive towards the "Strip" to see what we could find. At the first turning we found a very large supermarket – but this was called "Upper" – the same as the one on our site and guess what? The prices were the same, so we could shop on site in future if we wanted. Anyway, we bought a few things including some belly pork for tea and various toiletries we needed, but I couldn't find any Steradent or equivalent. Without taking my false teeth out to show an assistant, I didn't think I would be able to explain what I was looking for so I thought I would give that a miss, besides I had enough to last a week or so.

We drove down the strip and were amazed at the amount of shops and hotels there were. After parking up we had a walk round and found a newsagent's type shop where we made enquiries about top-up cards for our mobile phones. Yes, the man had one for Brian's Vodaphone which he registered for us but when I showed him mine which was with the Orange network, he said I would have to go to Cartegena which was about twenty miles away! So I would just have to save my euro coins to ring my Mum or better still use Brian's phone.

About two weeks before we left England I had realised that our Switch cards were due to expire in December, whilst we were away. So I called at the bank, explained the problem and they said they would get our new cards issued straight away. A week later, no sign of them, so I rang the bank who said they had been "activated" but not "used" so they appeared to have been intercepted in the post by someone so they would issue two more!

Three days before we were leaving, the replacement cards arrived, and so did the original ones! Again I rang the bank who said they didn't know how that had happened but we should only use the second ones and our new chip and PIN numbers would be in the post within the next ten days! Pardon? I explained that we were leaving home on Monday and travelling down to Dover then to France and Spain. They apologised again and said they would have the PIN numbers sent to the local branch and could I ring them from Dover on Monday or Tuesday and they would give me them over the phone provided I could answer several security questions when I rang.

Luckily when I rang the branch from Dover the following

Tuesday, they gave me the PIN numbers so we were OK. However, we had previously topped up our mobile phones using our old Switch cards and this was an automated system, which was very convenient and easy. We could no longer use this without registering our new cards and when I tried to ring the customer care departments from Spain I couldn't get through so that was tough luck! Valuable lesson learned- make sure nothing expires whilst you are away.

We were back at the site for lunchtime and it was a glorious day so we took Jack and Jill for a walk right down the beach and back over some fields. This covered about three and a half miles and Jack was very excited when he saw a hare in the long grass and gave chase. No chance of catching it but it certainly tired him out.

Calling at the phone booth on the way back we quickly called Brian's Dad Harry and also spoke to Pam who was there cleaning for her Dad. She said Gary, her husband, was pleased with his birthday card and present that I had left for him.

I made a belly pork casserole for tea and it was a lovely night so we ate outside and our Dutch neighbours came to talk to us as they washed up at the sinks opposite. Joop was the man who helped us put the awning up and he explained to Brian that when he was at school everyone was taught English and that's why the older Dutch people (he was in his late sixties) could converse with us. His wife was called Miep and she asked if I was going to Keep Fit on Tuesday. I said I could do with it!

Brian's sister Pam had bought us a Mediterranean cookbook to bring with us and it had some lovely recipes in it. At home we share the cooking as we both enjoy preparing and eating nice food – but I told Brian I would like to do most of the cooking whilst we were in Spain, as I would enjoy making different dishes from this lovely colour cook book and it would give me something to do.

Joop was very interested in what we were having to eat, as he had been a chef before he retired. He told us they had been coming here for a few years and they came in October and stayed for six months!

Things seemed better today, we both went to bed feeling a little more settled. It could have been the sunshine that cheered us up though it could have been the carton of red wine we finished off after tea!

Sunday 7th December 2003.

We were both awake at 7. 30 after a really good night's sleep. Sat outside the awning having breakfast in the morning sun seemed a perfect way to start a Sunday.

As we drank our tea, one of our other Dutch neighbours came to talk to us. Her name was Corrie and she invited me to Keep Fit classes. I was beginning to think I really was looking like a beached whale with new acquaintances almost immediately referring to the need for me to take up exercise! She explained that she took the classes on Tuesday and Thursday and it was just a gentle routine to music, which was a bit of fun and helped you to meet people. I said I might be there but didn't make any promises.

Whilst we were talking, she asked if we were going to the market – apparently there is a massive market every Sunday opposite the Upper supermarket and most people go to it for a look round. So that's where we had a run out to.

We took the dogs with us, which was a bit of a mistake as the market was indeed huge and Jack and Jill wanted to bark and run at every other dog they saw. There were hundreds of people and dogs there, but it was interesting to look round and we bought some nice fruit and vegetables and some roasted almonds. We also bought a cooked chicken, which we thought we could have for lunch later.

On the way back home (I was finding it easier to refer to our caravan as "home" rather than "the site"), we pulled off the road towards the National Park area and, as no one was about, the dogs had a great run around for almost an hour.

Our afternoon was spent sitting in the sun, eating chicken and salad and crusty bread and drinking a few glasses of white wine for a change.

An almost perfect day was ruined for me, as it was "that time of the month"!

Brian's late Mum Joan used to refer to it as "the visitor", and as I got into bed with stomach-ache, I said "Yes Joan – my visitor has even followed me to Spain". Good night!

Monday 8th December 2003.

Still feeling a bit sorry for myself, I decided to have a lie in. The gym was closed today as it was a national holiday – La Concepcion, which I understand translates as The Immaculate Conception, or Mother's Day.

Brian cooked a fry-up for breakfast, which was lovely and he then took the dogs for a walk along the beach. It was another gorgeous hot day and I finally got up around eleven after drinking endless cups of tea and snuggling back under the quilt. The day was too nice to miss.

Again we sat outside getting a bit of a tan and enjoying the fact that it would no doubt be raining back in England – this was the life. I had to be careful in the sun as I had a melanoma removed from my leg in 1995, which was cancerous, so another operation and skin graft followed. The surgeon said this had been caused by over exposure to the sun and, although I didn't need to sit in the shade, I had to use Factor 30 whenever I was in the sun in future. I was finally signed off from yearly check-ups in 2001 but it made me very grateful that it had been spotted in time.

Going through the trauma brought home to me what a pessimist Brian was. When I came home from the hospital with the devastating news that I had cancer and would be in hospital before the week was out, he said I should go straight to my Mum's as she'd know what to do! He also expressed concern about how terrible the parking situation was at Cookridge, which was the nearest "long term" cancer hospital, and was already worrying where he would park when I was dying in there!

After the lovely breakfast, we were discussing how disappointed we were that it looked unlikely we were going to be able to use the barbecue. I looked to see if we had brought the instruction book with the manufacturer's address and telephone number and was pleased to see we had. Their head office was in Halifax so I rang them on Brian's mobile and explained the problem. They told me we needed a different attachment if it was to be used abroad and if I gave them my credit card number and address in Spain they would post one out to me. Hooray! Another step forward.

Today was exactly sixteen years since our first date and we reminisced about the strange circumstances of our introduction. In

41

January 1987, after just three months of marriage, my first husband had beaten me up and broken my jaw in three places. I returned home to Mum and Dad's after a week in hospital with my jaws wired together and various other injuries stitched. I reported the assault to the police and the following day the local bobby came to take a statement. We had never had any dealings with the police, but this local chap, Brian, seemed very nice and he made my Mum and Dad feel much better with his down to earth attitude and lots of empathy.

He left after about an hour and a few cups of tea and biscuits. Several weeks later he called to let me know he had arrested my husband, taken his statement and the police were prosecuting him.

In November, I received a telephone call from this Brian bloke to tell me the court had found my husband guilty. He asked how I was doing and told me his wife has left him and somehow the conversation ended with him asking me if I wanted to go for a drink one evening! Due to work commitments on both sides, the first evening we were both free was Tuesday December the 8th so he said he would pick me up that night. And he did and the rest is history. Within three weeks, we were looking to buy a house together and moved into our house in Wakefield the following April. Brian still says the reason he was first attracted to me was because my jaws were wired together for six weeks, so he could "get a word in". He's always been romantic!

So, in July of this year when Brian reached 55 and had to retire from the police, I was still only 45. We still had another nine years to pay the mortgage and the only way we could both retire and enjoy some time together was to sell up and down-size, so we did. Moving to Lancashire was not really in our plans but the right place came along and I think Brian always fancied going back to his roots. He spent a lot of his younger days living at Carnforth, near Morecambe, and he only moved to Wakefield to join the police when he was married to his second wife, Liz. He's come full circle as we now live about ten minutes' drive from his teenage haunts.

By mid-afternoon I was feeling a bit better so, whilst Brian took the dogs for another walk, I prepared chicken thighs in lemon and garlic with rice. We ate outside again and spent time chatting to our neighbours and saying "ola" which was "hello" to everyone that passed by. We were talking to another Dutch neighbour, Henk, who was a few pitches further down from us.

Tummy ache subsided and we nearly went to a quiz night, down at the beach restaurant, which we had seen advertised on various posters around the site. But by eight o'clock we were worn out by the weather and agreed to go the following Monday night.

Tuesday 9th December 2003.

Although it was still warm, it rained most of the day. Joop warned us that there may be some winds and a bit of rain coming and advised us that we may like to invest in a heavy duty strap to put over the awning, just in case. So we went to the Ferreteria and bought ourselves a strap.

Whilst in the shop, I was again looking for a potato masher but couldn't see one. I even thought about buying a full 6-piece utensil set, but it didn't include a masher! What did they do in Spain when they wanted to have mash? I refused to resort to Smash so my quest continued.

We called at the large supermarket on the way back as I had seen a recipe for duck, my favourite. There were no pre-packed duck breasts in the freezers, so I took a ticket and waited my turn at the butcher's counter. A very friendly, smiling man asked what I would like. I said, "Do you have any duck, please?" To which he looked with that "haven't got a clue what you're talking about Mrs" look. I proceeded to flap my arms and quack at him, and he came round the other side of the counter and took me to the freezers, where he pointed out a full frozen duckling.

I pretended this was just what I was looking for and thanked him with a smile! By this time, Brian was almost under the counter with embarrassment! We vowed to get a phrase book so that I didn't have to go through that again. Needless to say I didn't buy a full duck, even though Brian thought we should in case the man that had served us thought we were ungrateful.

We drove down the strip again and found the Internet Café, which was shown in our reception as the nearest one to our site. I had never been in one before and wasn't sure what to expect. The price list was so many euros depending on the minutes you wanted to be on the internet, so I asked for an hour, which was 3 euros. I was shown to a seat and a table with screen and keyboard and off I went!

Neither of us are very good with computers in fact, Brian is from the "dinosaur" age and still to this day says computers won't catch on! We bought our first computer in 1996 and upgraded to a laptop this summer when we retired. The Internet access we have is only used about once a fortnight as neither of us really knows what we're doing, but before we left England, someone mentioned to me that if you don't access your Internet messages for three months, you lose the connection.

Panic stricken, I phoned Virgin net who told me not to worry I could go into an Internet café anywhere in the world and access my internet by typing wwwmail2web.com, then my password, and this would let me read any mail and email everyone!

So, here I was, feeling quite chuffed with myself that I was reading my mail and I then composed a "newsletter", to let friends and family know what we were up to. With just a few minutes to spare I had done it! My first Internet café experience would not be my last. It felt like a great achievement and before I came out of the shop, I was already looking forward to returning in a week or so to see if I had any replies.

On the way home, we got slightly lost but found a different supermarket called the "Mercadona", so we called in and found they had a lovely pack of two duck breasts. Even better was the fact that all their meat had a picture of the appropriate animal on so instead of guessing, we knew what we were buying!

Whilst Brian went to the gym in the afternoon and the dogs relaxed on their beds outside, I cooked duck breasts with spicy pears and it was delicious, even though I say it myself.

I felt we'd had quite a successful day and we went to bed after a night-cap of brandy for Brian and Muscatel for me.

Wednesday 10th December 2003.

What a night! The rain had finally arrived at midnight together with a howling wind and we were awake for the rest of the night.

Once we were awake listening to the awning being almost blown away, we realised that the awning strap, which Joop had advised us to buy, was in the back of the car. How silly was that? By this time it was too late to get it and secure it outside with tent pegs as Brian would have got soaked and probably blown into the sea. So we made cups of tea and cuddled up instead. Jack and Jill were allowed to come onto the bed for a cuddle as I thought they might be frightened! Although, as Brian pointed out, they were probably more frightened by seeing me in the middle of the night with no teeth in. How rude!

We listened to the radio from six o'clock to catch the hourly news and weather forecast. By eight o'clock, the rain had stopped and the wind had just about dropped.

The skies remained dull but the morning was still quite warm and the first job for Brian was to put the awning strap on. Talk about closing the gate after the horse has bolted. Most of the day we lazed about due to lack of sleep but we did take the dogs down to the beach early afternoon. The sea was very rough and even Jill wasn't tempted to go in.

When we got back from the beach I decided to take some washing to the launderette so I went to reception to buy a wash and dry token and some detergent tablets. On reaching the launderette with my two bags of washing, I realised it was closed and was only open from nine until one thirty. So I would have to come back tomorrow.

Tonight's tea was lamb with apricots, which was another triumph from Pam's recipe book. An early night was on the cards but I thought I would just ring my Mum before we went to sleep. Taking all my one-euro coins I walked round to the phone boxes and there were a few people queuing but after a few minutes one came free and me and Mum had a good chat for several minutes until my money had gone.

As I put the receiver back down, an English chap who had been on the phone behind me, asked if I was phoning home. He explained that the best way to ring home was to buy a phone card for 6 euros, which lasted 300 minutes! They were not available everywhere but he said the tobacconist's in the next village, Los Belones sold them. I thanked him for this information, and made a mental note to buy one as soon as I could.

Thursday 11th December 2003.

Having cooked a casserole-type meal almost every day in the oven in the caravan, I wasn't surprised when the gas finally ran out. Brian put a new cylinder on and we were quite pleased that it wasn't expensive to replace. However, Brian had brought with us a canister of propane gas, which he said he shouldn't have brought as it's really for colder climates, as it doesn't freeze.

He did decide that although camping gas is slightly more expensive than butane, we would be better using it whilst we were here, as the butane gas cylinders you could buy in Spain don't have a universal fitting. I don't think gas is something I should have to get involved with, its very confusing and its one area that Brian can be in sole charge of.

It was a gorgeous day the sun was out and the sky was once again a bright blue. I took the washing to the launderette expecting to be there some time, but found you couldn't do your own. You had to leave it with the tokens and washing tablets for the Spanish laundry lady to do for you. She didn't speak English, but I did manage to establish that it was too late for me to collect it today- I could come back tomorrow-manana! Not a bit like Pauline Fowler in the launderette in "Eastenders," but when in Rome…

A walk down the beach seemed in order as it was lovely and warm, and when we got back I went into Los Belones to look for the tobacconists, which I soon found but it was closed. I should have known it was siesta time and only a couple of shops were open. Back home I made a meat and potato pie for tea, and Brian asked for Yorkshire puddings but I had no baking tins with me so he had to fill up on pastry. Later I played Scrabble and read my book before another early night.

Friday 12th December 2003.

Another sunny day and as we sat eating breakfast outside we got talking to a couple who were washing up. We had now changed our view on the position of this plot and found that, being opposite the washing up area gave us lots of people to talk to. Ann and Derek were both retired teachers from Cockermouth and they had only been here a few days and were still finding their feet too.

They had two dogs but they were quite a bit older than ours and were reluctant to do much walking.

As we sat in the sun having a cold lager and some fruit for lunch, "Frank Cannon" the security man came round on his buggy. He seemed to be related to one of the cleaners as he would appear most mornings whilst the showers were being cleaned, and bring a drink for the cleaners and have a chat with them. They were all very friendly and always greeted us with "Ola" or "Buenas Dias", when they came three times each day to clean the showers, toilets and washing up areas.

He dismounted his buggy and brought me a parcel! How exciting, some mail. No one had said they were going to write so I almost ripped the package open in my eagerness to discover what it contained. There was a very welcome letter from my sister Janet which explained that the videocassette enclosed contained three hours of "Coronation Street" and "Eastenders". It was wonderful to receive some post from home and although we couldn't get any English television on our set, we had a TV/video combination so any videos were gratefully received.

At home, we do watch quite a lot of Telly and we especially enjoy the soaps. Within a few days of being here, we both said that although we weren't "missing" the television, we should really have brought some films with us or recorded some programmes just in case we fancied watching a bit of Telly one night. So Janet had saved the day and we looked forward to watching the tape another time.

My only disappointment was that the gas barbecue adapter hadn't yet arrived, but it was early days.

I collected my clean and dry washing and, after our usual walk along the beach, we decided that tonight we would go out for a meal just for a change. Off we went into Los Belones and after an hour tasting wine in the bodega and buying a couple of litres, I noticed a shop on the other side of the road which looked like our English "pound shops" and couldn't resist a quick look round. They had everything you could want and hundreds of things you didn't! But I found a swimming cap and asked how much. "One euro" came the reply so I was thrilled with my bargain. We found an Asian restaurant which looked very nice. We each chose a dish and some rice and had a couple of drinks and the bill was 40 Euros which we thought was quite expensive, but although the portions weren't big, the food was top quality, so we didn't mind.

Home by 9.30, a coffee and a liqueur and a marzipan sweet – which I had bought at the supermarket – delicious! What a lovely day this had been. It was maybe the fact that Janet had written but for some reason I felt more settled today than I had since we left England, and I slept like a log.

Saturday 13th December 2003.

Feeling quite giddy what with the sun out again, I thought I would go for a swim in my new yellow cap. We walked up to the gym and pool together as it was quite a good walk and Brian went into the gym whilst I tried the pool. It wasn't very big but was quite warm and there was only one lady in it, who was German. At the end of the pool was a jacuzzi which I enjoyed for ten minutes before getting a shower and waiting for Brian. The attendant marked my card to show I had had one swimming session – only 29 to go!

Another trip into Los Belones found the tobacconist's open and I bought one of the blue phone cards for 6 euros and then we called at the supermarket for something for tea. Rabbit is something I can eat but don't really like to cook but there were whole fresh rabbits available so we bought one. The assistant asked if I wanted the head removing and I said yes but then he was asking if I wanted it wrapping up with the rest of the rabbit! Not likely!

I soon had all the preparation done for "Rabbit salmorejo" and put the dish in the oven to cook slowly for a few hours. It was such a glorious day we sat in the sunshine from 1 o'clock until gone five.

After tea, we walked to the phone booths and Brian rang his Dad. The conversation lasted around ten minutes with such interesting topics as the weather and what the time difference was!

I then rang my Mum using our phone card, and it was lovely to know I could talk for five hours for 6 euros. After five minutes Brian indicated that he was making his way back as he could somehow sense that this conversation might go on for a while. And how right he was. Mum said I sounded very different from the previous week and I told her I was feeling much more at home and really enjoying it. After about half an hour, I rang Janet and thanked her for her parcel. She was relieved to hear it had arrived as she had given it to her husband Jimmy to post for her. On his return, she checked he'd asked for air mail. No, he hadn't because she didn't tell him to. Why do men sometimes need everything writing down? Anyway, it had arrived in one piece so we should be thankful that he'd posted it at all.

A quick call to Pam ended after around forty-five minutes and by the time I got back Brian had walked the dogs and washed up. Like most men, he can't imagine what women find to talk about for so long. It's no use explaining we talk about shopping, hair, soaps, her down the road and all sorts of irrelevant topics!

All that conversation had tired me out.

Sunday 14th December 2003.

A lovely drying day awaited us when we got up so I washed the bedding in my little hand-operated washer. I put it on the table in front of the awning and it usually attracted some interest as passers by wondered what I was doing.

An English lady came to talk to us and she was commenting on England's performance in the latest cricket match. Well, Brian's ears were up! He loves cricket and still plays on Sundays in friendly matches, so he was chatting to Barbara who told us she had a satellite dish and had been watching the match earlier. Her husband John wasn't a sports fan and he preferred to mess about with his computer or make marmalade. But Brian was in his element talking to someone who knew about sport. She explained they had just arrived and were just a few pitches further down from us. The couple we had met earlier, Rod and Wendy, had moved to the top end of the site and John and Barbara were now in their old place.

They had been coming here for quite a few years and Barbara seems to know most people. She asked how far we had walked along the beach and we said to the end and back. She advised us to keep going another half a mile and we would come to a nice little bar where we could get drinks and snacks, in another village called Mar de Cristal.

We set off at eleven and reached the bar about fifty minutes later. It was nice to sit outside with Jack and Jill and have a coffee and some nuts and nibbles, before walking back again.

A large piece of steak each for tea with a fresh salad was then followed by three hours of soaps! We couldn't resist any longer and thoroughly enjoyed overdosing on television with a few glasses of wine. Rounding our day off was the thought of getting into bed with fresh clean sheets – what could be nicer?

Monday 15th December 2003.

Happy Birthday Dad! Before leaving home I had left my Dad's birthday present and card so I rang to wish him happy birthday. But Mum had a surprise for me. She'd booked their flights and they would be coming on January 6th for two weeks. I told her not to worry about accommodation as there were lots of places to rent and, at a push they could stay in one of the wooden chalets.

An early start to the day meant we had been to the gym and swimming before eleven, so we drove through one of the national parks and took the dogs onto the beach. Whilst we were walking on the sands I asked Brian what the people in the distance were wearing as they looked a bit strange. He confirmed they were nude, so we had stumbled onto a naturist beach. We have been nude ourselves in Croatia and Fuertaventura so it wasn't a shock as such, but I didn't think it was warm enough for us to strip off and swim in the nude with the dogs and not a pretty sight!

After a long walk back through the park we arrived home and made a chilli for tea.

At six o'clock, I drove to the Internet Café and was thrilled to have some replies to my e-mails from last week. Lots of gossip from my old work place and just a bit of news from one of Brian's friends Tom, who was keeping us informed about other police officers who were due to retire.

I bought twenty-one postcards before making my way back. We had agreed not to send Christmas cards as we were away, but I felt a few postcards would be nice to send in time for Christmas just to let family know we were thinking about them.

When I came back home I noticed that almost everyone had put up some Christmas decorations and there were lights along windbreaks and awnings and in trees. The site looked really very festive and I knew this would annoy Brian when he saw it! I was fascinated looking at the different ways people's pitches were decorated, and was surprised I got back without crashing the car! As soon as I got home, I unpacked my musical fibre optic miniature tree, which the girls at work had bought me a few years ago, when we spent Christmas in the caravan at Loosehill. It was soon revolving on the table with the lights twinkling.

Writing the cards occupied most of the evening, and I had them all ready to put stamps on and post the next day. Oh Julie – get a life!

Tuesday 16th December 2003.

Warm but cloudy so we sat in the awning having breakfast, when I saw Derek come past with his reluctant dog. It made me smile as he was virtually dragging it along and he kept stopping to give it a gentle kick up the bum to make it move!

I made the "brave" decision to start Keep Fit with Corrie at ten, over at the football pitch. I spoke to a few English ladies and, although most of the participants were Dutch or German, Corrie gave out instructions in English, which was great.

The first half an hour were exercises whilst on our feet and the second half hour we did floor movements. Unfortunately I didn't realise that we really needed a floor mat but I managed. At the end of the session I asked one of the ladies where to buy a floor mat and she advised me to go to the "pound shop" in Los Belones. Although it was quite hard work, I really enjoyed the Keep Fit and the music that we used, and I promised to go again on Thursday.

Tuesday was market day at Los Belones so we went there as soon as I'd had a shower. The market was very small compared to the last one we had been to – about eight fruit and veg stalls and six others selling underwear, sweets and coats.

Of course I needed to go to the "pound shop" for a mat which was one euro, and whilst in there we bought two more swimming caps (for Mum and Dad), a windbreak and a fruit bowl. I did ask for a potato masher but they didn't have one and couldn't suggest where to buy one.

We were passing the chemist's so I popped in to see if they sold Steradent or the equivalent, as I was almost out. Yes, the assistant offered me a pack of two tubes of thirty. I usually buy Asda's own brand which are about fifty pence a tube. She wrapped them and rang them into the till. "Ten euros please."

"Pardon?" I couldn't believe I was being charged seven English pounds but paid so as not to embarrass Brian! That was an item that I would definitely bring with us if we came back to Spain next year.

Was this really me talking? Only two weeks ago I didn't like it here, then last week it was a bit better and now I'm planning for our return next winter!

Our afternoon walk down the beach was lovely, as a lot of the beach had been cleaned. On our return, I drove up to the supermarket to get some stamps and post my cards and I had a wander into reception to see if there was anything of interest.

The first thing I noticed was a large clear sign which said "Please collect your post any day, but only between five and seven o'clock". This was news to me. I thought Frank Cannon delivered everyone's post – perhaps this was because we were new but I realised that was not normal policy. I did ask but we didn't have any

51

to collect. We were still hoping for the gas fitting from England.

Back home, I cooked pork loin stuffed with figs and almonds, which we had bought fresh at this morning's market. It was eight o'clock before we ate our evening meal but it was worth waiting for.

Wednesday 17th December 2003.

The early morning sun encouraged me to go swimming again and Brian spent an hour at the gym. Although the equipment wasn't very good, Brian liked the fact that there was usually no one else there so he could use whatever he wanted.

The afternoon was quite cloudy so we just took the dogs on a short walk across the fields near the beach, and they chased each other, which made them quite tired.

Whilst making a chicken curry, I felt a sore throat coming on, so after tea and a few glasses of wine for medicinal purposes of course I snuggled into our bed and soon fell asleep.

Thursday 18th December 2003.

I was quite determined to keep up with my new found fitness regime but the rain meant that the Keep Fit was cancelled for today.

We went to the big Upper supermarket and got quite a big shop. I liked this supermarket as they accepted switch cards so I could keep my euros for longer. Our caravan only has a small fridge and a tiny freezer compartment, so we have to be careful what we buy that needs to go in the fridge or freezer.

At the Upper there is a cafeteria, so Brian said he would treat us to breakfast out! Whoopee – last of the big spenders. Unfortunately, neither of us had any idea what the food was that was being served or on display, so we ended up with a coffee and chocolate croissant – very healthy!

By one o'clock the sun was out again but my sore throat was getting worse and I felt a bit flu-like so I went to bed and left Brian to take the dogs out and do some tea. He made a very tasty casserole but neither of us was sure if the meat was lamb or pork. But who cares, it was lovely. He also washed up. Isn't he a gem?

Feeling a bit better in the evening, I went to the phone and rang Pam, Janet and my Mum. Sore throat or not, I managed to talk for an hour and a half in total – women just sail through the pain barrier!

Friday 19th December 2003.

Plenty of sunshine whilst we were sitting outside eating our breakfasts, and we got talking to another English chap called Clive and his wife Karen, whilst they were washing up. They had a large camper van and we were discussing the pros and cons of camper vans against caravans. We had almost bought a camper van instead of a new caravan, but didn't want to be stranded on sites with no transport. A lot of people have bikes to get about, which is great, but we didn't think that was practical for us and the dogs. Neither of them was small enough or indeed well behaved enough to sit in a basket at the front of a bike.

Clive explained that they had been enjoying this life for a couple of years and they towed a Smart car with them to use during their stay. We later realised this was quite common practice and what a good idea if you were staying for a month or two. We asked whereabouts they were on the site and they explained they were near to the site road next to Hazel the hairdresser. What, we have our own hairdresser on site? Yes, she is English and once you've made an appointment she will come to your pitch and do your hair in the sun for a small fee. This place was getting better every day! Her husband Mike is apparently a really nice chap who will teach you windsurfing. What a couple.

Not wanting to miss the heat, we sat in the sun until three and then walked on the beach, even though I was feeling quite groggy. I went to reception at five and was amazed to see about thirty campers, giving their pitch number and name, but we still had no post.

Friday night was "fish and chip" night at the restaurant and they were served with mushy peas and a drink for seven euros. Excellent. On the way back, we rang Brian's cousin Dave and his wife Gill but they were engaged. How dare they! I was still a bit mardy so we made our way back to the caravan and I had another early night. I know what you're thinking – if she gets any more early nights, she'll have sleeping sickness!

Saturday 20th December 2003.

Gorgeous day but I felt awful and although I hadn't got flu, I did have a bad cold. I know that's another woman thing, we get colds but men always get flu. How sad.

Brian went up to our small supermarket and treated us to a Saturday newspaper which I read from cover to cover. When we were working full-time, it was very rare that either of us got the time to read much of the daily paper, even though we had one delivered. One of the great things about being retired is having the time to read every article if you want to.

Tucked up for the rest of the day after taking a couple of tablets, good old Brian took the dogs for their walk and then came back and made meatballs in his own garlic and tomato sauce, and he cooked some garlic bread and spaghetti to have with them. It was very spicy which I felt would be good for my cold.

Early evening, Brian rang his Dad Harry and apparently it had been raining most of the day in Congleton. Well I never!

Sunday 21st December 2003.

I stayed in bed until ten thirty and got up to a really warm sunny day, too good a drying day to miss. Brian went to the supermarket for the Sunday paper whilst I got on with washing a few loads in my faithful Wonderwash. As people passed, I'm sure they were expecting music to eventually come out, as the winding action I had to do was reminiscent of the old gramophones.

Brian had rigged up a washing line for me across the corner of our pitch and I soon had lots of clean but quite damp clothes hanging out to dry.

As I sat down for a coffee with Brian on his return, Barbara came round for a chat. She and John were walking down to Mar de Cristal and would we like to go with them? I thanked her for the offer but after not feeling well the last couple of days I thought I would just take it easy today. It's amazing how easily I had slipped into this retirement lark at my age. I'd only done a bit of washing and was now ready for a rest! When I was working full-time a few months ago, I would be washing, ironing, feeding the dogs and ringing my Mum all at the same time, and still have the energy to go shopping later!

Whilst Barbara was chatting to Brian about England's terrible performance at cricket, I was squeezing more water from the clothes on the line. She said she had bought a spin dryer here in Spain the previous year; otherwise it takes days for the washing to dry. I went round to see it and was very impressed at its size and weight and apparently they were only about £100.

I went back home to Brian and we talked about whether it would be worth investing in one and we agreed it would. Not only would it save on launderette bills but also it would make life easier if the clothes dried quicker. Decision made we would buy one the next day.

After sitting in the sun discussing the news from England in today's paper until gone three o'clock, I felt much better and said I fancied resuming my daily walk exercise with Jack and Jill. I am not one of life's natural fitness folk and have to be nudged into any form of exertion and I mean any! Earlier this year I had joined a local gym with Brian but after two months of going twice a week, I had to confess that I only ever used the massage therapy chair, and then had a shower and came home saying how much better I felt after a good work out! I cancelled my membership and stopped feeling guilty immediately.

Today's tea was chicken with walnuts and pomegranates. Pam's Mediterranean cookbook was well thumbed, and bits of grease and dried onion remained on most of the pages that I had followed. Brian got the task of cracking the walnuts and when one rolled onto the floor, Jill picked it up, cracked it with her teeth and patiently took out every bit of nut, ate it, and discarded the shell. If we could train her to crack them and take out the nut without eating it, she may have come in useful for this recipe.

It was almost eight o'clock when we sat down to this wonderful meal and we splashed out on two bottles of wine to celebrate my recovery – who needs an excuse?

Monday 22nd December 2003.

Almost Christmas and the sun was out again. We were up and off to the gym and swimming quite early as we wanted to go shopping and try to buy a spin dryer.

We found just the one and paid out one hundred and sixty

euros and brought it home together with a reasonable shop from the supermarket. This included a turkey crown, some cheap champagne for Christmas Day, pigs in blankets and we finally purchased a light for the awning.

On our way back we called at the Chinese restaurant opposite the Mercadona supermarket and we paid ten euros deposit for New Year's Eve. We had agreed we would like Christmas dinner at home in the sun if possible but New Year's Eve we would treat ourselves to a meal out. Several people we had spoken to recommended this Chinese so we were booked in!

Later in the afternoon I drove to the Internet Café and sent Christmas greetings to everyone. I was thrilled to open an e-mail Christmas card from my oldest (as in known her longest) mate Gill. I had never seen one before and I think it was probably musical but there was no sound switched on at the Internet Café. There was also an e-mail from another mate Gill (from work) and I was shocked to hear that my former boss and friend Julia had been made redundant. Gill said that Julia was fine with the decision and was having a few weeks rest before deciding what she was going to do.

On my way back I called at reception and was delighted that not only had the bit for the barbecue arrived but also a couple of cards and a letter.

When I got home, I let Brian open the package with the adapter in and I opened the cards. Christmas cards from Janet and Pam, and a letter from Janet telling me all the latest news about the school where she teaches, and also what Jake and Connor had been up to. I read the letter a few times as it made me laugh and Brian was quite giddy with the part that had arrived and we finally had a barbecue that we could use.

I told him about Julia and he was shocked but said I should give her a ring one night to make sure she was OK. We had been friends through work since I started there over fifteen years ago. Julia had lost her partner Mark to meningitis less than two years ago, so I knew Christmas was going to be especially hard for her again this year.

Whilst Brian was making a meat and potato pie not out of Pam's book but the one out of his memory like his Mum used to make, I went to the phone to ring my Mum. We had quite a long chat and I was telling her all my news and about the new friends we were making. She was worrying about whether everyone would like what she'd bought them for Christmas and did I think a Marks and

Spencer's medium shirt would fit my Dad? How the hell would I know! But this was the part of Christmas that I wasn't missing – the worry and the build up to two days of overeating, too much drink and a Visa bill to make your hair curl in January!

On my return home, Brian asked me two things – could I make a crust for his pie no problem and what was the weather like in England. He couldn't believe that I had been on the phone nearly an hour and hadn't asked if it was raining. Who gives a damn?

After tea, we both reflected on what a lovely day we'd had and how we were now dropping into our conversations suggestions for "when we come back next year". I wondered if I was enjoying it more because I was looking forward to my Mum and Dad coming on January 6th, but it seemed more than that. We found everyone so friendly and helpful and it was like living in a sunny community where everyone had the same amount of possessions and lived the same sort of relaxed life. All we knew was we were looking forward to Christmas without the possibility of snow or an overdraft!

Tuesday 23rd December 2003.

Wind during the night meant a cold start to the day. However, it did get nicer as the day progressed. Tuesday was Keep Fit day and I was there again.

We then drove to Los Belones market, had a look at the stalls but didn't buy anything, and then had a coffee in the square.

Yesterday, we had bought a bulb to go with the light that we got at the Ferreteria. But it was the wrong size so we took it back and exchanged it for the correct one.

I was disappointed that I didn't have much washing as I was looking forward to trying out my new spin dryer, but decided to wait a day or two.

Brian, on the other hand, was able to use the barbecue at last. It was quite small but came with a griddle and a grill and the lid could be turned upside down and used as a wok. This is what he made paella in and it was great.

After a late walk down the beach I rang Janet and managed to gossip for over half an hour so that when I got back the washing up had all been done. What a shame.

As we sat in the awning admiring our new light, our friend Derek walked past, dragging his dog! He stopped for a chat as the dog was in no mood to go anywhere, and he mentioned that his daughter and her boyfriend were coming over on the 21st of January and would need some accommodation on the site.

We had both noticed at the bottom of our "avenue" was a Spanish bungalow which had a notice on "Se alquilar" which Derek informed me meant "To rent". Apparently Derek could speak some Spanish and when I explained that my Mum and Dad would also be looking for somewhere, he offered to ring the telephone number given and arrange a viewing for us both. What a good idea.

Ten minutes later Derek came back round to say that the owner, Diego, lived in Cartegena and would meet us at the bungalow at ten o'clock tomorrow morning.

Wednesday 24th December 2003.

Diego arrived on time and we were waiting at the bungalow. Derek was very competent with his conversational Spanish and, after we had been shown round the two bedrooms, lounge, bathroom and kitchen, the owner advised us that the rent was the equivalent of £30 per night, regardless of occupancy. The bungalow was free on the dates we required and there would be just one day between our respective families' visits so Diego said his wife would clean the bungalow and change the bedding on that date.

After handing over our deposits and getting a receipt, we shook hands with Diego and he said he would meet me there at nine o'clock on the morning of January 6th to hand over the keys. He reminded me very much of Walter Matthau and he seemed a very nice chap.

On my return home I told Brian that I had booked the bungalow for Mum and Dad, and we agreed to pay the rent. This was because my Dad had built some decking for us at our new home and although we had paid for the materials, he refused to accept anything for all his hard work, labour and travelling. I would keep this for a surprise when they arrived.

I couldn't resist any longer and soon had a small washer load spinning round in the sunshine on my table. After rinsing, they went into the spin dryer and came out two minutes later almost dry. Fantastic. Whilst I was doing this, Brian was smiling to himself. He explained this had just brought back memories of this second wife Liz's late father, as he used to do all the spin drying at home when

Brian and Liz lived with them years before, when they were first married.

It seemed strange to think it was Christmas Eve and we were still wearing shorts and T-shirts. Our usual walk down the beach seemed extra special as Christmas was almost here.

The barbecue was in demand again and we had two large pieces of steak, medium to well done, with salad and potatoes.

Barbara came over to ask if we would like to borrow any DVDs to play on our laptop. She said they had quite a lot with them so we walked to their motor home a few pitches away and Brian selected around half a dozen thriller type films to watch when we got time! Don't ask where the time goes it just does. And all the fresh air seems to make us more tired than we would be at home.

Usually on Christmas Eve, I don't sleep very well, as I am too excited about Santa coming! Believe it or believe it not, I was almost thirteen before I found out there wasn't a Santa. Janet and Christopher who are eighteen months and four years younger than me knew years before I did. My Mum and Dad had to make them promise not to tell me. I told you I live in a bit of a fantasy world.

So it was 1970 when Santa brought me some roller skates and I went into the street with them on, only to be told by Michael Fox, who was two years older than me, that there was no such person as Santa and that my Mum and Dad bought everything. I was mortified and went straight back into the house to ask Janet and she confirmed it! All these years waking up with a pillow case filled with toys, dragging them all into Mum and Dad's bedroom and shouting. "Look what he's bought me!" as though they had no idea. I still think it's wonderful for kids whilst they believe.

About seven years ago when Janet's boys were around five and eight, they were stopping with Janet and Jimmy at our house for Christmas. On Christmas morning, I went into Janet's bedroom about five o'clock and she was awake waiting for the boys to wake up. We both crept into the boys' room and tried not to giggle too loudly but were secretly furious that they were fast asleep on the most exciting morning of the year! They woke up soon after and I will never forget following them downstairs as they held onto each other asking "Do you think he's been?" Jake was at the age where he knew there wasn't a Santa but he still wanted to believe and Connor was just convinced he did exist. It took them about five full minutes to pluck up the courage to go into the lounge, still holding hands. But as soon as they put the light on, all we could hear was

"Mum, he's been! Auntie Julie, look what he's left for us!" It was a magical moment that I will always remember.

Thursday 25th December 2003.

Santa's been. Well, he hasn't really, because we had agreed not to buy each other presents as we were now living on Brian's pension and it did seem a bit daft buying each other things when we had virtually everything we needed. However, I couldn't resist and had brought a funny book wrapped up for Brian to open but it was from the dogs not me.

Brian's cousin David and his wife Gill had given us a small gift before we left England as Gill said she couldn't bear to think of us having nothing to open at all! She obviously knows Brian well and guessed correctly that he wouldn't think to buy even a bar of chocolate for me to open. He's tight but predictable.

Also, before we left, my Mum had given me a Christmas card with strict instructions we must not open it until Christmas morning.

So at eight o'clock with a cup of tea each, Brian opened his book from the dogs. I think he was secretly very pleased with me for not spending much and just buying a token gift. He always felt he was competing when it came to present buying and as I've mentioned previously, he's a poor loser!

I opened Gill and David's present, which was a lovely handmade wooden calendar, which I will keep in the caravan so I know what the date is!

Finally, I opened my Mum and Dad's card and was speechless for a few seconds! Inside the card were the forms to sign for each of us to get £2,500 of premium bonds! I asked Brian to come and look as I thought it must be £250 but no, he confirmed I had read it correctly the first time. I said I thought it was too much, but wasn't at all surprised when Brian said we should accept them, otherwise my parents might be upset! He's all heart.

Knowing that Janet and Jimmy would have been given exactly the same, Brian did suggest I text Janet with "What a lovely gesture, £4000 of premium bonds each from Mum and Dad!" just to see if she believed me. Mum and Dad were stopping at Janet's so I said I would ring later and didn't text her in case they hadn't yet opened theirs.

Outside was very sunny, and everyone was wishing each other

"Felice NaviDad," which roughly translates as Merry Christmas. We were surprised to see the cleaners at work as usual, smiling and cheerful.

We had quite a few texts from family and friends and I was waiting for one from my Dad, as I knew my Mum had bought him a mobile phone for Christmas. Now he had never used one before so we didn't know what he would think. Also he is quite deaf (which like most older people he denies, saying we all mutter instead of speaking properly!), so it would be interesting to see if he liked it and if he could hear it.

Brian took the dogs for a morning walk to the beach but not before I had put some green tinsel around their collars. I prepared the vegetables whilst they were gone and it took ages, as everyone that passed by stopped to say Merry Christmas and have a chat.

At twelve we went to the phones, armed with phone cards to call everyone. Brian rang his lads Simon and Ian to wish them Merry Christmas. At twenty-nine, Simon was finally in his first teaching post. He had studied at Lancaster for some years and achieved his master's degree. Illness had held his career up for a couple of years but he was now in good health and living only two miles from us. He was teaching at Kirby Lonsdale and had met another teacher, Lorraine, whom he seemed quite smitten with. She was from Scotland and was very easy to get on with, and it was the happiest we had seen Simon for some years.

Ian, the youngest at twenty-six, was a different lad altogether! Still living at home in Wakefield with his long-suffering Mum, he was at last working hard and earning an honest living. He had fallen by the wayside in his youth, and let's just say that Brian being in the police force ensured he could keep an eye on Ian's most recent escapades. Luckily, he was now doing really well and we were proud of the way he had changed his life around.

We rang Mum and Dad at Janet's, and Harry who was at Pam and Gary's for the day. It was great to share the chatter about who got what but even better to hear how cold it was over there! We couldn't help mentioning that we would be having lunch outside wearing our best shorts.

Lunch was served at two, and we had everything we usually had on Christmas Day, except I couldn't find any Christmas crackers, and there were only seven sprouts left when I bought them so we had three and a half each. The two bottles of bubbly were very nice and we were pleased we hadn't got a pudding, as we didn't have room for any.

Later on we phoned Gill and Dave and then we came back home and rounded the day off with coffee and marzipan sweets.

By eight o'clock, Brian said he didn't feel well and went to bed feeling sick. I didn't think it could be anything we'd eaten as I was fine but it could have been the fizzy drink, which he's not used to. Whereas I've always led a champagne lifestyle!

Friday 26th December 2003.

Boxing Day already and it started off cool but became sunnier after lunch. Brian had been up in the night being sick but was feeling a bit better now. He didn't get up until eleven, so I made him boiled eggs with soldiers to dip in! This is one of the "comfort" foods that I associate with being poorly along with Heinz tomato soup and stew and dumplings. One thing that I never liked was Lucozade and I can remember when we were young my Mum used to buy it as a treat if we were ill as it was very expensive, but I didn't like the taste at all. Sorry Mum!

Just before mid-day, Joop came past and said "Don't forget to be on the beach at twelve". "OK" we replied without thinking! What was he talking about? A minute later, Corrie came round. She asked if we were going to the beach and explained there was a sponsored swim for charity setting off at twelve, and everyone turns out to cheer the swimmers on. There must have been about four hundred people on the beach and maybe ten brave souls who were going to swim in the Mar Menor. Out to sea on a small boat, was a man dressed as Santa waving at us. He was the destination for the swimmers and at twelve o'clock, a whistle blew and they were off. We recognised one of the participants as Hazel the hairdresser's husband Mike, and he was dressed up as Santa!

Because the Mar Menor is so shallow, it was more like a sponsored paddle, but it was all in a good cause and there were several volunteers on the beach with collection tins for the English children's charities which stood to benefit. We heard later that around a thousand pounds had been raised. Well done.

Our walk was through the fields near the beach so the dogs didn't get wet. Usually, if they had been swimming, we had to wash them off with warm water when we got back and then, after towelling them dry we would put their beds in front of the fan heater in the awning which would help to dry their coats.

Turkey pasta was a light meal for tea after eating like pigs on Christmas Day, and we settled down with some wine and decided to watch one of the DVDs that John had lent us.

This was a new experience for us and we opened the laptop and positioned it so we could each lie on the settees and see the screen. We put the disc in and pressed "Play" and the film started. After a few seconds I asked Brian if he could hear it. No he couldn't, so I tried to adjust the volume on the computer. We seemed to be on full volume but were both straining to hear what was going on! After half an hour we gave it up as a bad job as we had no idea what was happening in the film and Brian was annoying me as he is a bit deaf and every few minutes was asking "What did he just say?"

More wine and we stayed up quite late just talking and drinking. Some of our friends have asked how we manage without a television for weeks on end and are interested to know what we actually do in a confined space and what we find to talk about without falling out. Well, I would say that this lifestyle is only suitable for couples who are very compatible and, more importantly who are at ease in each other's company without conversation. We can sit together reading our books or me playing Scrabble for a few hours in the evening with just the odd conversation like "Do you fancy a drink?" or "Shall we have some supper?"

If one of you is not happy with this type of life then it's not going to work for any length of time. Luckily we love it and we also enjoy "people watching". We can sit outside and say hello to passing fellow campers and then we will analyse them each saying what we think like "He seems a lot younger than her. I bet it's her second marriage" or "She's very friendly but he's a bit miserable maybe he doesn't speak much English or he might just be quite shy". We can have these discussions for hours and quite enjoy discovering our different opinions.

Almost midnight before we got to bed – would I ever recover from such a late night?

Saturday 27th December 2003.

Happy Birthday Pam. Brian's sister is forty-nine today and I had left her present and card before we set off.

As it was very warm I decided to do some washing. Brian went up to the gym leaving me to get on with some work. When he got back an hour and a half later, I had only washed about half a dozen things! I don't know why but I spent most of the morning talking to people as they passed by. This was an ideal pitch to meet people and pass the time of day as everyone seemed to stop and chat, but not a good spot if you needed to "crack on". Fortunately, the pace of life is so laid back, no one is in a rush to go anywhere or do anything so it doesn't matter how long it takes to do the washing.

On our way back from the afternoon walk we stopped at the phone booth and I rang Pam to wish her a happy birthday.

Barbecue for tea included some spicy Spanish sausages, which were lovely, and some very cheap sangria to wash it down.

Later, as we settled down for the evening after our showers, my mobile phone beeped and I was thrilled when it indicated that I'd had a text – from my Dad! I was with my Mum in October when she had bought my Dad the mobile, and I made a note of the telephone number from the box and put it into my phone ready to text him. Opening the message I was not surprised to find that he had typed his message using deliberately miss-spelt words as that's just my Dad's daft sense of humour. The message read "Wee R howm frome Janits hat mancheystur hand hits bin rayning".

I realised that this was going to be how my Dad's messages would be typed and because we have a very similar sense of humour, I would soon be able to understand them.

My reply was something along the lines of "Message received and understood! Welcome to the world of texting, Dad. Tell Mum I will ring her in next few days or if you text me to say you are in, I can go to phone and ring her. Merry Xmas. Love from me xx"

Five minutes later, another message received. Again this was from my Dad, but when I read it, it was exactly the same message as the first one so I ignored it. Within the next ten minutes, the same message was sent to me again. So I texted him back to say "Stop sending the same message – I heard you the first time – I'm not deaf!"

Ten minutes later – I received it again! So I then texted Janet, to tell her to ring him up and explain you only send each message once. This must have worked, as I didn't get it again. Whose stupid idea was it to get him a mobile? Oh yes, it was mine.

Sunday 28th December 2003.

We were woken up around five this morning by some activity in the pitch belonging to our neighbours to our left. They were a German couple who didn't speak English and they were both in their late seventies. Although they would both say "Good Morgan", that was about the extent of their socialising. An ambulance was outside their motor home and as we watched through our awning curtains, the gentleman walked into the ambulance and was driven away.

At least we knew he was walking so we assumed he wasn't at deaths door. After a cup of tea we went back to sleep until nine when we woke to another really sunny day. I thought today would be a good day to colour my hair and cover up the ever-increasing grey.

Whilst I was in the shower rooms, Barbara came in and I asked her what was wrong with our neighbour. She said he'd had a small stroke and had been taken into hospital for a few days.

An hour later I looked ten years younger or so Brian told me! No sign of any grey hair but my dressing gown was ruined. I had not secured the old towel I was using around my shoulders so the dye had gone all over the collar of my thick white full-length dressing gown. On reflection this was the most impractical item I had brought to Spain. Everyone else seemed to wear knee length, light-weight towelling, dark coloured wraps and Brian had commented that I looked like some old failed drama queen from the fifties, swanning around like Barbara Cartland's cleaner! Oh, how I love him!

A few hours sunbathing and reading The News Of The World whilst Brian washed the car. Luxury.

Although I wasn't cooking a Sunday dinner, I thought we could have a whole chicken cooked on the barbecue with the wok part inverted to act as a lid, as shown on the box that the barbecue came in! It did take almost three hours to cook but it was worth waiting for, and we had some nice fresh green beans, carrots and cabbage to go with it.

We had still not watched a film so we thought we'd have another go. Once again we set up the laptop, settled down with a drink and put the DVD in. This time, there was no sound at all, so the next half an hour we spent each trying to find a volume button and blaming one another for being so thick we couldn't even set it up to watch a film.

Brian became increasingly frustrated and stormed off into the awning in a temper! I was snuggled up warm in the caravan with Jack and Jill so I didn't bother following him to see if he was all right- I just left him to his own company! He very rarely is bad tempered, more often than not he is in a very silly mood and annoys me first thing on a morning when I'm trying to wake up and he is singing, whistling and messing about. The odd occasions when he's in a mood I find it's best to leave him to come round himself, which he usually does very quickly. We have never gone to bed not speaking and would honestly say that since we met in 1987 we have had less than a dozen "arguments". Brian's Mum Joan always used to say "Never go to bed on an argument – stay up and fight!"

Also, there was lots of cheap red wine in the awning so I knew he could have a few drinks if it made him feel better!

Monday 29ᵗʰ December 2003.

What a lovely warm night for Jack, Jill and me. I had let them sleep on the bed with me and I heard Brian getting into bed about four o'clock, moaning that he had fallen asleep in the awning after drinking loads of cheap red wine and was now frozen and had a terrible headache. Ha ha serves him right, and I pretended to be asleep.

The bedding and towels were ready for a wash so I dropped them off at the launderette and then went swimming. I was back for ten thirty and Brian still hadn't got up so I took the car and went to the Mercadona to do some shopping.

It's amazing how you soon get used to driving on the right hand side of the road and how familiar you become with the rules at junctions and roundabouts.

My most confusing experience whilst on the road was the drive down the Strip. It is a dual carriageway and there are road signs showing no U-turns onto the opposite side of the road so how could you get across to come back? There didn't appear to be any roundabouts for miles. On one of our first drives down the Strip we parked up and watched how others got across. There were what looked like bus lanes at frequent intervals, and we realised these were side roads for you to pull into on your right, then you came to a stop sign and traffic lights. When your green light showed, traffic on both sides of the dual carriageway stopped so you could drive across the road and turn round. It now seemed simple but at first it was baffling.

When I got back Brian was up and preparing a rabbit casserole for tea. As usual he had been listening to Spectrum Radio which has world news every hour, and he told me the sad news that Bob Monkhouse had died. It always seems extra sad to me when people that make us laugh die. Tonight seemed to get darker earlier and the sky was bright red. As my Dad always said "Red sky at night – shepherds cottage on fire!"

With my most patient head on, after tea I tried the DVD in the computer again and it took me a few minutes to work out why there was no sound – one of us has pressed "mute". I wonder which one of us that would have been? So, with quiet but audible sound we watched a very forgettable film. Just before bedtime I texted my Dad to tell him what we had been up to.

Tuesday 30ᵗʰ December 2003.

Tuesday already. These Keep Fit days seem to come round quickly. As usual, whilst I was at Keep Fit Brian went to the gym. The lady at the gym was always very pleasant but couldn't speak English so Brian was trying to strike up conversations with her about whether the gym would be closed for the bank holiday. Needless to say, he had no idea what she had said and he was none the wiser. She probably thought he was asking her out and for all we knew she could be meeting him in the bar later! We must at least get a phrase book for next year.

After collecting my washing from the launderette, we drove to Cabo De Palos and walked along the harbour. It was a lovely setting and on such a sunny day it seemed a shame not to stop for a light lunch. We had sardines, garlic prawns and a salad. I am not a salad lover – but I will pick out onions and any tomatoes without their hard "middle" bits in. How's that for awkward?

Calling at the Upper on the way back we bought quite a few extras like a new pillow for Brian's sweaty head and a large casserole dish for when Mum and Dad come.

Back home, Brian said he would pop round to John and Barbara's for the up to date cricket commentary and to ask John why we couldn't hear the films properly. It turned out that we needed two small speakers to get better sound, and John thought we already had some. Brian explained how gormless we were when it comes to computers so John leant us his speakers so we could watch another film, and he said he would go with Brian to get a couple of speakers in a day or two.

I went up to reception and at last – we had mail! A parcel had arrived which I took home and opened rather hurriedly. I knew it was from my Mum but I wasn't sure what was in it. There was a rather disjointed letter written in several different pens over a few days from Mum with lots of news about the weather and how her hair was looking without me being there to do it for her.

Inside the parcel were a video of recent "Coronation Streets," "Eastenders" and "Emmerdale" and a recording of the Christmas pantomime from Empire Stores where I used to work. Every Christmas, the managers and team leaders would put on a show for the staff to watch whilst they were having their Christmas lunch. For quite a few years, I had been responsible for writing a play or script for the Christmas show and when I had left in July, my fellow team leaders said they would miss me but would do their best to come up with ideas for the show without me.

I really enjoyed watching their production of "The Weakest Link" and it was nice to spot lots of friends in the recently refurbished canteen. Apparently, my Dad had made the podiums for the show. He still came in handy even though I didn't work there! One of the women I worked with, Sheila, lived next door to my Mum and Dad and she knew he wouldn't mind helping out. It was Sheila who had thought to video the show to send to me and it really meant a lot that she had been so thoughtful.

Also in the parcel were several things I had mentioned to my Mum that we were finding difficult to buy: - a potato masher, an oven glove, some nappy sacks (which we use as poo bags for the dogs), a spare fitted bottom sheet for the fixed bed and some pot pourri to hang in the wardrobe! There were also some items I had not requested like the glittery Santa tea towel and matching pan stand, but gratefully accepted.

Just soup for tea after our nice lunch out and we were all ready for a film at seven o'clock. At last all set up with John's speakers we could now hear the sound.

We sat through two hours of the most badly acted, poorly scripted B movie we could imagine but at least we knew what they were saying so we were able to follow the ludicrous plot!

Still only nine o'clock, so it would be eight in England. I texted my Dad to see if they were in and he texted me back almost immediately but the message was blank. A few minutes later I received the same blank message so I assumed that they must be in if he was using his mobile.

At the phone booth, I rang Mum and thanked her for the parcel and letter, etc. I asked her to get Sheila next door to give my Dad some lessons with his phone as I explained he was being charged for sending blank messages to Spain. Unless this was his way of telling me he'd lost his voice?

Wednesday 31st December 2003.

It was quite early when John called to see if Brian wanted to go to the computer shop down the Strip to buy a couple of speakers for the laptop. They were off before we knew it. John and Barbara have a camper van and bikes but no car whilst they are here. But they are friends with Marie and Richard and when they go home for Christmas, John takes them to the airport in their car and they let John and Barbara use it whilst they are back in England.

Whilst they were out I enjoyed a quiet half-hour sitting in the sun having a cup of tea and reading the previous day's newspaper.

In the afternoon I gave Brian a hair cut, but he didn't let me near his sideburns as he had decided to grow a beard whilst we were in Spain, and he took ages trimming it and shaping it!

New Year's Eve was never one of my favourite days of the year. In my younger days, I was a disc jockey for ten years and consequently was always working until one and two in the morning on this day. Now that I could enjoy myself without working, I was looking forward to our meal at the Chinese.

At seven o'clock I rang Janet and they were all OK and then I called Julia. She was really pleased to hear from me and we had a good chat. She didn't seem upset about the redundancy and was looking forward to taking her time finding a job that she really wanted, as opposed to needed. I wished her Happy New Year and told her we were both thinking about her.

Putting make-up on for the first time in weeks seemed strange, but we both looked well when we went out. We were both a little apprehensive about leaving Jack and Jill in the caravan whilst we were out. Jack had been quite destructive up until about a year ago, so we weren't at all confident that they would be OK. We did agree that if the dogs were staying in the caravan whilst we were out, we wouldn't lock the door just in case there was a fire. Don't ask me why we thought there might be a fire as we're confident that neither Jack nor Jill smokes, but I wanted to know that they could both be rescued easily.

So we enjoyed a lovely banquet at the restaurant. It was a set menu of eight different dishes plus rice and noodles, wine and champagne and liqueurs and we thoroughly enjoyed it. But by half past ten we were both feeling tired and I am ashamed to say we couldn't stay awake for the midnight toast and were home for eleven! We need not have worried as Jack and Jill seemed to have been asleep since we left and were both fine. No sign of a fire!

I put my pyjamas on and we opened a bottle of champagne and drank a toast together. We managed to stay up until midnight but were asleep within a few minutes. Brian had driven so I could have a drink so it would be my turn next time we went out and he never forgets when it's my turn to drive! Like most men, he is quite critical of my driving, until I am picking him up or driving when he's had a few drinks and then I suddenly become the best woman driver he has ever seen. How strange!

Thursday 1st January 2004.

Happy New Year. Well, it serves me right! Have I got a hangover, or what? I did manage to struggle outside and sit in the sun for a few hours with endless glasses of tonic water. Brian had to take the dogs on his own and make meatballs for tea. I was pretty useless apart from going to the phone to ring Mum.

Everyone that passed wished us Happy New Year, and Brian took great delight in mentioning to most people that I was suffering with a bad head as I didn't know when to stop drinking.

During the afternoon my "visitor" arrived, so I felt a little more justified in being pathetic and lazy.

John came round to help Brian connect the speakers to the laptop. Strictly speaking he didn't "help" Brian – he did it all himself whilst Brian watched him!

Brian rang his Dad and we settled down to watch the video of soaps which Mum had sent. It was nice to catch up with the story lines.

Friday 2nd January 2004.

A breezy but sunny day and I was feeling much better, so I did some spring-cleaning. Brian went to the gym and when he got back I was polishing everything and shampooing the carpet, cleaning the awning and ground sheet and doing washing in between. By the end of the day I was shattered but felt much better. Cleaning can blow away the cobwebs and make me feel wonderful. How sad!

After a nice easy spaghetti Bolognese tea, we watched another one of John's films and were in bed for nine.

Saturday 3rd January 2004.

Behind our pitch was an English bloke called Chris who had a chat with Brian most mornings when he came to the sinks to empty his coffee percolator. He was staying in a camper van and also had a tent set up on his pitch. We thought at first that he was on his own, but it turned out his wife Dawn and two kids were here but they were renting a static caravan on the next avenue. Her father was a retired policeman who was also staying on this site, whilst looking for a property to buy in this area of Spain. It all seemed a bit confusing and complicated to me.

After breakfast, we drove to the Portman Guns. This was only about ten minutes drive, but you had to park the car and then walk up a steep hill to see the guns which were like huge cannons. History is not one of my best subjects and I was struggling to look enthusiastic as Brian went into detail about how the cannons would have been loaded and what they were capable of doing. He was madly taking photographs of the cannons. I can not get my head round this type of photography! Why would anyone be interested in seeing an old cannon, just as I can't understand why he takes lots of scenery without including a person. Anyway, he did ask me to be in one of the photos of the cannon but after four attempts at trying to climb astride it and looking like Billy Bunter on a bad day, I gave up and insisted he just took the cannon without me on it!

The walk back down the hill was much better than the walk up it and Jack and Jill enjoyed the exercise.

Brian dropped me off at the phone booths on the way home so I rang Mum. She was very excited about coming. I told her not to bring any dressing-up clothes and explained it was a very casual life-style and a nice tracksuit would be as posh as she would get.

As I approached our caravan, I could see that Brian was sunning himself and he was giggling like a schoolboy. He explained that as he'd sat there, someone had brought an old saucepan, a rusty old table and some plastic plates to throw away and had put them on the floor to the side of the bins. Within a minute, three different people had been round, examined them and between them had taken all three items of rubbish! He said they were like a plague of locusts, and was fascinated that anyone would want to take someone's discarded trash. It takes all sorts!

Pork and Spanish sausage casserole with mashed potatoes, green beans and carrots rounded off a tiring day for all of us.

Sunday 4th January 2004.

Could the weather get any better? It was a gorgeous day again and must have been around twenty-two degrees, which we thought was great for January.

We had boiled eggs and soldiers and whilst we were drinking our tea, Barbara called and invited us to the Chinese restaurant for their Chinese New Year party which was on January 21st. There were quite a few others going and it sounded a good night so we said we'd love to go. What a pity Mum and Dad were leaving the day before, otherwise they would have enjoyed that.

On such a warm day, we couldn't resist the walk down the beach, as we knew Jill would have a swim and she did. Whilst she was swimming after sticks that we were throwing in, Jack was fascinated by a seagull that was diving into the shallow waters and he was tiring himself out by chasing it.

Back home, we were catching the last afternoon rays and having a drink, when Clive and Karen called. They asked if we wanted any water fetching from the mountain in Los Belones. We told them we didn't know what they meant as we bought our drinking water at the shop. They explained there was no need – you just took your empty water containers to the bottom of the mountain and there was a tap where everyone got free pure water – except us 'cos we didn't know about it!

They brought us a five-litre bottle back and it was lovely. This also explained why we had seen people rooting empty water containers out of the bins.

I made a beef and chickpea curry, which was loosely based on a recipe from the Mediterranean cookbook and was very spicy. I explained this would balance out the binding qualities of the boiled eggs we had for breakfast but in reality my hand had slipped with the chilli powder and mustard seeds! Lots of mountain water to cool our tongues.

Monday 5th January 2004.

Mum and Dad would be here tomorrow so whilst Brian was at the gym I did some washing and a quick tidy round before going to the Upper to get a "welcome pack" for their arrival. I got them some coffee, tea, bread, butter and jam, wine and cold drinks, lots of chocolate and marzipan for my Dad's sweet tooth and plenty of loo rolls for my Mum's big bum!

When I got back, Brian was round at John's having a "lesson" on how to use the computer and was being shown how to make a CD of his favourite tracks.

Barbara stopped for a chat and told me that Corrie, who takes Keep Fit, had flown back to Holland, as her father was ill. I had been looking forward to introducing Mum to Corrie but maybe this was not to be. I had thought about Mum coming to Keep Fit with me to see if she could do some of the exercises, but that would now be put on hold until Corrie came back to Spain.

After walking the dogs in the fields, we got back and Derek came round to say he'd got a message for me from Diego who we were hiring the bungalow from. Apparently he couldn't meet me tomorrow, the sixth, as it was a bank holiday – "Dia de Reyes" or Epiphany. He would meet me today at five at the bungalow so I went to reception and withdrew the cash to pay him. We met as arranged and he handed over the keys and did a final tour round showing me where things were and how various fixtures worked.

Later I went round with my welcome pack and put the fridge on and made sure it looked welcoming.

Brian made sweet and sour pork for tea whilst I went to the Internet Café and replied to my e-mails.

What a busy day we'd had. Is this really retirement? Yes and it's great!

Bank holiday or not, Mum and Dad were coming today! We drove to Alicante airport where parking was no problem as the signs were clear and you paid on leaving for the time you had been parked.

Their flight landed twenty minutes early and they both looked tired and in need of some rest and sunshine.

We chatted all the way back to the site and after ninety minutes we were home. Mum was quite excited about seeing our winter lifestyle, and was eager to see the accommodation I had reserved for them. Firstly we went to our caravan and had a cup of tea in the sunshine. Dad had a coffee, as he doesn't drink tea. Then we walked down to their Spanish bungalow with their luggage, which took us less than a minute.

They were very pleased with my choice and Mum was immediately wanting to sort out what she owed me for the deposit I had paid and asking who she was to pay the balance to. I told her there were to be no arguments as Brian and I had paid it all, to repay my Dad for his weeks of hard work back home. Both of them tried to argue but it was no good, our decision was final!

Dad was unpacking the "welcome pack" which I had bought for them I could see his eyes lighting up when he saw the chocolates and marzipan sweets. The inside of the bungalow was very pleasant but not posh and Dad was having a look at the washer and cooker to see how they worked.

During our many telephone conversations prior to them arriving, I had repeatedly told Mum not to bring any dressed-up clothes, as she wouldn't need them. I had explained this is a very laid-back lifestyle where we tend to wear casual dress, tracksuit bottoms, T-shirts, fleeces, etc and although I had an iron in the caravan, I had never used it! How many women dream of a world with no ironing? Except my Mum who still irons dusters, dishcloths and knickers! My Dad says she's short of something to do and he's probably right!

She opened her suitcase and the first thing that emerged was a lovely cerise pink skirt and matching jacket with diamante trim. Several other similar outfits followed this and the look on my face must have said it all. Mum was muttering things like "Well, you never know where you might be going" and I assured her that, wherever she had in mind we wouldn't be going! Luckily, Janet had bought her a new tracksuit for Christmas and Mum had a couple of different tops to go with it. I felt sure this would be worn most days.

After unpacking, we walked up to the indoor pool and had a look at the supermarket. It was a lovely day and I think the sunshine made them both feel better. We sat outside during the afternoon and several of our friends called and welcomed them to Spain.

For our meal we went down to the site restaurant and enjoyed three courses and drinks for less than forty euros. Very good value. Dad insisted on paying and we had to agree to Mum and Dad paying for the supermarket shopping whilst they were here, as I had said I would make the meals for us all each night. Of course, we would eat out some nights but generally we would enjoy a home cooked "Mediterranean" evening meal in our awning.

An early night was in order as the travelling can be tiring, so after the meal we walked home and called at the phone booths to ring Janet and let her know that they had arrived safely.

Wednesday 7th January 2004.

By half past nine we had showered, had breakfast and still no sign of Mum and Dad- so I went round to see if they were OK. They were just getting up! Dad likes to stay in bed and when he retired seven years ago at 65, he said the thing he was most looking forward to was not having to get up each morning. But Mum is a different matter. She is usually up in the night for a few hours as she can't sleep, then she'll go back to bed in the early hours after watching a recording of "Murder She Wrote" then she's up again at seven drinking tea. She would describe this as a "good nights sleep" as she'd only got up once in the night.

Anyway, I was surprised that Mum was still in bed at this time, but they were both fine and had slept well, although Mum was a bit cold. She emerged from the bed wearing more clothes than she'd worn to travel in. A long-sleeved nightie over her vest and pants, thick bed socks and a cardigan Dad always joked that she's never get raped as he would have forgotten what he was doing by the time he got all her night clothes off!

I helped her get dressed whilst Dad went into the kitchen to make a drink. He quickly discovered that there were no cups or mugs and no kettle! So we settled for some fruit juice as there were about thirty glasses in the cupboard. I began to realise that although the bungalow was very pretty and authentic as a Spanish holiday home, it was quite impractical for Mum's needs.

The one electric heater was not very powerful. Dad said he'd switched it on last night when they got home and the electric had fused. Luckily, John and Barbara were only next door and they sorted the trip switch out and the power was soon restored. Dad left the heater on all night to warm the place up and decided to leave it on for their whole stay.

The kitchen was very small and although there were two little stools under the table, it certainly was not big enough to sit down and enjoy a meal in. Outside, there was a lovely marble patio area with a table and four chairs, and a large statue, which was the centrepiece of a water feature. Beautiful bougainvillaea covered the overhead trellis but this meant that the whole area was in the shade. For the Spanish owners I would imagine that during the summer months when they would use their second home, they would need the shade to get out of the intense heat. However, for January when temperatures would be around 65-70 Fahrenheit, this outside area would be brilliant to sit in, if it wasn't in the shade. What a shame.

The other thing that I should have considered was Mum's failing eyesight. She has suffered from glaucoma for around twenty years and although she has received fantastic care under the National Health Service, her eyesight is deteriorating and there is little that can be done. She struggles to see steps, unless the edges of them are clearly defined and I now realised that the kitchen in the bungalow was down three steps, and the door from the lounge onto the patio also led onto three steps. The kitchen steps would stop her getting up in the night to make a cup of tea, as she wouldn't be safe. Dad had a brainwave, and using some bright red tape that we had in the caravan, he edged each step with the tape so Mum could see them.

It was quite a cloudy day so we went to the supermarket to buy food and some mugs for Mum's kitchen. Dad had decided they could boil a pan of water for cups of tea and coffee but the grill wasn't working on the cooker so he bought a toaster to use whilst they were here. He said we could have it when they went home, as we didn't have one.

Brian went to the gym and then he took the dogs for a walk whilst we were shopping.

For tea I made lemon and garlic chicken – but didn't tell Dad about the garlic as he thinks he doesn't like it. We had the heating on in the caravan, and after tea in the awning, we went inside and played cards all night. It was lovely and warm and we enjoyed having some company and Brian enjoyed the cards as he won probably by cheating but at least he played.

It was nearly half past eleven when they went back to their bungalow and I knew we would sleep well after such a late night. I was disappointed that it had been cloudy but hopeful that the sun would return before long.

Thursday 8th January 2004.

A much better sunny day was on the horizon. I was just making a cup of tea when I heard the awning being unzipped and there she was – a vision to behold. Mother in her dressing gown! When I had told Mum over the phone to bring a decent dressing gown she didn't quite believe that people walked to the shower blocks in their nightwear to get washed and showered. It doesn't seem to happen on English sites. I know it's never really warm enough to swan about in your night shirt, but in England, people tend to get dressed to go to the showers, and then get dressed again to go back to their caravans. On reflection, this strikes me as quite bizarre.

We had a cup of tea in our warm caravan and Mum told me she had been a bit cold in the night but had slept reasonably well. The bungalow had its own bathroom with shower but it was not very inviting, so I had told Mum to call for me and I would take her to the shower rooms and show her how things worked.

After our showers, I dried Mum's hair for her and helped her get dressed. She commented that it would be an idea if they had a couple of stools or chairs for people to sit on whilst they were drying their feet etc. What a good idea. I would mention this the next time I was at reception, as they welcome comments and suggestions.

Brian went to the gym and the three of us went swimming and then had another shower! The pool was small but adequate for twenty minutes' exercise and the Jacuzzi was welcoming and warm. As usual, there were only two other people in the pool and the sun was shining overhead.

Some toast for breakfast, then we drove into Los Belones and had a look round the shops. We found a small local bakery and brought some cakes back for lunch. On the way home we drove towards the mountains and filled a few large water bottles as Clive had suggested.

We sat in the sun in the afternoon and Dad was content to do his puzzle book He enjoys doing "tsunami" puzzles, which appear to be a type of colouring-in, that eventually becomes a picture of something. Yes, I know how it sounds, but he is mentally sound, honest!

Our next door neighbour was brought home from hospital mid-afternoon by a friend and appeared to be all right. He was eighty years old but managed to walk unaided into his camper van.

Tea tonight was pork and sausage casserole, and we played cards again but only until ten thirty, as we were all quite tired after being in the sun.

Friday 9th January 2004.

No sign of Mum for her cup of tea so I went down to the bungalow to see if they were OK. Mum was just getting up and had hurt her back. She wasn't sure if it was sleeping in a different bed that had caused it, as she couldn't recall anything that would have hurt it. Anyway, she was OK- just having a bit of a moan.

About twelve years ago, Mum had a heart by-pass operation and again, she has received first class treatment from the National Health Service at all stages. She now is limited in the amount and type of exercise she can do, but one of the best things for her heart is gentle walking where it's flat. This site is ideal, so I suggested we walked up to the supermarket and back, which we did.

Our side of the site is mainly tourers and each "avenue" runs from one end of the campsite to the other. There are five "avenues" on this side, each with vans at both sides. It is very easy to get lost if you are not familiar with the layout, but there are sporadic signs to tell you which "block" you are on. Mum commented that you could go to the supermarket every day for the next two weeks and take a different route each time, and she's right. As we walked along, Mum was fascinated by the different ways people make their caravans homely, with flowers in tubs, signs hanging in front of their pitch telling you their names, and at several points there were hand made "street signs", like "Happy Oldies Avenue". We bought a few things in the supermarket and Mum insisted on getting Brian a Daily Mail even though it was two euros.

The fruit and vegetables are displayed in open boxes, and you weigh your own and put the printed ticket, including price, on the plastic bag. I thought this was a very "trusting" method as I pointed out that you could weigh your products, stick the label on, then add more items to your plastic bag before tying it up. Maybe I just have a suspicious mind?

Back home the sun was beckoning us to sit out, so I put our barbecue on, and cooked breakfast-cum-lunch of Spanish sausages, bacon and eggs.

The three of us had a game of Scrabble whilst Brian took the dogs for a walk on the beach. Mum and Dad both said they weren't bothered about dashing around sight seeing, they had come to relax in the sun and to see us, so that's what we intended doing.

Fish is not one of my favourite foods and I'm not ashamed to say I prefer fish from the fish shop as I know it won't have bones in. However, Brian loves fish and he was glad that my Mum had come as she likes fish but my Dad isn't keen, so she doesn't get much chance to have it at home. Tonight, Brian said he would make prawn cocktails for himself, Mum and Dad, then we would have a lasagne. We left Brian to make the starters with the frozen bag of king prawns we had bought at the supermarket and which were now defrosted.

We sat down for tea and as they began eating their starters, my Dad asked, "Are these prawns cooked?" I sprung to Brian's defence. "Of course they are, Dad, do you think he's stupid?" But, as I watched them eating the prawns in the sauce and lettuce, I did wonder. At home, we are used to buying frozen bags of "cooked and peeled prawns". But I realised that the ones we had bought were grey in colour, not pink. As they tucked into their food I decided it was best to change the subject and not confirm or discuss their doubts! I could see tomorrow's headlines – "Pensioners poisoned by their son-in law!"

After polishing off the lasagne, we sat talking and laughing, and when Mum and Dad left to go home, I had a quiet word with Mum about the prawns. She also thought they should have been cooked but didn't like to say anything, as Brian had put so much effort into preparing the prawn cocktails.

Saturday 10th January 2004.

A scorching day and what a joy to see Mum at our caravan door with her toilet bag! They had both slept better and had not died in the night. It was such a relief, as I had been worrying how I would break the news to Janet and Chris, if Brian had killed them off with food poisoning!

I saw Jean-Pierre who was Corrie's husband and asked how her father was. He said he was very poorly and that it might be some time before she was back here in Spain.

We went to the Mercadona supermarket to stock up on food and drink. I also commented that the dog food was more expensive than in England – maybe something else for my list of things to bring next year. Whilst shopping I bought a get well card for our next door-neighbour. It was a choice of English or Spanish so I opted for English and hoped he understood the message!

The afternoon was glorious without a cloud in the sky so we sat about getting slowly bronzed. As we relaxed, one of our neighbours from Happy Oldies Avenue, Bill, called round to ask if he could have a look at the Spanish bungalow as his son and girlfriend were coming in March, and may be interested in renting it. Mum and I said no problem; we would go round with him now. So he fetched his wife Evelyn, and we met them at the bungalow. As we were showing them the rooms and equipment, who should appear at the kitchen door but Diego the owner! He had just called to see if everything was OK. He didn't speak much English and I didn't have my friend Derek here to speak Spanish, but Diego asked "Parlez-vous francais?" To which my mother replied "Je parlez un petite Francais!" You could have knocked me down with a feather-I had no idea that Mum could speak any French, and I stood open-mouthed as she proceeded to have a conversation in French with Diego! The gist of the exchange was Mum explaining that Bill and Evelyn would be interested in booking the bungalow for two weeks, and within five minutes, a deal was struck. Well done Mum.

Back home, we relayed her foreign negotiating skills, much to the amusement of Dad and Brian. Fish was on tonight's menu but not for Dad and me. We had bought a ready made cannelloni for us two, but Brian was pleased that he could cook a fish dish that Mum would love to share with him provided it was cooked as opposed to raw this time!

I wrote the get well card and took it next door, and the wife came to the door and was very touched that we had sent a card.

We sat down later than usual at around seven o'clock and whilst Dad and I enjoyed our "boring" tea, Brian and Mum tucked into trout with almonds in butter sauce. It did look nice but I

80

couldn't help but wonder how many bones would be in it!

Playing cards until eleven o'clock and then it was time for bed. How the days just race by – without feeling you've actually done very much.

Sunday 11th January 2004.

Another gloriously warm day, but Sundays was "huge market" day, so off we went after breakfast. We bought a cooked chicken on the market for six euros, which we could have for lunch with some salad. I also bought some fruit and vegetables from the market, but I was quite taken aback at the price. I had foolishly chosen a stall that didn't have any prices shown, and I had got carried away and bought bananas, oranges, onions, a cabbage, some tomatoes, and a lettuce. For this bag I was charged eleven euros, which was nearly eight English pounds! When I thought what I could get at the Asda for this amount I realised that I had been charged tourist prices and promised myself to only buy from stalls displaying prices in future. We live and learn.

After lunch back home, Mum told me she had put a load of washing in the automatic washer at the bungalow, so I went with her to hang it out. Most of the afternoon we played Scrabble it was lovely to have someone to play against instead of trying to beat myself!

We had agreed that we would go out tonight for a Chinese so no one had any cooking to do.

Brian went to the phone and rang his Dad, Simon and Ian and was pleased that everyone at home was well.

Mum came round about six o'clock to say she couldn't find the iron. Did I have one to iron Dad's shirt! I told her I didn't do ironing but would make an exception for my Dad.

The Chinese meal was wonderful and Dad tried duck with pancakes for the first time and thought it was great. Brian had prawn curry, Mum had king prawn chow mein and I chose fillet steak in OK sauce. We ordered a couple of different rice dishes and some noodles and everyone tried bits of everything. At the end of the meal, we were offered apple schnapps or a Chinese liqueur, both of which were very nice.

Dad insisted on paying and, I must say, Brian didn't put up much of a fight! We had all had a starter and drinks and the bill was very reasonable at forty-six euros.

We all arrived home feeling well fed and tired and we were tucked up in bed for ten thirty.

Monday 12th January 2004.

Today was the day Brian had been worrying about for weeks. Our new car needed a 10,000 mile service, which we knew would be due whilst we were in Spain. We had spotted a Kia garage some time ago, when we got lost in Alicante looking for the gas fitting shop, so said we'd come back whilst Mum and Dad were here. Brian was convinced we wouldn't be able to get the service done there and then, ever the pessimist. He was sure they would need to book it in for two weeks time, like we have to in England.

We set off with Mum and Dad along for the ride, to San Pedro which was only about half an hour's drive away, called at the garage and they said to leave the car and they would service it within the next two hours! Easy as that.

As luck would have it, just at the back of the garage, was a huge outdoor market, which we sauntered round to pass the time. We called for a coffee at one of the pavement cafes, and watched as the traffic police towed away several cars that were parked on yellow lines!

On our return to the garage, we were delighted that the service was complete and the charge was one hundred and eight euros – cheaper than England. Once the service record book was duly stamped, we returned home.

I was making duck with spicy pears for tea so I proceeded to prepare the meal whilst Brian, Mum and Dad sat in the sun. Brian had bought an English paper and was reading out most of the stories and passing his comments! Mum really enjoyed this as she is not able to read the newspapers herself and, even with Brian's opinionated waffling, she could keep up to date with stories in the papers.

Tonight was to be a first for us. We had decided to go to the Monday night English quiz, in the games room near the restaurant. Brian and I had kept threatening to go, but were always too tired, so Mum and Dad gave us the kick up the bum we needed to go.

It was quite well attended and was just one euro for each player to enter your team. The questions were very difficult and, not being very good at general knowledge, I offered to write down the answers as my contribution. Ted was the quizmaster, and it became apparent as the night went on that he was slightly dyslexic though we couldn't hold that against him as he was a Lancashire man like Brian. But some of the pronunciations he came out with were hilarious and he took it all in good part.

At the end of the night, we had scored only 42 out of 60, but had ranked about fourth. The winning team won all the euros paid on entrance and Ted did the quiz night just because he enjoyed it. What a nice bloke.

We walked Mum and Dad home and had a quick nightcap with them before retiring.

Tuesday 13th January 2004.

Los Belones market was each Tuesday, so I took Mum and Dad for a trip out. After looking round the stalls we sat in the open air at a little café and ordered three hot chocolates. When they arrived we couldn't believe how thick the drink was – it was like eating a bar of delicious chocolate. Sitting in the sun we savoured every mouthful, then Dad paid the bill of four and a half euros.

We called at the tobacconists and bought a new phone card, then went home to pizza for lunch. More sunbathing was on the agenda and whilst we relaxed, a Dutchman stopped to chat to us. After ten minutes, he said he had to go as he was having his evening meal early before going to play bridge. Mums eyes lit up and she asked him who could go to bridge, as she played a lot at home with her friend Barbara. He said everyone was welcome on Tuesday and Thursday evenings in the games room and he looked forward to seeing her later!

I knew what she was thinking – a chance to wear one of her glittery posh outfits, and play bridge at the same time!

After a lovely tea of homemade meatballs in a spicy tomato sauce with pasta, I walked down to the games room with Mum to see if she could join in the bridge. My Dad always refused to play as he says they are too serious and it's only a game! Martin, a Dutchman who spoke very good English and ran the bridge evenings, made Mum very welcome. Although there were no other English people there, she was soon sat at a table talking in depth about which type of bridge was played. She instructed me to ask Dad to come and collect her at half past ten, and that was that! I had been dismissed.

When I got back, Brian had gone to ring Ian, and when he came back I went to ring Janet and Pam.

Brian and I then played cards with Dad, and he left later to go and fetch Mum from her bridge evening.

Wednesday 14th January 2004.

We have been so lucky with the weather, and woke to another warm sunny day. I took some washing round to Mum's bungalow to do in her automatic washer, and after breakfast we had a walk around the site, stopping to talk to many people. She had really enjoyed her bridge evening and couldn't wait to go again on Thursday.

Calling at our supermarket for a few bits, Mum again insisted on treating Brian to an English newspaper. As I took it from the counter, I did a double take. The picture on the front page looked just like Brian, now that he had grown a beard. We read that this was Harold Shipman, mass murderer, who had committed suicide the day before! I must ask Brian to shave his beard off and stop wearing his glasses.

As we walked back to our caravan, two gentlemen approached us. They were pointing at Mum and then one of them said in a Dutch accent, "Veronica, hello we have been talking about you this morning!" Mum couldn't recognise who they were, but they explained that they had been at the bridge evening and were very impressed with her card skills! They were asking if she would be there on Thursday as they looked forward to seeing her again! An instant fan club! She couldn't wait to tell her friend Barbara when she got home.

Later in the afternoon, John and Barbara came round and invited us to go and play boules. We had never played before, but John explained the rules as we went along, and Mum and Dad watched as Brian and I were beaten two games to one.

For tea today I made a lamb and broad bean casserole, which was a bit silly, as Dad and I don't like broad beans! However, they are favourites of Mum and Brian so when I served it up, I made sure that they got the lion's share of beans.

When Mum and I had walked around earlier, we had noticed a couple of posters for bingo, in the games room on Wednesday evenings. So we decided to leave the men at home and go for a laugh.

When we arrived, we realised that most of the people were German and Dutch, but we asked how it worked, i.e. how much each bingo book was, etc. After buying two books each, for five games, we sat down at a table with some Dutch ladies and I went to the bar to get a jug of sangria.

As the bingo was about to begin, the organiser asked over the microphone, "Where are the two English ladies who have never played bingo before and need all the rules explaining?" We both blushed and raised our hands! Of course we knew how to play bingo but were too embarrassed to tell him, so we let him proceed with five minutes of broken English, giving the Idiots Guide to Bingo!

The first game was for a top line so we all had our pens at the ready as the caller pulled out the first number. It soon dawned on me why this was called "International Bingo" – every number was called out in German, French, Dutch, then English. It was about twenty minutes before the first line was won, and we settled down for a long night!

We didn't win anything but, as I said to Mum; it was probably because we didn't know how to play properly! Everyone was very friendly and we had enjoyed our little night out.

Thursday 15th January 2004.

We packed a picnic and prepared to go to the beach for a few hours. Although the sun was out it felt a little cooler, but we knew the dogs would enjoy a swim in the sea so we wrapped up and set off.

On the way, we called at the Ferreteria and my Dad bought himself a hand saw, with which he wanted to cut down tree branches in his garden at home. We would bring it home with us in the caravan, as we didn't think he would be allowed on the plane with it in his luggage!

Dad also bought a piece of the padded table protector for the caravan table. He had mentioned when we first played cards that our fixed table in the caravan had a groove at the outer edge and this made it tricky to pick your cards up! He would cut this to fit and it would be just the right thickness to rectify the problem and it was.

He has always fixed things. I can recall Dad mending broken dolls, hairdryers, bikes, typewriters you name it, Dad could usually mend it. When I was in my teens, I can remember our next door neighbour's little girl Susannah, when she was about six years old, coming round one Sunday lunchtime with her Mum. Apparently, her Mum's Yorkshire puddings had failed to rise and Susannah had said "Take them round to David – he can mend anything". Some things are even beyond my Dad!

The beach was deserted and we set up chairs for Mum and me whilst Brian and Dad threw sticks in the sea for Jack and Jill to fetch. It was breezy but sunny and we had sandwiches and crisps, and cups of tea from the flask.

On our return, I made a beef, tomato and pea stew and whilst that was cooking slowly in the oven, I dyed Mum's hair.

After tea, Mum and I walked to bridge via the phone booths so she could ring her friend Kathy for a chat. I got her settled at bridge before returning home to play Scrabble with Dad, as Brian didn't feel like cards tonight.

Friday 16th January 2004.

Whilst Brian went to the gym, I took Mum and Dad down to the harbour at Cabo de Palos for a coffee. We watched the world go by for a while and then called at a pottery shop on the way back where Mum bought a couple of trinkets to take home.

We also called at the supermarket to do the shopping, as I wanted to make chicken with walnuts and pomegranate for tea. We couldn't find the pomegranates at first but eventually we had all the ingredients and a few marzipan treats for me and Dad fell into the trolley!

Another afternoon of sheer laziness spent lounging about in the sun. Our friends Rod and Wendy called to see us with Wendy's Mum Beryl, who had come to stay with them for a few weeks. We had a natter and a few drinks and before we knew it, it was time for tea- again! I made a Spanish potato dish which John had given me a recipe for, and this really complemented the chicken dish.

Brian was back on form and fancied cheating again at cards, so we played until midnight! However, his cheating can't have been that good as he didn't win one game all night.

Saturday 17th January 2004.

Each Saturday, our chosen radio station, Spectrum, broadcasts "Talksport" from England for most of the day, and Brian enjoys catching up with the football and general sports results and gossip.

Brian is still a bit of a Preston supporter from his younger days when he lived in Lancashire, and he likes to hear how they have done. My Dad, on the other hand, supports Doncaster Rovers, as he played for them in his very young days and I believe the Yorkshire comedian Charlie Williams was playing for them about the same time.

So we knew they would be happy sitting around, listening to sport and talking about football, even though it was very unlikely that Doncaster Rovers would get a mention.

Although it started off cloudy, it turned into a lovely day so Mum and I had a gentle stroll to the supermarket on site, bought a few bits and had a leisurely walk back. We then went down to the beach restaurant and had a coffee whilst watching people wind surfing and drifting about in boats. The winds had picked up, so that was great for the people that wanted to windsurf.

When we got back, Brian wasn't feeling too well so Dad took the dogs for a walk and Mum helped me prepare dinner, which was calf's liver in honey served with savoury rice. Gorgeous. What she actually did was sit down and have a brandy whilst I prepared the meal but I insisted that she had a rest whilst I had the chance to look after her.

Mum came with me to ring Janet, who was very excited and told me she had seen some really cheap flights on the Internet, for her and the two boys to come for a weekend on January 30th. Also, these were to Murcia airport, which is much nearer to us at La Manga than Alicante. I had to break the news gently to her that we were leaving here on January 30th to come home. Thank goodness she hadn't booked the flights. But I was very disappointed, as it would have been lovely to see them.

Sunday 18th January 2004.

The wind had picked up during the night, but the day started off sunny and warm. I took Mum to the market and we again brought a cooked chicken back for lunch. She also bought herself a long sleeved, three-quarter length, winceyette nightshirt with teddy bears on. I could imagine the excitement when she showed my Dad. She would have to beat him off with a stick!

Dad had requested that we return to the lovely Chinese for another meal before they went home, so we decided tonight would be good.

As the day progressed, the weather got worse, and by the afternoon it had clouded over and was quite cool. We moved into the awning and put the fan heater on, so we could play cards and have a few glasses of Muscatel to warm us up.

We showered at six o'clock, and I did Mum's hair ready for going out. As a special treat, I also gave her a foot massage, which she loves! This is Mum's idea of heaven having her feet rubbed.

The Chinese did not disappoint. Another really nice meal, which Brian said was made even better when Dad insisted on paying again. Somebody once said Brian's that tight, he only breathes in – and I think they're right!

Monday 19th January 2004.

Last day! The weather was disappointing, as it had turned a top coat colder. This didn't put us off our planned swim in the indoor pool so we all walked up together as Brian was going to the gym.

Later in the day, Dad and Brian took the dogs for a walk, but came back quite flustered. Apparently, a dog the size of an Alsatian had appeared which was off the lead and unaccompanied. Jack and Jill had had a bit of a fight with it and it had then backed off, but was not injured. We had heard stories about packs of wild dogs roaming around the national park areas, but Brian thought this was just someone's pet which had got off its lead.

Mum and I were having a cup of tea when Dawn came past – she was the lady renting a nearby caravan with her two children, whilst her husband Chris stayed in a tent at the back of us. We had just been discussing the possibility of Mum renting somewhere other than the bungalow if they came out to see us again, so we asked Dawn if we could just have a quick look round the caravan she was renting. It was only a few pitches away so we walked round and could tell as soon as we walked in that this would be much more suitable. It was warm, the patio would get the sun all afternoon and the caravan itself, though not posh, was certainly more homely and comfortable. Dawn gave me the telephone number of Gwen, the English owner so I could ring her if we decided to rent.

I went round to the bungalow with Mum to help her get most of the packing done ready for their lunchtime flight tomorrow. I gave Mum two birthday cards to post for me – one was for my friend Jill from the old cricket club and the other was for my friend Daniela who was the gorgeous receptionist where I used to work. Mum promised to post them when she got back to England.

We had decided to eat at our restaurant tonight and then go straight into Ted's quiz. An excellent meal again and, for the quiz we had persuaded Derek and Ann to join our team. As we were getting ready for the quiz to start, a couple came into the games room looking a bit lost. I asked if they would like to join us and they sat down and we soon got chatting. Yvonne and Michael were both very good at general knowledge, and our team only lost by two points. But there were eight of us!

Tuesday 20th January 2004.

Setting off at 9.30 am, we had a clear run to Alicante airport, and Mum and Dad both looked much better than when they had arrived. On the journey, Mum said she hadn't known what to expect when they came out to Spain, as neither of them had ever been caravanners. But she could now see why we enjoyed the lifestyle so much and was quite envious of the community spirit and friendship which seems to exist. We said our goodbyes and we were back home just after twelve.

We called at the supermarket and it felt strange at the checkout, having to pay again! I had got used to Mum paying for the last two weeks. Brian made a spaghetti bolognese for tea, and I did bugger all! I was really tired after looking after Mum and Dad but it had been brilliant to see them. Mum said it had been a real rest for my Dad, as she is very dependent on him as her eyesight deteriorates, but he'd had a break as I looked after her a lot of the time.

I received a text from Dad whilst we were watching a film on DVD, to say they were home safe, it was cold in England but they'd had a great holiday. It read "Om sayf, tis cowd an wett. av putt eatin on. Fanks 4 grate olidi x bye."

I was asleep for eight o'clock! Back to the early nights.

Wednesday 21ˢᵗ January 2004.

We had arranged to go to Lidl's supermarket at San Xavier with John and Barbara, and the half-hour drive was very pleasant and the sun shone. Quite a few bargains were available and we stocked up on cans of beer and pop and bought a few nice bottles of red wine as well as some food, of course.

Our afternoon walk was over the fields and it was nice not having to make any tea as we were going to the Chinese New Year party. Of course it was my turn to drive as Brian had driven home on January 1ˢᵗ.

This restaurant is well known for its gin and tonics, and when Brian was served with his first one, we realised why. They were served in glasses which could easily have been used as goldfish bowls without getting any complaints from the RSPCA! Each one must have contained at least three usual measures of gin and a bottle of tonic, together with the obligatory ice and lemon.

Everyone ordered what they fancied to eat from the extensive menu. There were eleven of us at our table Wendy and Rod, Wendy's Mum Beryl, Chris and Angie, Marie and Richard, John and Barbara and us two. A chap playing the organ and singing a variety of easy listening songs provided the entertainment. After we had eaten, he changed the tempo and we were soon up dancing and having a laugh. At midnight, there was a fireworks display outside and then we continued dancing and drinking.

After paying the bill between us, each of the ladies was given a small bottle of Chinese liqueur to take home.

It was after 1am when I drove home and we parked the car in the car park at the entrance to the site. There is a rule that no cars can be driven on site between midnight and 7.30am and I think this is a good idea.

We set off walking the half a mile towards our caravan, hoping that Jack and Jill had been OK whilst we were out. Brian had drunk seven gin and tonics and some wine during the night, so I was holding him by his arm as we walked. As we neared our area of the site, I could hear someone singing. It was Chris, the chap in the pitch behind us, and he appeared to be completely lost and very drunk! So I now had Brian on one arm and Chris on the other, as we walked home together. Brian took Chris to his pitch and said goodnight but Chris wanted to talk about life as we often do when we've had a few too many. So Brian came back for a few cans of beer to take round and I said I was going to bed and told him not to be up all night!

As I lay in bed, I could hear them putting the world to rights and talking the biggest load of nonsense I've heard in a long time. It was almost five before Brian came to bed and I knew he would not be feeling too well tomorrow. Serves him right!

Thursday 22nd January 2004.

As I expected, Brian was too ill to come outside and see the lovely sunshine. I did some washing and left him in bed. Most of our neighbours who came by asked where Brian was, and I took great delight in telling them he was in bed nursing a hangover.

Derek came past dragging his dog, and we were chatting about vaccinations that the dogs need. I told Derek we had a list of vets in France that DEFRA had kindly sent to me, but we were still unsure where to stay overnight so that we could see an English-speaking vet. Derek had just the solution! They use a vet at Eperlecques, who speaks really good English and is familiar with all the relevant paperwork. There was also a good caravan site not far away in Ardres where we could stay, and this was only half an hour from Calais.

Five minutes later he returned with the address and telephone number for the vet and the page number of the Caravan Club Europe book where we would find "Bal Parc" camping. This part of the return journey was quite daunting in that the timing for the vets visit was crucial. The dogs had to have been seen by a vet more than 24 hours but less than 48 hours before we got on the ferry. Another consideration that occurred to me was not to book a return ferry on a Tuesday otherwise we would need to seek out a vet on a Sunday. By good luck rather than good management, our return ferry was on a Friday so this would be fine.

At half past ten Brian appeared at the caravan door in his underpants, with a facial expression that said "Oh my god, why did you let me drink seven gin and tonics?" As often is the case the morning after the night before, he announced that he was starving so I made him three slices of cheese on toast. I used the toaster that my Dad had given us when they went home, and I laid the toaster on its side to brown the cheese! What a good idea.

He wolfed down the toast, couldn't face a cup of tea and

promptly went back to bed for the rest of the day. I walked up to the top of the site to fetch the car back and called at our supermarket for some liver for tea.

After ringing Mum and Janet, we had tea at six and were both fast asleep for eight o'clock.

Friday 23rd January 2004.

I knew it was still dark when I woke up, and Brian was asking "Are you awake?" Well, I was now that he'd woken me! He announced that it was half past four and he was feeling much better and fancied a cup of tea. There wasn't much point trying to get back to sleep when Brian wants to chat, he's like an old woman nattering on. So he made us both a cup of tea, Jack and Jill came to lie on the bed and we sat talking about never having another gin and tonic and generally putting the world to rights. I suppose after eight and a half hours sleep it wasn't surprising that we were awake.

Our caravan had two very large skylights in the roof and they were great when the sun was coming up in the early mornings. We could see a small tree that was overhanging the roof and we watched the birds landing on the branches above our heads. This would be another very sunny day and the general talk on the site was that this was the warmest December and January they had had for years.

We were up and dressed and driving to Los Belones at half past nine. We called for a drink in the square. Brian always moans that we can come home for a "free" coffee and doesn't see why we have to sit outside a café. But he usually gives in quite easily and I thoroughly enjoyed my cup of hot chocolate and Brian did enjoy his coffee, which came with a free biscuit.

After calling for another phone card, we were back home for half past ten when Barbara called round to see if we wanted to play boules later. We agreed to be ready for half past one – she explained that the Dutch and German always played at two o'clock for some reason and if we waited until two we might not get a place to play!

As we sat eating a sandwich for our lunch, an ambulance arrived at the pitch next door. We both assumed that the gentleman was ill again, so were taken aback when the lady from next door was helped into the ambulance, and her husband then got in the back with what appeared to be her overnight bag!

92

We took Jack and Jill over to the boules pitches as we could tether them to a tree whilst we played and then take them for a walk when we had finished. Barbara said the lady next door had been taken to hospital with breathing difficulties. Although I hadn't seen her with a cigarette, she did sound as though she had a smoker's cough most mornings. We talked about how awful it must be to be ill whilst you are away from home, and Barbara said "It's a good job we all bring an E111 with us". I had no idea what she was talking about! She explained that this was a form which you filled out and got stamped and signed at the post office before coming to Spain, and this entitled you to treatment in an emergency, in any other country in the EU. She was quite horrified that we had neither heard of it, nor obtained one!

When Brian had retired from the police, we continued our subscriptions to a company which insured our lives, and we also paid for annual travel insurance with them. Just before we had left England, I had rung them to check we would be covered for our trip to Spain. They advised me that the maximum cover had changed from ninety to thirty days, but as we had been with them for years and the new rule was only just being introduced, they would cover us on this occasion for our trip. However, there would be an additional premium of £70, which I duly paid, and it was made clear that this could not be done for any subsequent trips of more than thirty days without a very expensive additional premium. What a shock! I made a mental note to find out about this E111 form when we got back to England.

Anyway, we had a great game of boules, and Brian and I were very much improved in our performance. We beat John and Barbara six five the first game and upheld our lead when we played the best of three.

We returned home later after walking the dogs. I went along the strip to the Internet café at teatime, leaving Brian to make a nice beef curry.

The evening was quite balmy and although we were ready for an early night, as we'd been up since half past four, it was uncomfortably warm for sleeping. Perhaps air-conditioning should be a consideration for our next caravan?

Saturday 24th January 2004.

Another early start after a good night's sleep, so we were at the Mercadona for ten o'clock. We bought some freshly made croissants, some mackerel and mussels for Brian and a lasagne for me.

When we got back we sat in the sun having coffee and croissants – very slimming, I'm sure and then I walked down to the games room at the restaurant, which I had heard was also a small library. I took some books that we had read and a few that my Mum had left to pass on. Hers were all large print but she thought someone might like them. Well, the library was certainly small, and consisted of three shelves on the wall, with a variety of books, old and new, some English but mostly German and in no particular order. I toyed with the idea of putting them in some sort of order and tidying the display and then thought "Get a life!" So I put my books on a shelf and picked out a tatty-looking Catherine Cookson book which I thought I might have read but wasn't sure. All of her novels seem to have a similar theme so it's difficult to tell which you've read, especially when you have a terrible memory as I have.

On my way back, I rang Gill and Dave who were at home for a change, and I then rang Pam. She told me that Harry had a hospital appointment on the afternoon of February 3rd for a scan, to see why he was having abdominal pains. Being abroad can put you on a guilt trip if you have relatives at home that are having health problems. Luckily for Brian, Pam copes very well, but after nursing her Mum when she was dying; Brian feels that Pam has done more than her fair share. We all agree however, that you can't put your lives on hold, and that if Harry were very ill, Brian would be there immediately.

Returning home, I called to see Hazel the hairdresser and I made an appointment for my hair cutting next Tuesday at ten.

Brian had barbecued mackerel and I enjoyed my lasagne. He made phone calls in the evening to his Dad and to Simon, and we watched another one of Johns DVD's before bed.

Sunday 25th January 2004.

Mum's birthday was coming up on February ninth which was the day we would be arriving home. I thought it would be nice to send her a card from Spain but was very disappointed at the selection available in the shops! Next year I might bring some with me to send home. I found one that was awful with a Spanish dancer in a bright red flamenco dress that was made of red and black stiff netting, and glued to the front of the card. Yes, my Mum likes this sort of thing! Maybe, with her failing eyesight, she likes it as she can feel the design? So I posted that to her together with a letter in large print so she could read it.

We walked along the beach to Mar de Cristal, and decided to have a bite to eat at Pepe's on the sea front. We had a Spanish omelette, a cheeseburger, a beer, a coffee and a coke and this was eleven euros. Very good value, lovely food and surroundings.

After our walk back we called for a paper and then sat in the sun all afternoon.

Our neighbour Chris was packing up to fly back to England. He said some work had come up and he didn't think he would be coming back to Spain for quite a few months. His wife and children weren't going with him, which seemed odd, but it takes all sorts to make a world.

He was bringing lots of things to the bins that he'd used whilst here but couldn't take on a plane. I spied a decent-looking three tier vegetable rack, but this was snapped up almost immediately. Then he brought round an old-looking sun lounger, and he'd no sooner put it down than my friend Barbara checked it over and picked it up! She explained that if people are throwing things away, which they feel other people may get even a few weeks use out of, they put them in front of the bins so passers by can take what they want. It seemed like a free jumble sale to me and I couldn't imagine wanting anyone else's cast offs but you never know!

I made tea quite early and after finishing the chicken and almonds with chickpeas, we read our books and relaxed. What a hard life this is.

Monday 26th January 2004.

Ready for action this morning, Brian was off to the gym at half past nine. That was the opening time, but sometimes the lady that opened up was a few minutes late. She didn't speak any English but Brian was embarrassed that the only thing he could say to her was "Hello" and every time he got back from the gym he would remind me that he must learn to speak Spanish! He said she was always smiling and pleasant. I think he had a bit of a thing for her – she was much younger than him, and he sometimes lives in a bit of a fantasy land, like most men his age! Some days, he would come home and say she'd said a really long sentence to him in Spanish so he'd just nodded. He wondered if she was asking him to take her for lunch. But deep down he knew it was more likely she was saying, "Aren't you a bit old to be lifting weights!"

I did a few washes and when he got back about eleven, we had a barbecued brunch. Another game of boules and a walk through the fields seemed to fill our day.

We had decided that, on the journey home, we would stop at a site in England for a couple of days, in order to clean the caravan and wash all of the bedding etc ready for winter storage. Our friend Derek recommended a site at Peterborough called Ferry Meadows. This was about half way home for us and sounded just what we needed- laundry facilities, dog walk nearby, pubs and eating-places within walking distance. So I rang them to book a pitch and they were pleased to take the booking and wished us a safe journey home.

We ate chicken with tomatoes and honey, and then headed for Ted's Monday night quiz. Yvonne and Michael had saved us two seats and although we didn't win again we came sixth out of around fourteen teams.

Tuesday 27th January 2004.

Hazel arrived as promised at ten and gave me a smashing haircut and blow dry for ten euros. Brian took the dogs on an early walk whilst I was having my haircut. He was quite upset when he came back as he had lost his designer sunglasses in the fields. I had asked him not to waste his money the previous year in Northern Cyprus on sunglasses, which were for young lads to pose in. But he wanted them so he had them and now he'd lost them. Oh dear, how sad!

My "visitor" arrived later in the day so Brian made a chilli for tea, after which he rang Simon and Ian. I then went to ring Janet, and she was snuggled up at home in Manchester, on the settee with a quilt, as it was snowing! I told her we would be home in two weeks and didn't want any snow hampering our journey, so she said she would see what she could do.

Walking back, I saw Barbara and she told me that Corrie's Dad had died so I wouldn't get chance to see her before we left for England. I asked Barbara if I could just leave a card with her to give to Corrie when she finally got back to Spain. I wanted her to know I was thinking of her, and to thank her for being so welcoming and making me feel at home. Barbara promised to do that for me.

Brian's mobile phone rang and it was his friend Norman who had just retired from the police, and he and his wife Lynn had left England and bought a house in Murcia only about 60 miles from here. Norman was asking if Brian could do some plastering for him. He had served his apprenticeship before joining the police and did do occasional bits of plastering as favours for friends–but Brian explained we were almost ready for leaving. Maybe next year, who knows?

Wednesday 28th January 2004.

It was slowly dawning on us that we were leaving soon, and neither of us relished the task of taking down the awning and packing up. Besides leaving this lovely weather, we would miss everyone and the lifestyle we had adopted.

Although it had rained for an hour during the night, the rest of the day was bright and dry. Brian suggested we take the awning down today instead of waiting until tomorrow just in case it rained again. Another disadvantage of not having the caravan at home was that you didn't get the chance to dry the awning out when you got back home. So it was essential it was dry when we packed it away. We began emptying the awning and then took it down, packing it away as neatly as we could. At least the job of dismantling it seems to be three times quicker than erecting it!

The lady from next door was brought home by a friend, and she smiled and waved as she went inside their camper van. Our neighbour Joop told us she was now fine and had been treated for a chest infection.

Joop asked when we were leaving and we told him Friday. The rule on the site for booking is you can book your own pitch for next year by leaving a deposit of 360 euros, and no one else can reserve your pitch until you leave. Joop explained he had a Dutch friend who was in another part of the camp, but who would like to move onto our pitch when we left on Friday. He would need to come to reception with me when I settled the bill to secure this particular pitch. I said I could go now, so he rang his friend and we arranged to meet at reception.

I settled our bill, which was 690 euros up until Friday, and the Dutchman would be able to transfer onto our pitch as soon as we left. I also paid 360 euros to reserve the same pitch for next year. You could leave 100 euros to reserve a pitch but it would be potluck as to which pitch you were given on arrival. Alternatively you could just turn up and hope there was room.

The disadvantage of booking the same pitch was that you had to reserve it from October 1st, so even if you didn't arrive until November you still had to pay for each night from October 1st. Whereas, if you just paid 100 euros deposit, you were guaranteed a pitch somewhere and you only paid from the day you arrived. There was however method in my madness I knew that tight old Brian would come as early as we could to get his money's worth so we would get here much sooner. Let's hope it works!

Our main reasons for booking the same pitch was familiarity and laziness! Although we were opposite the sinks and showers, it was really handy. Also, Jack and Jill were on a long tether outside most days getting some sunshine and fresh air. They would bark at passing dogs but were well behaved if they knew where we were, so keeping them in sight was a consideration. Our lovely neighbours were also a deciding factor. Although they weren't English, we felt they had made us very welcome and been very helpful and we would look forward to seeing them again.

We had agreed that we would eat at our restaurant tonight so we didn't have to think about cooking whilst we had the task of packing up.

Derek's wife Ann was washing up around teatime and she came across to wish us a safe journey home. I said we were going to the restaurant for a meal and she suggested I had an aceatica coffee. Apparently, it's a Spanish speciality coffee that has brandy, another spirit and evaporated milk in it and sounded just up my street. Why hadn't I discovered them whilst I had been here, she asked. Probably 'cos tight Brian thinks sitting about having coffees is a bit decadent!

After our three-course meal with wine, I asked for an aceatica coffee. Brian wanted to know what it was. I told him to order one and see! It was delicious. Typical I find something I really like two days before leaving. I will be back!

Thursday 29th January 2004.

This threatened to be a rather industrious day, as we were leaving in the morning. Luckily the sun was out, so we busied ourselves with all sorts of mundane but necessary tasks. Our shopping list was made up of items we thought we would need for to the journey home and cleaning the caravan so it had on it milk, bread, water, ham, cheese, dog food, carpet shampoo and diesel!

Brian did the heavier cleaning like the groundsheet and water barrels whilst I concentrated on tidying and cleaning the cupboards inside the caravan.

Mid-afternoon we had done enough, so we took Jack and Jill for their final beach walk. We wondered if we would be back in October and if the dogs would remember? We just don't know what's round the corner for any of us. Certainly not Brian's sunglasses, which were nowhere to be seen!

As we walked back through the site, we said goodbye to lots of people we had met and whom we hoped to see again. Clive and Karen came to chat with us and quite unexpectedly, their huge Alsatian, Boston, escaped from behind their secured windbreak. Before we knew what was happening, he bounded over towards Jack and Jill, Jack was shivering behind Brian, and Jill let out a loud cry and jumped into my arms! If I didn't know better, I would think that Boston had bitten her but I know Jill quite well and it was all dramatics! He hadn't been near enough to touch her and besides, he is a lovely soft dog. Drama over although Brian admitted later he was thinking the worse – all these weeks with no pet problems then on the last day they are both savaged and have to go to the vets to be put to sleep! Oh, prophet of doom.

Again, we ate at the site restaurant and the meal was lovely. We were in bed at nine o'clock, as we wanted an early start for the first leg of our journey home.

Friday 30th January 2004.

A seven-thirty start was good, and we were very organised in the final packing up procedure. The whole street turned out to wave us off! We imagined they would be in bed but no, they all got up to help us push the heavy laden caravan onto the tow bar and Derek and Ann and John and Barbara were giving us cuddles and wishing us well. Derek mentioned to Brian that although he didn't have a mover on his caravan as it was only small, if he had an outfit this size, he would definitely buy one. They are around a thousand pounds but can make the job of moving and manoeuvring a caravan much easier. Maybe he has planted a seed in Brian's mind?

At nine o'clock, just as we planned, we were off. It was sad to be leaving everyone but, like most holidays, once they are at an end, we were looking forward to getting home.

As we joined the main road at the top of the site, I looked at Brian and asked, "What's that noise?" He seemed as mesmerised as I was and he soon realised that the car wouldn't go above twenty miles an hour! A light on the dashboard read "In Low 4wd". So we were in four wheel drive but no matter what Brian did, we couldn't cancel it, and he was ranting about not being able to drive thirteen hundred miles back to England at twenty miles an hour!

I tried to keep calm and told him to come off the road at the next exit, which fortunately was only a mile away. We pulled up and had to get the car manual out. After five minutes, I found the correct page. If the four-wheel drive needs to be cancelled, you must stop, turn the ignition off, put the car into "Stop", then "Neutral", then cancel the four-wheel drive and then Bob's your uncle! Hooray we were OK again! Nightmare over.

Not a good start, but at least we were off in good time towards L'Ametlla, where we shouldn't have a repeat puncture!

What a lovely day for travelling. Warm and sunny with clear roads and we stopped for a toilet break at half past eleven. The rest of the journey was a doddle, and we arrived at the campsite at three thirty.

It was slightly cooler here than at La Manga, but still nice enough to take Jack and Jill down to the beach for a walk.

The German couple who has kindly helped us in November were still here. They came round to chat with us, and said they were going back to Germany in a week or two. They were only young maybe mid-thirties–and we wondered how they could afford to be here not working for a few months. We did gather that they had their own plant hire company, and they had left it in capable hands whilst they took a holiday. Nice work if you can get it!

We set up for the night and made a quick pasta dish and garlic bread for tea, washed down with a nice bottle of red wine.

Saturday 31st January 2004.

The gym here was far superior to the one we had left at La Manga, so Brian was off first thing! It was a lovely day so I did two loads of washing at the laundrette and we then went into the village for a few things. We bought two T-bone steaks for fifteen euros and a couple of duck breasts. Also we replenished our stocks of fresh vegetables and wine, and Brian treated himself to a Daily Mail.

We called at the garage where we had met the helpful policeman previously, and filled up with diesel.

On our return, we took the dogs for a two-hour walk along the beach and into the woods. There was no one else in sight so they were able to run about off the leads and tire themselves out.

A light shower appeared at five o'clock, so I made a duck casserole for tea. We could save the barbecue steaks for tomorrow.

Brian sat outside with the dogs around six o'clock having a cool beer, and a German chap came past with his golden retriever. He was on the site a few pitches up and he tried to introduce his dog Shirley, to Jack and Jill! Jack just hid behind Brian's chair but Jill seemed to like Shirley so they had a bit of a play together.

Luckily, this chap spoke good English, and he was telling Brian that during the war, when he was a little boy, he lived in Lancashire with a lady he called "Auntie Doris". When Brian told him he was from Lancashire, he asked if Brian knew his Auntie Doris. It's a small world but not that small. He was on route to a site called Marjal Camping, which we gathered was near Alicante, and he brought us a leaflet about it. If ever we went there, he said, we must ask to be near him on pitch 55, as he would love to see us again. You may laugh but what a lovely friendly chap he was.

Sunday 1st February 2004.

Our last full day in Spain, so we made the best of it. The weather yet again had been kind to us, and we walked along the beach and up into the woods.

The afternoon we spent soaking up the final rays of the sun and Brian lit the barbecue around four o'clock. I made some chunky chilli chips in the oven and a salad whilst the steaks were cooking. We were able to sit outside until just after seven and it was Brian's turn to wash up whilst I put up sandwiches for the long day ahead.

I went to reception to pay the bill, which was 48 euros for three nights. Later I received a text from Dad, which basically wished us a good journey and told us they still had some snow. Then we had a text from David and Gill to say they were skiing somewhere in France.

Later in the evening I was feeling quite cold (as usual) so I switched the heating up. This blew the electric, which Brian was not very pleased about. He made me get dressed and go to reception even though he was fully dressed and I was in my pyjamas and dressing gown – he's such a love! The girl from reception came with a key for the power boxes and reset the electricity. The site at La Manga had been 10 amp but this one was only 5 amp – you soon get used to luxury!

Finally I was lovely and warm and we snuggled down for an early night. We were hoping to be off for seven in the morning and as we talked about the journey home, I forgot that I wasn't speaking to him!

Monday 2nd February 2004.

As agreed, we were up, showered and almost ready for the off at seven o'clock. We pulled the caravan out and lined it up with the tow bar and hitched up no problem. The next job, as always, was to plug in the connectors from the car to the caravan for the lights. Brian always did this task but this morning he seemed to be struggling. After ten minutes of him muttering and swearing under his breath, I asked if I could help. And to my surprise he said yes.

I knelt on the floor and asked for the torch so I could see what I was supposed to be doing. Why don't men ever seem to have the right tools for the job? Pardon!!

There are two connectors on the car one is grey, the other is black and grey. They should fit into the two "corresponding" connectors on a caravan one of which is grey, the other being black. Confused? You will be! I could see that the reason they weren't fitting was that one of them had been forced and had subsequently bent. I tried to muster up all my patience and asked Brian which ones went into which? His reply was, "How am I supposed to know, they're similar colours and I can't remember which goes into which". Why can't they be made so that one is red and the other is green on all cars and caravans? This would seem quite logical to me but then what do women know?

I asked for his trusty Swiss army knife and explained that somehow, they had been buckled and I would now try to straighten them out. Who could have done such a thing, I wondered as I knelt next to the most heavy-handed man I had ever met! The same man that admits he always manages to finish jigsaws by cutting the edges of any pieces he can't get to fit!

Finally, after about half an hour, I had bent the plastic surrounds and got them to fit. I insisted on putting coloured tape on them at our next stop in France, so that this didn't happen again. I also made it a rule that on all future trips, I would couple the lights up as I couldn't trust Brian not to break them again. He was in full agreement with this suggestion!

At ten past nine, we checked as always that the lights were all working and we finally set off, after a cuddle of forgiveness and a promise not to mention this again.

This was to be a heavy driving day for Brian and we were stopping overnight at one of the services in France. We hadn't decided which one; we would see how the journey went.

As we drove into France, the temperature outside dropped a little and the day became dull and misty. We stopped at 1 o'clock and filled up with diesel. The price had increased from 69cents a litre in Spain, to 88 cents in France but was still much cheaper than England.

Whilst Brian gave the dogs a walk, I popped into the caravan for some coloured tape. We bought four rolls of different colours some years ago to colour code our old awning to help when putting it up. The tape had been really handy for many things and marking the bent light connectors would be another! Don't tell Brian I told you this but he bought some new caravan wing mirrors for the car earlier this year. They came in a pack of two- one left, one right. Now he will admit he is not the best at fixing things or logical thinking. (He has confessed that he threw the kids' Rubik cube in the bin as he couldn't do it!) The first time he put the mirrors onto the car, it took him about twenty minutes. He said he'd been trying to put them on the wrong side and was pleased with himself when he had the idea to put some red tape round the one that fixed to the right hand side, so he would not have this problem again. On closer examination, I could see that each side could only be fitted one way, otherwise they would be upside down! But he's happy so who I am

103

to throw logic into the equation?

It was half past four when we stopped again for a drink and sandwiches. We braced ourselves for the next leg, as we would be going through Lyon before we stopped for the night. Maybe it would be quiet, as we had missed the rush hour?

We hit Lyon just after six o'clock and it was dark. If anything, there seemed to be more traffic than in the daytime. I did my best to keep calm and sound as though I knew where we were going, until we were on a really busy road with traffic at both sides and we approached a huge fork in the road and I had no idea which way to go! Other drivers were tooting their horns at everyone and when Brian asked, "Which way left or right?" I had to be honest and say "I've no idea"! I knew this was no help and luckily Brian made a decision to go left and I could have kissed him – we were on the right road. This had been quite hair raising and I felt Brian was justified in calling me a "dozy cow" and other such terms of endearment!

By eight-thirty we had covered 550 miles and we pulled in to the services at Macon. We parked where there were quite a few lorries and as near as we could to the well lit restaurant and toilets. Unfortunately the only warm food available was from a French equivalent of a McDonald's and everything came with salad and mayonnaise. I tucked into some chips and a chocolate biscuit washed down with a horrible cup of tea. What a treat.

As we got into bed around ten o'clock, Brian decided he would take some additional security precautions. Whilst I drank a decent cup of tea in bed, he was using some string to tie the inside door handle to the cupboard and fridge doors. I could see that if someone did open the caravan door, the fridge door would just open up, and anyone breaking in would probably think they were being invited to stay for supper! I didn't mention this as Brian was doing his best to make us feel safe, but I think if the worst happened and someone did try to get in, Jack and Jill would probably have become entangled by the cats cradle of string which now adorned the living area!

Tuesday 3ʳᵈ February 2004.

A frosty morning, and I was shocked when I finally managed to undo all the string and open the door. A huge lorry had parked at the side of us in the night, and I could only just get out of the caravan. The lorry driver was stood having a cup of something hot, and he said, "Bonjour" as I alighted so I replied, "Bonjour, monsieur" in my best French accent. If only I could have seen an old biro on the floor, I could have picked it up and impressed him with my version of "Voici la plume de ma tante!" Remember? "Here is my auntie's pen."

Just before eight we were back on the road, stopping at eleven for diesel. It was quite a sunny day and we sat outside at the services, eating a cheese and ham baguette and drinking coffee.

No problems following the route today, and we arrived at Bal Parc at four o'clock. Were we in for a surprise!

The "write up" for the site includes the phrases "ideal for the family," "a paradise for the children," "an incomparable spot," "quiet and comfortable." The reality in winter is- "ideal setting for an Alfred Hitchcock movie," "like a ghost town," "unkempt and scruffy," "like stepping back in time twenty years."

At least we were here and what did it matter for a few nights? I went to reception at the adjoining hotel and was told we could park in any of the six available pitches. These were unmarked and the whole "touring" area was just a circular car park with electric hook ups. To the side was a falling down wooden construction which was probably a drinks bar many moons ago, and there were half empty bottles of spirits and beers covered in cobwebs with dead spiders floating inside.

Once we had got the electric on and briefly unpacked, we took the dogs for a walk round the rest of this "incomparable paradise". It was eerie. There was no one else on this site, just around fifty static caravans and constructions, none of which looked as though they had been lived in for at least five years. Some caravans had awnings erected, which looked to have been half blown down in a storm, torn and mouldy, but inside we could see microwaves, tables with mugs and plates on them, table lamps, fridges, bikes and children's toys. It was as though the occupants of every caravan had left in a hurry, never to return. Spooky.

We inspected the site washroom, which was a shared shower, sink and toilet - just the one! It was clean and there was hot water and a heater in there, so we collected our things and both showered and freshened up, whilst discussing possible scenarios for the sudden departure of our fellow guests.

At seven o'clock we went to the hotel to see if we could get something to eat without driving into the village. Yes, we were seated in a small clean dining room and ordered a bottle of wine. The chef, who was also the receptionist, barman and probably the cleaner, told us we could have fish starter, beef main course and lemon pudding. That was today's menu and there was no other food available. So we agreed to this meal and really had no idea what to expect. It was a surreal experience.

In fairness, the meal was excellent. Not huge portions but the food was well cooked and presented, and we thought the final bill of 47 euros, including wine and coffee, was good.

A few sherries in the caravan for me, and a large brandy for Brian before our heads hit the pillows.

Wednesday 4th February 2004.

Warm and breezy weather today and after some toast for breakfast we set off to find the vets', which Derek had drawn us a map of. We only got lost once and at eleven o'clock we pulled in to the driveway of the vet's practice. His wife made us an appointment for 3.15 and we then drove to a supermarket and did some shopping. Brian wanted to take some red wine home but decided he would wait until we saw a wine shop, rather than buy at the supermarket.

Harry had been to the hospital yesterday, so whilst we were out we were looking for a phone box to ring him and see how he had fared. Unlike in Spain, the phone boxes in this French village were very scarce. The ones we did find were out of order but we remembered we had seen a red phone box on the site near reception so we'd use that when we got back. Calling from our mobiles would be very expensive but we could use them as a last resort.

Back at the hotel, we soon discovered that the red phone box was empty completely, not even a shelf in it. So we walked into reception and asked if there was a phone we could use. The chef said we could use the hotel phone to call England, and there would be no charge as we were staying on the campsite. How kind.

Brian got through to his Dad and had a long chat about the scan. It had shown that he had an aneurysm that needed operating on as soon as possible. It was a blood clot that could burst at any time without warning and would kill him instantly. Harry's brother Bob had died with the same thing only two years ago and apparently it was hereditary. The hospital had told Harry that if he had any sons over 55 they should get a scan done, just to be on the safe side. Brian tried to make his Dad feel a bit more reassured that things would be fine, but ended up asking him what the weather was like in Congleton! He told Harry to ring Pam so she knew we'd called and said we would be home in less than a week and we'd come and stay with him as soon as we were back.

Of course, whilst Brian was relaying the conversation to me, he convinced himself that he'd not been feeling too good recently, and did I think I could feel a blood clot building up in his stomach? Are all men hypochondriacs or is it just the ones I've ever known?

Back at the vets' the procedure was straightforward and the vet spoke very good English. Jack and Jill were well behaved and I paid the bill of 78 euros. This didn't include the cost of "Frontline" drops as I had taken some with me.

The sun came out for an hour so we enjoyed it whilst we could with a glass of wine each.

We decided to eat at the hotel again, as Brian was worrying about his Dad and himself, and didn't fancy driving anywhere. The menu was different and the food was excellent and we were back in the caravan at eight. Just after we got in, Pam rang Brian on his mobile to tell him how Harry had gone on at the hospital. Obviously Harry hadn't rung Pam but it didn't matter- it was something they should be discussing together. The phone call lasted just eleven minutes and cost us £11. We didn't realise that it was a pound a minute to receive a call!

Ideally, we would have liked to get the ferry home tomorrow, but we now had to wait until 24 hours had elapsed before taking the dogs on the ferry so we would spend Thursday looking round Calais.

Thursday 5th February 2004.

No chance of sitting in the sun today – what a cold and dull morning it was. We drove into Calais centre and stopped at the Tourist Office to ask where Cité Europe was. They gave us directions and a leaflet about all the shops that were there. Brian drove through Calais in his usual calm manner (!) and we arrived at Cité Europe almost an hour later.

It was a huge shopping complex and we parked in the car park and went into the nearest entrance. Two hours later, we still hadn't bought anything except two coffees and two sandwiches. I had tried some clothes on in a few shops as we were going to a Valentine's dance on February 14th and I had nothing to wear that fit me. Of course, my bum looked massive in everything and I refused to buy anything. Brian is an excellent shopper and has lots of patience and very good taste, but I just wasn't in the mood for buying clothes today.

On our way back to the "incomparable paradise", we called at a wine shop for Brian to buy some wine to take home. It was quite a small shop and I soon realised that rather than a warehouse type place, we appeared to be in a rather upmarket store.

It took Brian nearly an hour to choose eighteen bottles of wine, and just one minute to pay 118 euros for them! This was not the "cheap" wine we had in mind, but time was running out and we didn't fancy driving about much longer.

Back at the site, I went to reception and paid the bill, which was 30 euros for three nights. We made spaghetti bolognese for tea and had two bottles of the wine we'd bought! Later, I checked all the documents we needed for the ferry tomorrow and we set the alarm on the mobile phone for six thirty. The ferry was at ten o'clock but we had to check in an hour before sailing to allow time for the dogs to be checked.

To be on the safe side, Brian wanted to be there ninety minutes before the sailing, just in case. So that was the plan.

Friday 6th February 2004.

Up at six thirty, we were showered and dressed and getting on with our usual packing up procedure, in a timely fashion, whilst having a cup of tea and some toast, all very civilised. At half past seven, Brian announced that he couldn't find the caravan keys to open the front box. We needed to get in there to disconnect the gas, and get to lots of things that were essential to setting off! He said he'd had the keys earlier and must have put them down. I had probably tidied up and moved them! What? I knew I hadn't seen them, but as we didn't know where the spare key was, it was important that we stayed calm and didn't fall out in the panic!

Everything was packed into boxes on the floor, so we began quickly unpacking to see if the keys had fallen into one of the boxes. I looked in the most unlikely places the fridge, the oven, the wardrobe, my handbag but they were nowhere to be found. We took the torch outside to see if he had dropped them earlier, but couldn't find them. By now it was eight o'clock and I suggested we retraced Brian's steps since he got up at half past six. Ten minutes later, I had found them. Where? In his dressing gown pocket which was hung in the wardrobe! We were so relieved that we could still get to the ferry on time, that I resisted the temptation to ask unhelpful questions like "Why did you take them to the showers?" or "Why didn't you put them somewhere you would remember?"

We drove to Calais and arrived just before nine o'clock – perfect timing. The dogs were scanned to check their microchips, and their papers were examined and found to be in order. One of the officials asked if he could have a look inside the caravan, so Brian got out of the car to open the door to let him in. He looked inside the wardrobe and the shower cubicle and explained they were checking for stowaways.

Another very straightforward boarding procedure and we set sail on time. Breakfast in the restaurant and a quick look round the shop and we were soon back in Dover.

We were reminded to put our watches back an hour and we were on the road to Peterborough at ten thirty. We could tell we were back in England as it was raining heavily, and the skies were dark and grey. Despite the fairly heavy traffic we had a good journey and arrived at Ferry Meadows at 2 o'clock. It was nice to be back in England, and within an hour we were set up and the caravan was lovely and warm.

Jack and Jill were ready for their long walk round a lake and through some woodland. Later, we walked to a pub for a meal, which was very average but filled a hole. On the walk back, I rang Mum and Brian rang Harry, and then I tuned the television in so we could watch "Coronation Street" – now it felt like we were home!

Saturday 7ᵗʰ February 2004.

The rain had stopped and the day looked as though it would remain dry. I began the task of cleaning the caravan, shampooing the carpet and washing everything in sight! The laundry facilities were good and I made sure I had enough correct English coins for the half a dozen washes and dries I would need to do. We had chosen a pitch that was not too far from the washing area, as I knew

I would be spending a large part of the day there.

Brian set about cleaning the outside of the caravan and generally tidying the external bits. He was interrupted twice during the morning by passing fellow caravanners asking him what he thought of his Kia Sorento car! Both of these chaps said they were thinking of getting one and would value Brian's opinion, so he was in his element. I was making cups of tea for these people as it was cold outside, and I felt like the receptionist at the Kia showroom!

By two o'clock we were well on with our chores, so we drove into Peterborough to look round the shops. We saw a sign for a multi-storey car park, and as we pulled in, we heard a loud bang. Brian put the brakes on, and we both realised what it was. Our top-box meant the car was too high to go under the barrier! Fortunately, there was no damage, but we then had to reverse out and of course there was already a queue of a dozen cars behind us! Eventually we drove to another car park with no height restrictions.

Peterborough has a lovely shopping centre, and I bought some trousers and a blouse at John Lewis for our Valentine's dinner, and Brian got himself some trousers.

We bought an Indian take-away meal for two and when we got back to the site, Brian took the dogs for a walk whilst I went to the phone and rang Janet and Pam. I asked Janet if she would ring her local Interflora florist and send Mum some flowers for her birthday on Monday and I would settle up with her later. No problem.

Sunday 8th February 2004.

A thin covering of snow was on the ground and we could feel that the temperature had gone down since yesterday. At least it was dry and we continued packing the van ready for storage. I had made a list in Spain of things we needed to take back home, and things that could stay in the caravan. Top of my list for taking home was Dad's saw that he'd bought in Spain and we gradually finished packing things and the caravan looked like a new pin.

We rewarded our hard work by driving to Marholm for a meal at the Fitzwilliam Arms. This had been advertised in a local magazine that I'd picked up in reception and we weren't disappointed. A few hours of telly when we got back had us drifting to sleep.

Monday 9th February 2004.

We set off at 9 o'clock after paying £28.80 for three nights at Ferry Meadows. Getting used to the pound again after using euros for so long was strange. It was a crisp sunny day, ideal for driving and we were back at Derrick's farm for 1 o'clock.

I texted my Dad to say we were almost home and to wish Mum a happy 69th birthday. He texted back thanking us for the lovely flowers and said Mum would ring me later.

Arriving home, we could hardly get through the door for the post. We had enjoyed our trip and it has been a great adventure that we both felt we were lucky to be in a position to experience. Since leaving on 24th November, we had driven 4,507 miles and, although it was great to be home, we were already looking forward to October when we'd be off again, armed with the lessons we had learned!

As I switched the central heating on to "constant", I wondered why we had come home so early. It was freezing!

David & Gill with Jack & Jill.

A gorgeous view down to the beach!

Brian &Barbara enjoy Christmas Lunch.

Me & Marie relax by the sinks!

Me, mum and Janet celebrate mum's 70th birthday.

Packing up, ready to go home.

Part Two

Friday 1st October 2004.

We seemed to have been so busy since we got back from Spain in February; we were looking forward to getting back there for a rest! As I predicted, Brian had agreed we should set off much earlier to get our money's worth, as we've reserved our pitch from October 1st. Our arrival date at La Manga should be next Friday 8th October.

The final day of packing up – boring chores like defrosting the freezer and spring-cleaning the home. Men never seem to understand why we have to clean the house and change the bedding before we go on holiday. They come out with statements like "You'll only have to clean it again when you get back so why bother?" If I thought about this for too long, I would find myself agreeing with the logic and all my hard work would have been for nothing!

We had been to Derrick's yesterday and packed the caravan ready for off tomorrow morning. There was so much to think about but I thought I'd covered most things. This year, we had our signed E111 forms and I'd checked that our bank card wouldn't run out whilst were away. The Visa cards didn't expire until the end of March 2005 so that would be OK. I had decided that, because we were going to be staying away longer this time, our mail would be redirected to my Mum's. I had told her she could open everything and let me know if there was anything I needed to know about.

The phone would be disconnected on Monday – no point paying line rental for six months when we can reconnect for free when we get home. There was a slight possibility that we may not get our original telephone number again, but I thought it was worth the risk. I also rang Television Licensing who confirmed I didn't need a licence whilst we were abroad and they would refund our bank account with the overpayment we had made of £29, as we pay by direct debit.

Earlier in the day I had picked up plenty of euros to keep us going on the journey there and hopefully for the first few weeks once we arrive at La Manga.

With all the washing and ironing done we had packed the caravan with enough clothes for the journey: - knickers, pyjamas, T-shirts, jumpers, jeans, socks etc. The top box on the car could now be packed with clothes, coats and footwear that we wouldn't need until we got to our final destination. Everything was going according to plan and we both felt much more organised than last year, probably because we knew what to expect.

I had virtually emptied all the cupboards of food and taken most things to Simon to use up instead of throwing them away. He had just bought his first house with Lorraine about twenty miles away from us, and they were very happy together.

Brian suggested that we could start our adventure with a meal out at the Bridge Inn at Wray, a short drive away. We had a great meal and were back home in bed for ten o'clock, ready for our early start the next day.

Saturday 2nd October 2004.

It rained all night and was still raining when we woke up at six. As we were packing the final things in the car, Brian suddenly decided he needed to take a tape measure to Spain in his tackle box. In the summer, he had decided that he might like to do some beach fishing when we got to Spain so he had bought a rod and some tackle and a few books telling him what to do! He had never had any interest in fishing before, but thought it would be something to fill his leisure time as we were going to be away for almost six months. When he asked if I knew where his steel tape measure was I burst out laughing. Did he honestly expect to be catching fish big enough to need a six metre steel tape to measure them? No, he explained, this was for him to measure the lines he would be making up! Silly me.

We were well on time as we hooked up at Derrick's and were on the road for 7.45am. Both of us had been weighed as we were determined to get some weight off whilst we were away. Brian was 17 stone 5lb and I was 11 stone 12lb. At six feet two and a bit, Brian was maybe a stone overweight but he could carry it. I on the other hand was at my heaviest ever! I was only 5 foot 4 inches and until I stopped smoking just over a year ago my average weight was around nine stone ten pounds.

On our return from Spain in February, we had registered at the new doctors and had both been given quite a thorough examination. Brian was found to have slightly high blood pressure for which he was prescribed some daily tablets. I was found to have a very under active thyroid which the doctor explained was one of the reasons I had put on so much weight. My tablets would need to be taken for the rest of my life and once he had got the dosage right, I began to

116

feel much better. We had both been given three months prescriptions before we set off and the doctor had said that if we couldn't get the tablets over the counter, we would need to see a doctor in Spain. Let's worry about that if and when we need to.

So we are off on our second winter trip, with a combined weight of almost thirty stone!

The rain stopped by mid-morning and apart from a few delays on the A1, we were making good time. After last year's awful journey down the M6, we decided to try the A1, A14 route, which was only five miles longer than using the motorway.

Just after lunch, my phone rang. It was our friend Tony asking if we were in! He and his wife Ann had come to Ingleton in their camper van and wanted to pop in and see us. I had to explain that we were on our way to Folkestone and we wouldn't be home until March. Tony said they would keep in touch and wished us a great trip and a warm winter.

The weather worsened, and when we arrived at the site in Folkestone at four o'clock it was raining heavily and the winds had picked up. Although we had arrived at a much more sensible time than last year, ie. in daylight, the weather was just the same – we couldn't believe we had chosen another wet and windy weekend.

However, we were soon set up and connected to the electric. Coffee and brandy warmed us up and after walking the dogs, we went round to see Janice and Malcolm. Still no chef at the pub on site so we had a few drinks and then got a taxi to Densole and had a really nice meal at the Black Horse. We caught up on each other's news and I was very impressed with Janice's weight loss, which she put down to using a hula-hoop.

We told them about Harry having his operation for an aneurysm and how the doctors were amazed by the speed of his recovery. Although he still relied heavily on Pam to help out, he was doing very well, but now had the added worry of a problem with his prostate. He was under the hospital for further checks and tests. Brian had been to hospital for a scan and was given the all clear for aneurysms. He would need to be checked again when he was sixty.

Between us we put the world to rights, got a taxi home and after a few drinks in the pub we went to our snuggly beds.

Sunday 3rd October 2004.

Happy Birthday Chris. My brother's card and present I had left with Mum to give him today. Eight-thirty and the morning looked promising- bright and dry but by ten-thirty dark clouds had arrived and it was pouring with rain. By lunchtime it was torrential rain but Jack and Jill needed to go out so Brian the Brave put on his waterproof jacket and hood and set off for a short walk with the dogs.

I busied myself drinking tea and reading a magazine, and I was starting to get worried when they hadn't returned half an hour later. I was just on the point of getting my coat and umbrella when I saw them walking towards the caravan all three of them soaked to the skin. Towels at the ready, I opened the door to find Brian with a face like thunder and green skid marks and mud covering the front of his jeans! I could tell that he wasn't pleased and as Jill jumped into the caravan her ears were pinned back so I knew she had done something naughty.

Brian stood for a few minutes in the rain, teeth chattering, holding his chest as though he couldn't breathe. I didn't dare ask what had happened until ten minutes later when the dogs were dried off and Brian had sat down and started to get warm.

Apparently, he had found a field with no one in sight, so had let the dogs off so they could have a quick run about. Jill had bolted into the next field and by the time Brian had spotted several sheep, it was too late! She had one cornered against a tree and was snapping at its legs. Looking round for the farmer and his gun, Brian put Jack back on his lead and hooked the handle of the lead over a gate post, whilst he concentrated on getting Jill back. She ignored his shouts and he ended up chasing her round the muddy field and every time he tried to grab her in a rugby tackle she slipped out of his grip, like a greasy pig! By the time he caught her when she was out of breath, Jack was on the point of being strangled by his collar as a huge sheep had him pinned against the gatepost and Jack was so frightened he was trying to climb over the gate to get away. What a nightmare.

When Brian had calmed down, he took his wet jeans off and I looked in the wardrobe for some clean jeans or trousers. All I could find were numerous pairs of shorts and when I questioned this Brian admitted that against my advice, he thought his jeans would do until we got to France tomorrow, when he was sure the sun would be out and he could put some shorts on! His other trousers were locked away in the top box on the car roof so he had to get wet again whilst trying to find a clean dry pair! Why don't they listen?

Later on, when tempers were restored, we went round to Janice and Malcolm's for a while and then we all trooped into the pub. The landlord insisted that we bring the dogs in so I went to the caravan to fetch them.

I was surprised to see another caravan parked in the field. They must have arrived whilst we were in the pub. It was a cold rainy day and as I passed their window I waved and said "Hello". That was it! The man opened the door and invited me in for a drink with him and his wife. He was quite insistent so I went inside and they seemed to be half way through a five-litre drum of red wine. A glass was thrust into my hand and although it wasn't the best wine it was palatable. The wife had no teeth in but this didn't seem to bother her and an hour later after hearing their life stories, I managed to make my excuses and continue my short trip to our caravan to get Jack and Jill.

Back at the pub, Brian didn't seem to notice that it had taken me over an hour to walk ten yards! I remember when we first started caravanning that Brian's Mum and Dad said you wouldn't meet a friendlier set of people, and they were right. They had both been keen caravanners and when they gave up in 1993 they asked if we wanted their caravan and all the bits that went with it. At the time, we had no interest at all and couldn't see that we would ever take it up. It was a couple of years later when Brian decided to retire from league cricket that he was looking for another hobby as he didn't want to spend every weekend watching cricket and drinking! His friend Tom at work happened to mention that he was selling his caravan and when Brian came home and asked me what I thought, I assumed he was joking. But he was quite serious so we bought Tom's caravan and have loved the lifestyle ever since.

Early evening we walked along the cliff tops and had a meal at a nice pub, which Malcolm insisted on treating us to. We had a nightcap and they wished us a safe journey, as we would be leaving just after five the next morning. We wished them a lovely time also, as they were going to Goa again early December for a couple of months. At nine o'clock we were tucked up in bed then the gale force winds started. It was just like a rerun of last year.

Monday 4th October 2004.

Not a good night's sleep so we were very tired when the alarm went off at quarter to four.

Everything went like clockwork and we left the site at 5.15, ready to catch the ferry at six, and still speaking to each other.

This year, I had taken more time to get different quotes for the ferry journey, and had booked with P&O through the Caravan Club. They gave the cheapest quote of £189 return including the two dogs. However, when I booked it, the girl taking the booking had told me we couldn't book for the return date we wanted, as the prices weren't available for 2005. She explained that normal procedure was for her to choose a return date in December, then a week before that date, I should ring up and ask to amend the date. This would incur a booking amendment fee of £10 and she warned there was a small possibility that there could be a slight increase in the price of maybe another £10. This was still a very favourable quote so I had booked it and made a note in my diary to phone on December 6th with our correct return date.

As we waited to board the ferry, I thought this was the ideal time to put on the headlight converters. I had studied the instructions before setting off and knew exactly where to place them. Who's a clever girl?

We were soon sitting in the restaurant looking at the breakfast menu. I commented that the steak breakfast looked good value at £2.95 whilst Brian was anticipating the taste of smoked haddock and eggs which was just £2.50. As we sat discussing the excellent value for money, a waiter appeared and asked if he could see our "Freight Card". He explained we were in the drivers' restaurant, which wasn't open to the public! We hurriedly found the correct dining area where we had to settle for the full English and pay six pounds each!

Arriving in Calais at 7.25 am, we put our watches forward an hour and were soon confidently driving along the quiet motorway. Both of our mobiles were bleeping with incoming messages, and we remembered not to get excited, as these would only be from our service providers welcoming us to France.

Brian kept the journey interesting again, by giving a running commentary as we passed through historical places like Cambrai where he explained tanks had first been used in a battle. Well, I didn't know that!

As you may recall, last year we had stayed on the services in France with no problems. But a few months ago on the local news, was a frightening story of a family from Lancashire who had stayed on the same services at Macon. Their camper van had gas put through the vents and they were robbed of money and passports. Thankfully, their children and themselves were unharmed but on the strength of it, we decided to stay at a couple of caravan sites on the way down, instead of sleeping at the services.

We were heading for our first overnight stop, which was at Beaune, and just for a change we got lost! After driving around a village for an hour with Brian frantic that we would get stuck down a side street, we arrived at the correct destination.

It was a nice dry day and we were shortly sitting outside having a coffee in the last rays of the day's sunshine. After showering and a change of clothing, we walked into the nearby village and found a small local restaurant. Meal of the day was excellent and the bill was 41 euros including a bottle of wine and coffee. This was much more civilised than parking up at the service stations!

When we arrived back at the site, we paid the fee of 15 euros for the night as we had enough to do the next day without trying to remember not to drive off without paying.

Tuesday 5th October 2004.

Up, washed and ready for off at ten past nine! I had even made sausage and egg butties for breakfast. What a team until we tried to get out of Beaune and we were lost for almost an hour again.

Before we knew it, the dreaded Lyon was approaching but we agreed to stay calm and not shout or swear at each other. We followed the signs for Lyon-Centre then kept to the left and headed towards Marseilles. Brilliant no problem!

At two o'clock we had a well-deserved rest at Montelimar and Jack and Jill were ready for a walk about. The temperature had risen to 28 degrees so Brian was right to have put his shorts on. As we headed south, the temperature cooled and we were looking forward to our next overnight stop at Boulou. No getting lost this time so we arrived at six o'clock and we got a lovely spot next to the woods. At the entrance to the site was a cheese stall so I went to buy a piece of horrible blue cheese for Brian, as he loves it.

Setting up was becoming second nature and after using the shower blocks, which were very clean and well equipped, we walked back towards reception to try the small restaurant. Brian had driven 411 miles today so he was ready for a good meal and a drink. Menu of the day was 10 euros and we were served with rabbit pate and salad, then fish and vegetables, a piece of cheese, and raspberry cake. The house red wine was good and we took our time over coffee as we chatted to a French couple who sat on the next table.

Back at the caravan, Brian took the dogs for a walk round the site and didn't return for nearly an hour! When he got back he was holding two mini snickers chocolate bars and a Bounty bar! He explained he had got talking to a French bloke called Dave who made him have a large glass of red wine and sent him home with some chocolate for me! !

It was now dark so we sat in the warmth of the caravan having a cup of tea before bed. It was a warm night so we slept with the roof windows fully open to let some air in. The large piece of cheese, which I had bought, was placed on a chair outside so that it didn't smell the caravan out.

At half past one, I woke up to a strange snorting sound. Brian wasn't snoring and neither were the dogs so I nudged Brian to wake him up. He confirmed he could hear a noise but didn't know what it was. It was however getting louder and we realised it sounded like pigs snorting in the ground. Suddenly, Brian yelled, "The pigs will be getting my cheese quick, get up and see what's happening". I was up and standing outside in my pyjamas in a flash! How sad is that? There I was, pyjamas on but no teeth in, guarding Brian's cheese like a mad woman. Why didn't he get up himself? Too late- I was up now and able to confirm that some wild pigs were in the wood behind, probably attracted by the smell of the cheese. Luckily there was a wire fence between the wood and the campsite so the cheese was safe! Hooray.

Wednesday 6th October 2004.

After a fitful night's sleep, we woke at 7.30 and set off leisurely at 9.20 after paying the one night fee of 15 euros. Today's journey was only about 200 miles so we knew there was no rush to get to our next destination of L'Ametlla where we had stayed last year. We stopped for a break around eleven o'clock and arrived at the site at 1 o'clock. Checking in for two nights, I paid the bill of 32 euros and ordered croissants for the next morning.

There were only a couple of others on the site and we backed into the same pitch we had used last year. It was a really hot day so we unhitched and got set up as quickly as we could and then drove into the village to get a few provisions. What are we like? We should have known better. Everywhere was closed for siesta as it was now 2.30.

Back at the camp, we had a beer then took Jack and Jill for a long walk along the deserted beach. They were soon in the cool waters of the sea and before long, Brian had joined them for a swim. A gorgeous afternoon and we all enjoyed our few hours in the sun.

On our return, we looked in the fridge and decided we would settle for a fry up for tea. So we barbecued bacon and sausage and had eggs and beans and a few homemade oven chips. A bottle of wine from reception was very nice and what a cheap meal. I did a small wash at the launderette in between Brian sorting out the tea.

Unexpectedly it rained at seven o'clock quite heavily and then there was a thunderstorm. Once again we were all snuggled up in the caravan and decided to watch a video. We still only had our TV/video set so could only use it to play videos, as we couldn't get a picture in Spain. The months up to October we had taped things onto video to bring to Spain with us in case we fancied watching some telly one night. Tonight we decided to watch an episode of "Frost," which we hadn't seen the first time it was on, so we settled down, me in my pyjamas as usual, and were soon engrossed in the plot. A friend of mine called Jean did some television work as an extra, and has been in most of the episodes of "Frost," playing a canteen lady! We always look out for her when the scene is in the police station canteen and can usually spot her desperately trying to get in the shot of the camera!

Thoroughly enjoying the story line, we were both left open-mouthed when the recording finished with the last five minutes of the episode missing! A big debate followed trying to establish blame. Who recorded it, who set the timer up incorrectly, which stupid idiot didn't leave the tape running? All to no avail as it didn't really matter. We didn't know who had committed the murder and Jean was nowhere in sight!

Thursday 7ᵗʰ October 2004.

A grey start to the day so we went to the market as soon as we were dressed. We returned with salad, bread, steak, brandy, muscatel and a pair of sandals for Brian – the Imelda Marco of Lancashire!

The English couple parked almost opposite us came over for a chat. They had until recently run a Caravan Club site near Clitheroe and they were now exploring a bit of Spain, together with the Smart car which they had on their trailer. When Brian told them we were on our way to La Manga, they told us to look out for a friend of theirs called Fred who would be wearing a cricket cap and had a small dog! Maybe we will run into him?

The day got better as the sun tried to get out so we all went to the beach, Brian with his new fishing gear that he was itching to try out. Whilst I kept the dogs entertained with various sticks, Brian spent the afternoon getting to know his rod and tackle. No fish to take home but he had enjoyed the fresh air or so he said.

Showers were very welcome when we got back and as Brian prepared a salad to have with the steaks, I decided to try our new printer. We had invested in a digital camera and then bought a small printer, which produced postcards of your chosen snaps. This idea appealed to me so that I could send them back to family and friends to show them what we were doing. I printed two of Brian fishing, which I would send to Simon and Ian when we arrived at La Manga the next day.

We sat in the evening sunshine eating our barbecued steaks and salad and said hello to the English couple who were behind us. They were touring Spain and were interested in the site at La Manga as it was one that had appealed to them and which they were considering visiting.

As darkness fell, we moved inside and settled down for the evening but we were disturbed by a loud rattling sound. Once again, Brian thought I should go outside and see what the noise was. He explained he'd done enough "investigating" when he was a policeman. I was quite amused to find it was the couple behind us who were chaining and padlocking their two sun chairs to the trees on the pitch. There were only three lots of campers there, we were all English and I thought they were being overcautious but as Brian says it's better to be safe than sorry. Maybe he was an ex-crime prevention officer, or perhaps he just got heavy chain and padlocks on the cheap?

Friday 8ᵗʰ October 2004.

The final leg of the journey would take around six or seven hours so we set off at 9.30, carefully following the diversion signs typical – the road out of the village was closed just for the day due to road works. But we were soon on the motorway and didn't stop until one o'clock for refreshments and to let the dogs out.

I opened the boot of the car to let the dogs out whilst Brian was getting their water and bowl out of the back seat. He didn't realise I had opened the boot, and he walked straight into the corner of the raised edge. Blood was pouring down his face and I could detect the anger in his taut face but he didn't speak for quite some time.

"Sorry" seemed inadequate but I couldn't think of anything else to say. After a few minutes he had calmed down and I got the first aid kit from the back seat. The cut on his forehead was deep but not too long and after a few minutes the blood flow lessened. Brian began rooting around in the first aid tin and took out a pair of scissors, which I assumed he was going to cut a length of sticking plaster with. Don't ask me how, but the scissors ended up in mid-air and whilst trying to catch them, they landed on Brian's face and cut his ear, which then bled quite profusely! Were we auditioning for an episode of "Casualty"? Luckily we could both see the funny side and when we realised he was not going to bleed to death we apologised to each other for getting annoyed. After applying plasters to both injuries, we walked the dogs and had a rest for ten minutes at one of the picnic tables.

The remainder of the journey was uneventful and we arrived at La Manga at four o'clock. We pulled into the car park and I went to reception whilst Brian gave the dogs a short walk. Driving to our reserved pitch was a doddle as we knew just which route to take and we were soon unhitching and using our remote controlled caravan mover to get the best position. Yes, we had taken Derek's advice and had a mover fitted earlier in the spring. It was worth every penny of the one thousand pounds it cost and on an earlier trip to North Wales we had learnt a valuable lesson!

We love caravanning in Wales, and decided to combine our trip in June with a weekend of six-a-side cricket at Hurst Green. After a really good weekend staying at Merrick's Farm, we packed up on the Monday morning to continue our journey to Red Wharf Bay, and were amazed how easily the caravan moved using the remote control. In no time at all we had the caravan in the correct position and we hooked up and set off feeling very pleased with our latest investment.

About an hour later and some fifty miles down the motorway, I asked Brian where the remote control was. He replied "I left it on the roof of the car at the farm!" He said there was no point saying otherwise because as soon as I had asked the question, he could remember where he'd left it. Don't you just love him?

We agreed to take the next junction off the motorway and drive back to Hurst Green. Although neither of us held out much hope of finding it there, we knew we had to at least try. Typically, the next exit off the motorway was bloody miles away but eventually we were retracing our tracks driving back into the village of Hurst Green. About a mile before we reached the farm, Brian shouted "It's there–on the grass verge!" He continued driving to the farm and we pulled in and turned round. Back on the main road he pulled over and sure enough, there it was. The back of the remote had come off and was a few feet away but other than a few scratches it was as good as new. From then on, we agreed we would always keep it in the glove compartment and would double check with each other before leaving a site.

This year, we decided to position the caravan parallel to the road as we realised that this would give us maximum sunshine on the pitch, whereas the previous year we had set the caravan up facing the road. We are learning all the time.

We hadn't been on the pitch half an hour when our first visitors arrived to welcome us back. Joop and Meip, Corrie and Jean-Pierre and Bill and Evelyn all greeted us, and of course, Jack and Jill. They were asking how we were, how my Mum and Dad were and generally making us feel like we had come home! Corrie gave me an extra cuddle and thanked me for the lovely card that I had left with Barbara. She took my hand and led me to her caravan and showed me the picture of a sunflower from the front of the card I had sent her, which was now permanently positioned in the awning, covering up a plug socket! How sweet.

We unpacked a few bits but decided we would put the awning up and unpack properly at our own pace. There was no rush; we were here until March this time.

Jack and Jill enjoyed a good run down the beach. I told Brian I was wondering if the dogs could remember being here. He said I must be short of something to think about!

There were quite a few fishermen on the beach so Brian was getting quite giddy about being able to fish in the Mar Menor.

We both went to get a shower and the first thing I noticed were four stools placed outside the shower stalls. I must tell Mum. After showering and changing we walked down to the restaurant for the meal of the day. It was fish and chips – Friday special and the price had only gone up by 80 cents to 9.80 euros. We remembered the waiters and a few familiar faces said hello.

Back home, we tuned the radio in to Spectrum and listened to it for an hour before getting into bed. It was a sad end to the day when it was announced on the ten o'clock world news that Ken Bigley had been executed.

Everyone had told us there hadn't been any serious rain since May and it was such a warm night that we put the fan heater on to blow cool.

And all four of us slept like logs.

Saturday 9th October 2004.

We couldn't have wished for better weather, sunny and warm ideal for putting up the awning. Within an hour we had it up and were feeling quite pleased with our efforts. The ground was very hard due to lack of rain and some of the metal pegs that Brian was trying to hammer in were bending. Bill was passing and he suggested pouring water onto the ground where we wanted the pegs to go in, and this made the task much easier. He also lent Brian his rake as the gravel on the pitches needs to be raised underneath the awning groundsheet to help keep it dry, in the event of rain.

Whilst Brian was securing the awning, I busied myself sorting out the cupboards and allocating wardrobe and drawer space. He took the top-box off the car roof so that I could unpack and we kept stopping for a cup of tea or a beer to keep us going. Jack and Jill were basking in the temperatures of 32 degrees.

Early afternoon I walked up to the supermarket and bought some steak, a few beers, a newspaper and some milk. I also bought two stamps and sent the postcards to Simon and Ian. On the way back, I rang Mum and she was pleased to hear from me as usual.

Back home, Bill's wife Evelyn called round and invited us for nibbles and a drink on Tuesday about 3 o'clock. How nice. She was making a fuss of Jack and Jill and she explained that they had now lost both of their dogs and she really missed them. Any time we wanted to go off for the day, she would be happy to "dogsit" for us. We said we would take her up on the kind offer as soon as the situation arose.

The permanent Spanish homes just along from our pitch seemed very quiet except for the one next door but one, where they had an African Grey parrot, two cats and a dog called "Rocky". We hadn't previously noticed any cats on the site, but this time there seemed to be quite a few, though they mostly looked clean and well fed and were all wearing "flea" collars.

Brian set his barbecue up outside and we had juicy steaks, salad and jacket potatoes together with a great bottle of red wine.

Quite a tiring day and we'd both worked fairly hard so after a warm shower we snuggled up with Jack and Jill to watch a video we had brought with us of "Emmerdale." How sad is that? Well, we don't care!

Sunday 10ᵗʰ October 2004.

Oh no, my visitor has arrived again. Never mind, I would still start my diet as planned so I had an orange for breakfast.

We had bought a new Isabella windbreak in the summer and we put it up for the first time this morning. We also erected the cheap one we had bought in Los Belones last year and we were feeling quite territorial as the edge of our pitch became defined. Each of the pitches has trees and hedges on three sides which makes them quite private. Brian had brought his secateurs this year and was soon pruning the branches around our boundary. The sun was out and as the temperature reached 33 degrees he took off his T-shirt and enjoyed the warmth- and I was enjoying the view! The working woman's Percy Thrower – there's no accounting for taste!

Last year, we had both noticed that most people had bought some green plastic floor covering to lay over the gravel, which was a bit like a ground sheet. We had seen this on the roll at the Ferreteria but had talked ourselves out of buying any, as we weren't here so long last time.

Anyway, as we were pottering about doing the "garden", Brian noticed that someone had just left some of this sheeting at the side of the bins, so he fetched it over to see if we could use it. I was horrified! Taking things from the bins was something we had previously scoffed at, but as he laid it out we could see that there was nothing wrong with it and although it only measured around three square metres, it would certainly come in handy. This time, we would do things properly and have our gravel covered with this "carpet effect" like other more experienced campers.

So Brian's tape measure came in handy as we worked out how much more we would need to complete our pitch – another 4 metres should do it.

A late morning walk along the beach, and Jill was soon swimming in the warm shallow waters. We would throw a stick into the sea and it was so shallow she could wade out most of the way before she had to start swimming. Jack was joining in periodically and generally having a wonderful time.

Back home, I sat in the sun with Jack and Jill whilst Brian made a chicken and chickpea curry. He enjoys cooking and had brought with him a box full of spices, everything you could think of but he had forgotten to bring some cloves so they would go on the shopping list. He made the curry in the wok part of the barbecue and as he was outside cooking it the aroma attracted many comments from people who were passing. Joop came over to ask what the lovely smell was. He reminded us that he was a chef before he retired and he was very interested in food.

I put my washing line up at the back of the caravan and I printed a dozen photographs to send to friends. Too lazy to go to the phone, I sent text messages to Pam, David and Gill, Dad and Connor. Janet has got a mobile phone, but it is usually in the bottom of her handbag in the wardrobe, or it needs charging or she's forgotten to put any credit on. So I usually get a better response if I text Connor and he passes the message on, when he remembers!

All this sun bathing had worn us out so after tea it was the usual shower, reading and an early night.

Monday 11th October 2004.

On the beach for half past eight even the dogs were surprised at this early morning walk. Next we went to the Ferreteria and bought four metres of the green covering, after spending an hour looking round the shop. We also bought four wineglasses and two brandy glasses, and a selection of good quality plastic containers for our tea, coffee, sugar and cereal.

We went shopping later to the Upper supermarket, not the one on site, the bigger one towards the strip. If you recall, I had used this one the most last year as they accepted Switch cards and I found this very convenient. What I hadn't realised until I got home and checked my bank statements was that every time I used my card, there was a standing charge of almost a pound. This doesn't sound much, but I was often popping in and spending five or six pounds and using the card, so it soon mounted up. This year I had a different plan I would use the cash point on site to withdraw cash when we needed it, and only use my Switch or Visa for unexpected expenses. There was a maximum charge by the bank of £4 for this service so I would withdraw the most I could each time, which turned out to be 450 euros. At least this way, I knew exactly what it was costing me.

On the way back I called and bought four telephone cards-the same ones as last year at six euros each. Brian asked why I had bought four. I told him they would probably last me until Christmas to which he replied "I've heard geese fart before!" He has some lovely sayings!

After posting the cards at reception, I called in to put up a small advert on the "For Sale" board. It read "Wonderwash–Table top pressure washer for sale. In good condition. ten euros. See Julie O93". I had brought with me my new electric washer. How extravagant is that? It only takes a small wash but the manual winding of the pressure washer had not helped my tennis elbow one bit, so I had spent £37 on a little electric one and thought I would see if I could sell my other one whilst we were here.

Once we were home, I began measuring the area where we were having the gravel covered and we laid out both sheets and secured them with tent pegs. How posh are we?

Whilst Brian started preparing the chicken in red wine for tea, I walked round to the static caravan that Mum had seen last year to see if it was still available to rent. I was pleased to see a poster in the window with a telephone number on. I went to the phone and was soon chatting to Gwen, the English owner who lived on the site at the other side of the camp. The caravan belonged to her son and she was letting it for him. I explained that my Mum and Dad wanted to come for a month in February and she said this was fine, she would book it for me and it would be around £80 a week. She said she would call at my pitch in the next few weeks to see me.

Mum was very excited when I rang her and she said she would

now get on with booking some flights. My friend Gill had said she would book the flights on the Internet for Mum, so they would discuss it at the slimming club tonight. Mum had been busy as her Auntie Joyce had been to stay for a few days but had now gone back home to Doncaster. She had been mugged a few months previously and it had really shaken her up. At seventy-five it must have been quite upsetting. Mum said she thought the change of scenery had done her good–although they had not slept well due to Joyce making thumping noises in the night. It turned out that she hadn't ever slept under a continental quilt and during the night she had become entangled in the quilt cover and ended up falling out of bed and then struggling to unravel herself to get back into bed! Auntie Joyce could always make us laugh!

I was very pleased to hear Mum say that her eyesight was the best it had been for a few years, since she'd had an operation just before we left. The specialist told Mum she might lose the sight in one eye altogether but he thought it was worth the risk as she could barely see anything through it as it was.

There was very little post for us so I asked her to just keep opening it and let us know if anything exciting came- like a win on the Premium Bonds!

Janet was next on my list for a phone call and she was pleased that I had booked the caravan for Mum, as it was a six berth and Janet was hoping to come for a week whilst Mum and Dad were here. Her school holidays were earlier than they had ever been. They would break up on February 4th but this meant that Janet, Jimmy and the lads would be here for Mum's 70th birthday on February 9th. I was already looking forward to seeing everyone.

After tea, Brian walked to the phone and rang Harry. He was doing really well and guess what, it was cold but dry in Congleton!

Tuesday 12th October 2004.

I was disappointed that it was a cloudy start to the day, but I carried on with my washing. I set up my electric washer and my spin dryer and proceeded to fill the washer with hot water from the sinks opposite, put the clothes and some detergent in, then set the timer for 15 minutes and wait! Much easier than turning that handle last year. Rinse, spin and hang out to dry what could be simpler? Apart from an automatic washer and a tumble dryer but this was still "camping", even if it was for six months. Brian says what he enjoys about caravanning is the outdoor living. He says it's like being a Boy Scout at fifty-six!

The washing was all done and hung out by twelve and the clouds cleared to make way for some gorgeous sunshine.

Today was a bank holiday- The Virgin of the Pillar day according to a book I had brought with me. Yes, we remembered to bring a phrase book and a Spanish/English dictionary and also a CD with accompanying book to learn Spanish. The phrase book was one I found in Brian's Mum's bookcase when we stayed at his Dad's in August. Pam's name was scribbled in the front and when I asked her if we could have it, she was delighted we would use it but warned me it was very old, probably from the early seventies. She was right! It contains some very useful everyday phrases like "Es un maricon" "He is a pansy" and "Ese hombre me sigue por todas" "That man is following me everywhere." You should be so lucky!!

Corrie came past as we sat having a lunchtime coffee and she said it was a bank holiday in honour of all the policemen in Spain, so she'd heard.

We both showered and got ready to go to Evelyn and Bill's at 3 o'clock. When we arrived, we were surprised to see about a dozen other people sitting outside. Evelyn introduced us to everyone–they were all Dutch and mostly from their "street" Happy Oldies Avenue. We recognised Henk from last year and he was with his wife Ria whom we didn't recall seeing before. Also Wim and Emmy who were next door to Evelyn and Bill and who had become firm friends to them after being next door neighbours for the last four winters.

Everyone made us very welcome and we enjoyed some nice nibbles and drinks as we sat in the glorious sunshine. Evelyn explained that in previous years, each couple had taken their turn at inviting the others round and making a meal for everyone. But it had become very hard work so they had all agreed it would just be nibbles in future and good conversation!

Back home at six o'clock and Brian made a spaghetti bolognese whilst I went to ring Pam. But all the lines to England were busy so that would have to wait for another day.

Wednesday 13ᵗʰ October 2004.

The evenings and nights were still very warm so we woke quite early most mornings. The beach looked lovely at 9.20 this morning and the dogs were swimming and playing in the sea for ages. Back home, we gave them both a shampoo, towelled them off and let them dry in the sun.

Later, at the Ferreteria we bought a peg bag, a paella pan and a length of hose and connector for our tap. Each pitch on the site has its own water tap and last year we had used it as it was. But watching other people we saw that we could buy a cheap fitting and attach a hose so we could use it more effectively. We had also set up the waste water container, which Brian was emptying down our drain every couple of days until Bill advised us to run a length of hose from the waste outlet straight into the drain! Why didn't we think of that? So no need to use the wastewater container at all.

Calling at the Upper we bought some fresh vegetables, salad and fruit and some beefburgers to barbecue for lunch. Yes, I know I am on a diet but I will only have one and I will give most of the bread to the dogs, so there.

As we sat in the sun, a German lady called to ask to see my Wonderwash. I showed her it and she seemed very pleased and she said her husband would come down on his bike and buy it from me. Half an hour later he duly arrived and was pleased that I still had the box and all the bits that went with it. Deal done for ten euros.

Good old Brian prepared tea which was a veal and potato casserole, but he wanted a crust on it so I made some pastry for him and that was another very tasty tea. I didn't eat any pastry but filled up on nice fresh vegetables. Although Brian had said he wanted to do most of the cooking, and I was enjoying having food cooked for me, I told him to let me know if he wanted me to make a meal for a change.

Pastry and Yorkshire puddings are the only two things he's not good at making – oh, and white sauce. He once made a Sunday dinner years ago when I was working, and the meal was lovely and I was very impressed that he had found my Be-Ro book and made some Yorkshire puddings. However, when I ate one it tasted quite "cloggy" and stuck to my teeth so I questioned how he had made them. Brian explained that the book listed the ingredients – flour, eggs, milk, water, salt, two ounces of lard and told you to beat all the ingredients together! I had to explain that the lard was for putting in the tins, not beating into the mixture, and he said he thought it didn't look like the batter I usually made! At least he'd tried.

We watched an episode of "Heartbeat" that we had taped followed by a two-hour drama with Brenda Blethyn called "Belonging," which was quite funny and very easy watching. Up until eleven-thirty – what will the neighbours say!

Thursday 14th October 2004.

Another early morning walk along the beach meant there were no other dogs about so Jack and Jill could run about and play.

Brian decided to try a swim in the outdoor pool. It was closed last year when we got here in November but it would stay open until the end of October so off he went. The indoor pool and gym wouldn't open until the outdoor pool closed. I didn't fancy it as Meip and her friend Lineker had been and told me it was quite cool.

Just as Brian arrived back, Rod and Wendy called to see us. It was lovely to see them again and they explained that they now had a permanent static over on C Block at the other side and they would be spending most of the year here from now on. They invited us for a drink on Sunday evening and we said we'd love to go.

The pool was cool but very refreshing, according to Brian. I would take his word for it. He had also said hello to the lady that he'd taken a shine to last year at the gym- she must work at the outdoor pool in the summer, then the gym–and indoor pool from November onwards. Anyway, he explained that when he saw her she smiled as she recognised him and he went over to her and noticed she was pregnant. When he pointed to her tummy and said Bambino" she said "No" then explained in broken English this was due to too much food! How embarrassing.

As we enjoyed our lunchtime refreshment, a German lady came past and left a box at the side of the bins. She said "Nothing wrong with them, we just have too many!" But what were they? As soon as she was out of sight, Brian dashed across and brought the box back. There were four small glass trifle dishes, four tiny coffee cups and saucers and a pair of walking boots which were as new and had never been worn. We decided to keep the crockery- we could always put it back by the bin again if we didn't use it. I could see Brian's eyes light up when he saw the boots- this footwear fetish of his is quite obvious! He once bought some size eight and a half shoes in a sale because he liked them and they were cheap. He takes a ten and a half or eleven. Needless to say they eventually went to the hospice shop unworn! What a bargain. Anyway, these walking boots were a size nine so we were just about to put them back when two older couples walking past stopped to have a chat. They were with the camping and caravanning club rally and they were just finding their way around the site. Brian asked the men if they wanted the walking boots before we put them back next to the bin. One of the blokes was like Cinderella! Yes, the shoe fits, and he was thrilled to bits with his "gift". Glad to be of service.

At the Mercadona we bought some fish to barbecue- I know I should eat more fish so I am going to try. We called at the pound shop in Los Belones and splashed out on a white plastic table and two chairs to keep outside. Last year, we only had one table so we would carry it out each morning, then drag it back into the awning at teatime. This table and chairs were only 30 euros and even if we threw them away when we left it would be money well spent if we got six months continuous use out of them. Of course I would need a new tablecloth and a set of those tacky looking clips to hold the cloth on in windy weather!

After a nice tea of fish, salad and potatoes, I set off to the phone booths with my phone card and our list of numbers. Mum was in and she said Gill would book their flights soon and she would let me know as soon as she had their flight dates and times. Her eyesight was so improved that she could now see who the characters were in "Coronation Street," instead of just recognising their voices. I told her Brian Tilsley had sold the garage but this went over her head.

Next I rang Pam but she wasn't in. David and Gill were at home and they were looking forward to coming to see us on November 7th and staying for a week. I tried Pam again–still no one home. All week I had been texting her but I had not had any replies. She is a bit slack like Janet when it comes to her mobile but I thought she would have picked up her messages. When I got back home, I sent a text to Hannah asking if her Mum was OK. Hannah replied yes, all was well. She thought her Mum was probably out shopping but she wasn't sure as she was just at the airport waiting for a flight to Kos with her mate!

Oh to be young and carefree!

Friday 15th October 2004.

These early morning walks are becoming a habit probably because it gets so hot by the afternoon we are all flagging! We bumped into Martin on our way back. He's the Dutch man who runs the bridge nights. He remembered that I had said I would like to learn bridge this year, but he explained that there needs to be at least six or eight people wanting to learn, otherwise it's impossible to teach. So far, there were just Wendy and me wanting to learn but he would let me know if there were any others. He asked if Mum was coming this year and when I told him she would be here in February he said he looked forward to seeing her again.

I remembered that Derek had also said last year that he would like to learn bridge, but he and Anne hadn't arrived yet so I would just have to wait and see.

On our way back, we called at the phone and rang David's Mum, Brian's Auntie Eleanor, to wish her happy 80th birthday. She was thrilled that we had rung her and we were sorry we would miss her party. I had left a card and gift for her with Gill and David before we set off. We knew she was getting a hot air balloon ride from her family so we kept the surprise and didn't mention it. We asked her to give our regards to everyone at the party, including of course Brian's Dad Harry, Eleanor's only surviving brother, and Pam and Gary.

Once back home Brian sent a text to Ian as it was his birthday today as well. Twenty-seven and never been kissed! Ian sent a text back to say he was working but hoping to go for a drink later.

Two loads of washing were soon hung out in the sun again, before I gave Brian a hair cut – number four all over. One thing about men getting older and losing their hair is it becomes so easy to keep short and tidy.

A relaxing afternoon, is there any other sort? And Brian made a creamy prawn and coconut curry. Evelyn called round with some leftovers for the dogs, which they wolfed down. All this exercise on the beach was tiring them out.

Ted came past and told us the Monday night quiz had started this week and there would also be English bingo on Wednesday nights down at the function room above the restaurant. It was nice to see an old face if you know what I mean!

Before retiring for the evening, I sent a text to my Dad and one to my old mate Noz who regularly sends me jokes via text and she always makes me smile.

Saturday 16th October 2004.

We thought we had better take advantage of this lovely weather so we drove a couple of miles to Calblanque beach. Jack and Jill knew we were at the seaside and couldn't wait to run on the sand. Apart from a white horse, which was wandering near the beach, there was no one in sight.

What a lovely day this was and all four of us were in the sea swimming – that's the dogs and us, not the horse! At one o'clock we drove back home as Jack and Jill were worn out and we relaxed for the rest of the afternoon in the sun.

Although we had two very comfortable lightweight relaxer chairs, we knew we needed some new sun loungers that we could lie on for the purpose of sunbathing. We would keep our eyes open for some here in Spain.

Pork and apple casserole was tonight's meal and whilst that was cooking, we walked to the phone and rang Simon and Pam. They were both at home. Simon was having a night in with Lorraine and Pam was cleaning Hannah's bedroom whilst she was on holiday in Kos. What a life! And yes, Pam hadn't checked her mobile phone and wasn't even sure where it was. What's she like!

Our evening meal was very tasty and had been cooking slowly in our electric pan, which we had bought to bring here. Last year, we did most of the cooking in the oven in the caravan, which used our gas. But the pitch fees include electricity and most people thought we were mad using our gas so we had invested in an electric pan and it was very versatile. We could cook a breakfast in it, or do a curry or a chilli or a casserole. Great value for money at just under £40 from Argos.

Brian's choice for tonight's video was a two-hour special called "Arthur's Dyke", starring, among others Pauline Quirke. A very well acted television comedy, which we had recorded some weeks before we set off. A few glasses of muscatel before bed sent me to sleep nicely.

Sunday 17th October 2004.

Mum and Dad's 51st wedding anniversary. Last time I was at

Mum's, I had left a card with Sheila next door and asked her to post it through the letterbox today. I was usually the only one that remembered their anniversary including Mum and Dad. But last year had been their golden anniversary and they didn't want a party so my Dad took all of us to Tenerife for a week's all-inclusive holiday. There were thirteen of us and we had a really good time. Brian enjoyed it 'cos Dad insisted on paying for us all!

Janet had come up with a novel idea for a present. Like most couples who have been together for fifty years, they had everything they wanted or needed. So we decided to buy them fifty individual presents, one for each year of marriage, and each item had to include the word "gold". We ended up with a jar of Nescafe Gold Blend, a Kodak Gold film, a pair of Marigold gloves, an Abba Gold CD, the DVD of "Goldfinger", a jar of Golden Shred and so on! I was given the task of wrapping all fifty items in gold paper and presenting them in a gold themed hamper, and the three of us shared the total cost. Mum and Dad were thrilled with this and it took them over a week to open everything – they were spinning it out to make it last – a bit like their marriage!

For a change I decided to ring Mum in the morning to wish them happy anniversary. She was pleased with her card but I could tell she was upset on the phone. Janet had been burgled in the night and they were getting ready to go to Manchester so Dad could help Jimmy change all the locks. I said I would ring Janet straight away, which I did.

Well, Janet was a lot calmer than I had been led to believe by my dramatic mother she can make a drama out of a crisis! Janet was quite philosophical about everything and was just pleased that none of them were hurt. As she said, the burglars had taken the car, the house keys, Janet and Jimmy's mobiles, Connor's new watch that I had bought him for his birthday just before we left England and everything inside Janet's handbag but they were all replaceable.

She had been disturbed at four o'clock by a noise downstairs, which she thought at first was Jake on the computer. On checking his bedroom she found he was fast asleep and so was Connor ,so she realised someone was in the house. Unfortunately, Jimmy had been off work for a few days with a bad back so when she woke him up and he tried to get his boxer shorts on, he couldn't bend down to put his legs in! Janet said that on reflection it was quite an hilarious scene with Jimmy falling over and Janet not being able to see, as she didn't have her contact lenses in, and both of them stumbling

138

about trying to be quiet! By the time Jimmy got downstairs, the intruders were just reversing Janet's car out of the drive, so he chased them down the street, cursing as he ran.

Back home, the police came very quickly and Janet said the policeman that came was very sympathetic but she told him about Brian retiring and that we were in Spain for the winter, and she said he was more interested in our retirement lifestyle than the burglary!

They decided not to get Jake and Connor up as they had slept through everything, and the police told them not to move anything until the fingerprints team had been later in the morning. The front room looked like a bomb had dropped, as they had overturned the settees and coffee table, and the computer was on its head with the chair on its side. Janet heard Jake getting up about nine o'clock and when he hadn't gone into the kitchen ten minutes later, she found him sat in the front room, on the computer! She asked what he was doing and he replied "I'm on the Internet is there a problem?" When she pointed out that they had been burgled he looked around but still failed to notice anything different, as though they usually upturn furniture when they go to bed on a Saturday night.

At least she could laugh about it, but she was worried as they were due to go to Scotland the following Friday in the car, for a week's holiday. It is times like this when you wish you weren't so far away. I would have just driven over if I had been at home. But as Janet said "Calm down dear, it's only a burglary."

The rest of the day we didn't do much except we had a quick walk round the market where we bought two cushions for the new chairs and a tablecloth for the new table. Brian made liver and onions for tea before we walked up to Rod and Wendy's. Their static was very homely and they had bought two pitches next to each other so they had twice as much room. We had a few gin and tonics and it was nice to sit outside on their lovely patio having a good natter. Later we went inside as it got cooler and we walked home about half past eleven.

Monday 18th October 2004.

Not surprisingly, we slept in until 9. 20. A cloudy start to the day but I still did a few loads of washing and luckily the sun came out to dry it all.

I had a text from Dad which read-"Blowk corld Erni scent yu

fifti squid in powst" which translates as "A bloke called Ernie sent you £50 in the post", in other words I had won £50 on the premium bonds! Great. Brian was still trying to work out Dad's message an hour later, and declared that he was "off his trolley"!

Problem. Winning cheques have to be signed and paid in within three months, so I sent a text back asking Mum if she could post it to Gill and Dave. They could bring it here in November. I could then sign the cheque and pop it in the post with a paying in slip for my bank. Sorted.

I had my spring cleaning head on and decided to wash the awning floor and give the awning a really good tidy up and clean. Brian went to the Mercadona for some shopping- Isn't he a treasure?

When he returned after lunch, we walked the dogs and he made a large paella for tea. Unfortunately, we were too tired to go to the quiz after last nights late bedtime. Brian did manage to walk to the phone to ring Ian.

Tuesday 19th October 2004.

A cooler day but ideal for beach fishing- who said that? Well I got wrapped up and we all set off in the car to Calblanque Beach, just a five-minute drive away. Brian thought this beach might be good for fishing so off we went.

As soon as we arrived I could tell it was going to be too cold for me to stay, as there was quite a breeze on the beach. After letting the dogs have a run, we left Brian and he said he would text me when he was ready for picking up.

Back home, I read the paper in peace and made spicy meatballs for tea. At four o'clock I received a text. "Caught nothing. Can you come and get me? Love me" so that was a disappointing day for him.

After tea, I rang Janet who wasn't in, then I rang Mum and we chatted for half an hour about nothing much. On the way back, I could hear someone shouting "Rocky", which was the little Yorkshire terrier dog that lived next-door-but-one. When I went into the caravan and the shouting continued for five minutes, we realised it was the parrot imitating the owner's wife calling the dog! It sounded just like her, and I bet it drove the dog mad.

The evening was very warm and we again put the fan heater on to blow cool air. I thought about sleeping without my pyjamas on but couldn't quite do it.

Wednesday 20th October 2004.

Evelyn and Bill were having Jack and Jill today so we could go shopping to Lidls supermarket at San Xavier about half an hours drive away.

We had been with Barbara and John last year, but we weren't surprised when we got lost on the way to it. Eventually we arrived and stocked up on wine, beer, pop and some other essentials. This year I had brought with me enough toiletries to last a few months shower gel, deodorant, shampoo, toothpaste, and of course loads of Steradent! I also brought a couple of catering packs of tea bags and coffee and a couple of boxes of sachets of dog food and a box of 25 pig's ears! So shopping didn't seem as expensive as we weren't buying any of the boring stuff, ie. things you can't eat or drink.

Driving back, we agreed that although we didn't want to be out all day as it was the first time we had left the dogs, we should make the best of the freedom. So we called at Cabo de Palos and had lunch at the Miramar restaurant overlooking the lovely harbour. We had a couple of drinks, I had the lamb chops whilst Brian had mixed fish grill and with two coffees the bill was 40 euros. This was a bit expensive for what we had, but you pay for the setting in this restaurant and we did enjoy it.

Arriving home at three-thirty, we went round to Evelyn's to find Jack and Jill sitting in the sun with her and Bill. They said Jill had been fine, no problem, but Jack had fretted a bit but eventually calmed down and was now OK. We had arranged that the four of us would go to bingo later.

We were all ready with our bingo cards at eight o'clock eyes down, look in. It was Ted that was running the bingo and I soon realised he was a little bit "number dyslexic" too. The first game contained the following calls "One and Eight-Eighty one", "Just your age, thirty seven" and "On its own number ten"! But it was a good fun night and although we didn't win we enjoyed it and promised to come next week. Let's hope Ted gets some practice in before then!

Thursday 21st October 2004.

Despite a shower of rain at nine-thirty which lasted less than a minute–the day looked promising. We sat in the sun having fruit for breakfast when Corrie came past and reminded me that Keep Fit started next Tuesday, same times as last year, Tuesdays and Thursdays from ten until eleven. I promised I would be there.

A Welsh chap came to wash up and he asked us if we knew where the nearest vet's was. He had only arrived yesterday and didn't know his way about so we had a chat with him about the area and where to go. His name was John and he was asking where to buy a phone card and it was nice to be able to help someone who was in the same position as we were last year. He said they had brought their dog abroad for the first time but she hadn't travelled very well and was a bit off colour today.

Later in the day as we walked to the beach, we went past John's caravan and met his wife Joyce. I had with me a pig's ear for their dog to try and cheer her up.

Brian went up to the supermarket for some almonds, a paper and some milk. He made a beef and almond curry for tea, which was quite spicy but nice.

Bill called round to say he was about to throw three rugs out which had seen better days, and he wondered if we wanted them for the dogs to lie on. We certainly did, and took them off him gratefully. We seem to be taking in all sorts of rubbish this year!

It was Harry's turn for a call from Brian and I knew before he told me that it had been raining again in Congleton.

Friday 22nd October 2004.

An overcast start to the day as we set off to the Mercadona, and we filled up with diesel and put the car through the car wash. It was only one euro for a wash and wax so Brian thought this was excellent value for money compared to England. It annoys him every time he uses the air pumps in England that you have to pay 20 pence for air.

At the supermarket we got a trolley as usual but we only bought a rabbit, some mince and some fresh fruit and vegetables. When we came out, I went to sit in the car whilst Brian returned the trolley and retrieved our one euro coin. What a scream!

I watched from the car as he pushed the trolley, which just had two carrier bags of shopping in it, towards the other stationary trolleys. He pushed his trolley into the row and took the euro coin out but the shopping was now stuck, still in the trolley. He tried to get his hand between the two trolleys and although he managed to grab the handles of the carriers, he couldn't get the shopping through the gap. Like lightening, he was struck by a brain-wave: he took the euro coin and just when I thought he was showing an unusual amount of common sense by starting again, he put the coin in a trolley three in front of his! So the shopping was now stuck in the end trolley, with three others joined to the front of it! How can he make life's simplest tasks look like the entrance exam for Mensa? I was about to get out of the car and help him, when the penny seemed to drop and he retrieved the shopping. He held the two carrier bags up to show me what he had finally achieved. I did promise not to tell anyone about this escapade but I couldn't keep it to myself. Sorry, Brian.

A very hot afternoon so we took the dogs for a cool swim in the sea and on the way back, Brian called at the phone booth. He rang his mate Tom who was still working for the police and had a chat with him just to catch up on any gossip.

I had a text from Dad to say Janet's car had been found the previous day and there was no damage so they had gone to Scotland as planned.

Rabbit casserole was done very slowly in the electric pan and Brian made it look very appetising by serving it with creamy mashed potatoes, cabbage and bacon and green beans. Yummy.

Saturday 23rd October 2004.

An early morning burst of rain, which lasted under a minute, didn't deter Brian from going fishing at half past eight on our beach. The bed was stripped and the bedding washed before I set about cleaning the awning out and generally sprucing the place up a bit.

I walked the dogs down to the beach at noon and Brian was still fishing but hadn't caught anything. He introduced me to his friend Helmut who spoke very good English and was giving him lots of hints and tips about beach fishing and what sort of bait to use. Very interesting I'm sure! On the way back I stopped to ring

Mum who told me she was quite tired as her and Dad had got Chris's baby son Joshua for a couple of days, and he was very clingy with her. But a gorgeous little boy who was a pleasure to have.

We waited for Brian back home and weren't surprised when he returned at three o'clock with no fish. The two cats that belonged next-door-but-one kept walking in front of Jack and Jill's beds as if to torment them, and after a while the dogs seemed to get more used to them. You never know, they may become friends.

Brian made a chilli for tea instead of fish, and we had just finished eating in the awning when an English couple came past and said hello. We got talking, as you do, and asked them if they wanted to come in for a drink. They were going down to the restaurant bar for a drink but said they would love to join us instead.

Les and Anita were in a camper van and were pitched on Happy Oldies Avenue opposite our friends Bill and Evelyn. The drinks flowed and the conversation went on and before we knew it, midnight was upon us! We finally got to bed at half past one, and the washing up had to wait.

Sunday 24th October 2004.

Emerging briefly from our beds at nine o'clock, we had a cup of tea, washed up in our pyjamas, and then went back to bed until eleven!

Today was very hot and after the dogs enjoyed a swim on the beach, we rang Dave and Gill who were looking forward to coming in two weeks' time. I made a roast chicken "dinner" but was disappointed that my Yorkshire puddings didn't rise. Yes, I brought some tins to cook them in, but no whisk, and for some reason they were awful.

Because it was so warm, we were inundated with flies so although we had planned to eat outside, we had to bring everything into the awning instead. A bottle of white wine that was less than a pound was wonderful very smooth and not too dry. We'll get some more of that.

After late showers, we settled down to watch an episode of "Heartbeat" from September 5th followed by a two-hour comedy thriller called "Quite Ugly One Morning" with James Nesbitt. This was a good idea to bring videos for those snuggly telly nights.

However, it was too warm to snuggle and we switched the cool blower on before getting into bed.

Monday 25th October 2004.

Another glorious day so after doing a small wash, we took the dogs for an early walk so we could relax in the sunshine for the afternoon. We still hadn't really looked for any sun-loungers but our chairs were very comfy so we made them do.

We ate our chicken pasta quite early so we could get ready to meet Les and Anita and go to the quiz. Just four of us in our team, but we only scored 33 out of 60 so that was quite poor.

One of the questions was about Yorkshire, and when we got it wrong thanks to "know all" Brian, the chap on the next table commented that we should have known the answer as he could tell we were from Yorkshire like he was. We struck up a conversation and to cut a long story short, he was also from Wakefield was called Ray and I had known him years ago through work but hadn't seen him since 1978! What a small world! He had been coming to the site for a few years and he and his wife always wintered here, but our paths hadn't crossed until now.

We enjoyed our night out and as we set off back at eleven we had just missed an hour's rain. What excellent timing.

Tuesday 26th October 2004.

Keep Fit beckoned at ten o'clock and when I arrived I saw Ray again. He was pitched opposite the Keep Fit and he was the chap who kindly let Corrie plug her music player into his electric every Tuesday and Thursday.

Enjoying the sunshine again, Evelyn and Bill called round and stayed for a beer in the warmth of the afternoon. I mentioned that I hadn't been to the Internet café since we arrived and Bill kindly offered to take me with him later as he was going about five o'clock.

I wasn't sure if I would have any emails, so when I signed in at the Internet café I was quite stunned to see I had over forty items in my "Inbox". Back in July, I had written to the Caravan Club

Magazine asking if anyone knew any sites in France, near the motorway, that accepted dogs and were open in winter. The Caravan Club had told me there was a few months' backlog with letters and up until we had left England I had forgotten about my letter. Reading some of the emails, I realised that my letter must have been printed in the October edition, which we hadn't seen. Whilst some of the replies were giving helpful information, the majority were asking if I could pass any replies on to them!

After reading most of the mail I sent general messages to everyone I could think of who might be interested and some that might not.

Bill brought us home and Brian had prepared another lovely meal, steamed salmon for me (the tail with hopefully no bones) and a huge piece of tuna for himself.

He told me that Joop had been across to ask what delights he was cooking and they were talking about fishing. Joop told Brian he had a friend Eric who went fishing and he would ask him to call round and maybe Brian could go fishing with him sometime.

I went to ring Mum and Pam and this got me out of doing the washing up. Pam was telling me all about their house being sold at last, and they were hoping to be moving before Christmas. Fingers crossed.

Wednesday 27th October 2004.

A breezy, cloudy but warm morning greeted us, and as we sat outside having breakfast we said hello to an English woman who we had seen arriving the previous day. But she completely ignored us.

We walked on the fields today for a change and when we came back, Brian prepared his beef curry outside whilst I sat with him and played Scrabble. The same English woman came to the sinks to wash up and was moaning to herself that she didn't like this site and she would be leaving before long. I tried to strike up a conversation with her and then realised she was quite deaf. She could lip-read when I stood facing her and she told me her and her husband were having an apartment built in Torrevieja so they were staying here in their caravan for a week or two, whilst they visited their builders. She didn't like the site, as there were a lot of foreigners on it! Why was she moving to Spain, I wondered!!

After tea, it was my turn to wash up whilst Brian took a new phone card to ring Harry and Simon. He was back before long and thought I had given him an old card as he said it only had 45 minutes on when he tapped the PIN in at the beginning of his calls. I told him he must have dialled a wrong number or done something stupid as it was a new card and would have 300 minutes on it.

It was cold but dry in Congleton and Harry was having problems with his waterworks again. Pam was going to ring the doctors and sort him out.

Thursday 28th October 2004.

Despite the wind and rain, which had kept us awake during the night, it was dry enough for Keep Fit. Halfway through, Brian came past walking the dogs, and waving at me.

When I got back, Brian was quite excited, as he'd salvaged a table from the bins that Wim was throwing out. It would just fit over my washer and spin dryer in the awning, hiding them from view – what a find!

Later we called at the Upper for a newspaper, milk and some chicken thighs. Of course I also had to buy a tablecloth for my "new" table and three stacking wine racks to go on the top of it!

My turn to make one of my favourite dishes from Pam's Mediterranean cookbook, chicken with garlic and lemon, served with boiled rice. Whilst I was preparing tea, Brian washed his car and, sod's law, it rained as soon as he had leathered it off! But the rain only lasted a few minutes before the sun came out again.

For some reason bingo had changed to Thursday so off we went with Bill and Evelyn. I was quite excited when I won a full house, but had to share it with someone else. Still, I won 54 euros so it was worth winning and I promised we would go for a Chinese meal with it.

Friday 29th October 2004.

Again it had rained in the night, but Brian was down on the beach by nine o'clock hoping to catch his first fish again.

It was quite cloudy so at twelve I took the dogs to see Brian and made him a flask of coffee and some sandwiches, which were gratefully received. On the way back I rang Mum, using a new phone card, just to prove that Brian had done something wrong the other evening when he rang his Dad. No, I think I owed him an apology, the recorded voice said I had 45minutes of calling time!

Mum still hadn't booked her flights as she said Gill was waiting for the prices to come down but they were just going up all the time. I told her to stop messing about and just get them booked so she said she would. She told me my Dad's sister, my Auntie Margaret, was not very well, and they would be going to visit her in Derbyshire soon.

Early afternoon, Brian was back without any fish, but with a list of things Helmut had suggested he needed to improve his chances! So we went to the Ferreteria, and bought some packets of hooks and various other bits, and a paella pan.

I had a text from Julia to say she was trying to get a flight out to see us at Christmas and one from Gill confirming their flight times on the 7th. I made a few postcards to send home, and posted one to Simon and one to Auntie Margaret to cheer her up.

Quite a hectic day, really, by our standards and we were soon eating Brian's latest made-up dish of pork and apple casserole.

A final text from Dad just before we went to bed read "Janits bak ome frome skotland gud nite". Thanks for the information Dad!

Saturday 30th October 2004.

When we were here last year, we had bumped into the "Saturday walking group" when we were at Portman Guns, and Corrie told us that whilst it was attended by mainly Dutch people, we would be made very welcome. So this year we said we would give it a go.

The posters round the site shower blocks told everyone to meet at the top car park at ten o'clock and to bring sandwiches, a drink and good walking shoes. We weren't sure if we would be driving somewhere before we started the walk, so we drove up to the car park. There were about twenty people there and three other dogs, and Corrie the organiser (another one, not my Keep Fit friend) told us the walk today would be about eight miles. And we didn't need the cars.

Rod and Wendy had turned up and I soon got talking to a lady called Margaret who was with her husband Norman and lovely old dog Misty. I knew that socialising with other dogs would be good for Jack and Jill and once we were on the beach, I let Jill have a run around with a very friendly German Shepherd. It was early days for Jack. Maybe next week I could trust him not to bite Misty? Margaret suggested I went to the vet's to get the dogs a white collar each, which protects them against fleas and mites that are peculiar to Spain. She gave me lots of recommendations for places to eat and things to do, and within half an hour she had recounted her virtual life story! The time flew and after stopping for an hour's break on a lovely beach to eat our sandwiches, we were back at the bottom end of the site at three o'clock.

Feeling very tired, we asked Rod and Wendy to stay for a drink at our pitch, as they had to walk back to the top of the site. We all sat in the sun and then I went to get some drinks from the fridge only to realise the caravan door was locked and guess where the keys were? In the car right at the top of the site! Good old Brian walked another half a mile and brought the car back by which time we were more than ready for a cool drink each.

After showering and getting dressed we drove to the Chinese and had a great meal, which cost us 32 euros and there was enough food in the doggie bags to feed the dogs the day after.

Back at the site for nine, we had promised Rod and Wendy we would go to the Halloween dance above the restaurant if we were back in time, so we finished our day off with a few drinks a good dance and another late night!

Sunday 31st October 2004.

The clocks went back an hour and Brian woke up with a sore throat probably due to his tuneless singing to the old records at last night's dance. He stayed in bed until twelve whilst I did some washing.

We walked up to our supermarket and bought two steaks and treated ourselves to a News of The World.

Back home, we sat in the sun reading the paper and having a glass of sangria. One of our Spanish neighbours, Antonio, came to talk to us but he couldn't speak any English and of course we hadn't even taken the wrapping off our Spanish Language CD. However, I brought the Spanish/English dictionary outside and, after about an hour and a few cans of beer, Brian and Antonio knew a little bit about each other! The barbecue was fired up by four o'clock and the steaks were really tender and juicy. Brian drew the short straw again and washed up whilst I rang Pam and Janet. I kept the conversations very brief as the phone cards were quickly running out. I would have to ask somebody what was happening with these cards.

Janet had enjoyed Scotland but was upset that the insurance company wouldn't pay out for the burglary as they had admitted leaving a small top window open in the room.

Pam was very excited as Gary was taking her to the Dominican Republic tomorrow for a week. This was for her 50th birthday, which would be December 27th, so she was busy packing.

Monday 1st November 2004.

Another bank holiday! Todos los Santos or All Saints Day.

Unlike England where bank holidays tended to have rain, Spanish Bank Holidays were usually glorious, and today was no exception. As we sat in the sun, Miep came over with the Dutch neighbours who were almost opposite us. They were getting ready to go home and wanted to ask if we would be interested in buying their two sun loungers for 50 euros, before they put them up for sale in reception. I fetched my purse immediately, as they were very light weight and good quality. Just what we needed.

The two neighbours' cats were getting closer to the dogs every day. They didn't run when the dogs came towards them- they rubbed past the dogs' faces and weren't bothered at all, probably because they were used to dogs.

Les and Anita called to tell us some friends of theirs, Fran and Geoff had just arrived and had invited us along to a barbecue later this evening. Anita said just to bring some drink but I felt a bit mean not taking any food especially as they had only arrived today. So I quickly made up a recipe for some garlic bread, using the packets of dried yeast that I brought with me. It turned out a treat and went down really well with the steak, sausages and salad.

After a few drinks we all walked down to the games room for the quiz, and because there were six of us we did better than previous weeks, scoring 45 out of 60, and we came in fourth.

Tuesday 2nd November 2004.

Brian went to the gym, but not before he had memorised a couple of phrases from Pam's book. He was trying to strike up a little conversation with the "tricky bird" at the gym, as he now referred to her! He would try to say "see you again soon" when he left the gym in his best Spanish accent.

I went to Keep Fit, and I walked back with Corrie. She speaks very good English and gives out most of the instructions in Dutch and English. Sometimes she gets her words mixed up and today she told us to stand up and move our heads to one side so the ear was touching the elbow! As all fifty of us looked puzzled she then corrected it to "the ear should be touching the shoulder, not the elbow".

She commented today that the dogs were "very brave" – I think she meant they are well behaved.

At lunchtime we made a quick trip to Los Belones market for some fruit and vegetables. We also called at the English Shop, as I couldn't get any bread flour anywhere. They had some in the English Shop and when I put it on the counter the owner told me it was free! Apparently it was just out of date so they let customers have it when they brought it to the counter. They didn't advertise it as people would just take it because it was free, and not because they wanted it.

We bought quite a few things at the Mercadona for sixty euros and were home and unpacking before two o'clock. But I couldn't find the cheese, the Oxos, the eggs or the butter and soon realised we must have left one carrier bag at the supermarket. It was also possible that Brian had left it trapped in a trolley so we said we'd forget it!

A walk down the beach and an hour in the sun gave us a good appetite and Brian set up his wok pan outside and cooked trout with almonds. He attracted the usual attention from neighbours and passers-by and the meal was lovely.

I joked that I would buy a blackboard and easel to put up announcing "Brian's cooking tonight.... ." and this would save him having to tell everyone what he was making.

Wednesday 3rd November 2004.

Today Brian decided to shave his beard off that he'd been growing since we got here, and I gave him a hair cut. He then went fishing for the morning.

I drove to the Ferreteria to buy some rope lights, which a lot of people had up in their awnings. I didn't mention it to Brian, as he would have argued they were too expensive or they would be too festive or something so I just went and bought some. I had them tied to the awning rails and working before lunchtime. Joop came over to see what I was doing and he asked if I wanted some for outside the awning too. He said they were going home for Christmas and if I wanted their outdoor Xmas lights I could have them for five euros! What a bargain.

So by the time Brian was back from fishing, it was like Santa's Grotto, but he said he quite liked it. Don't ask if he caught any fish.

Joop's friend Eric called to chat to Brian and he spoke good English. He told Brian he usually went fishing on Wednesdays and next time he was going Brian could go with him.

A quick tea tonight of sausage, mash, eggs and beans! How very English, but scrummy.

We had arranged to go to bingo with Bill and Evelyn, Les and Anita and Fran and Geoff who incidentally were only going to stay for two nights but had decided to stay until March! Les won 100 euros and Bill won 130 euros so our table had a good night.

On the way home, Brian rang Harry whilst Anita and Les came back to our awning for a nightcap.

Thursday 4th November 2004.

A cooler morning but I still went to Keep Fit. Whilst there, an elderly gentleman was taking a couple of photos of the group doing our exercises and I assumed he was here probably with his wife and was just taking a picture. But one of the English women took offence to this and was shouting "Get away, you pervert!" Most of the class felt as I did that if he really were a pervert, he wouldn't be taking photographs of a group of generally overweight women in old tracksuits! But there we are.

Wendy came over after Keep Fit finished to ask if I'd had any problems ringing home. Corrie also heard us talking and before long we realised that everyone had the same problem the calling time had gone from 300 minutes to 45, just like that! So it wasn't silly Brian, it was the phone company! One of the ladies said she had seen a poster in the supermarket telling people that the times had changed, so that was that. We thought it was too good to last.

It started to rain at twelve o'clock and I went up to the supermarket to buy a stamp to post a card that I had made for my Mum of Jack and Jill watching Brian make his trout dish. The girls in the supermarket were quite fascinated by the picture and the fact that it had now become a postcard. The checkout queue was building up as they took the photo around the shop to show everyone!

At two o'clock as we sat in the awning watching the rain, who should call but Barbara and John! We had kept in touch by email so I knew they weren't arriving until November. It was lovely to see them both again and they said they were just walking up to the supermarket. I was glad they had called as I was able to tell them that the shop now closed for lunch from two until three every day, whereas last year it stayed open all day. So they stayed for a chat and a cup of tea before venturing back out into the rain.

Whilst Brian prepared meatballs and spaghetti I took the umbrella to the phone and rang Mum and Gill.

Tonight's television treat was an old film that Brian had taped called "The Fiend". It was so badly written and acted that it was hilarious. We were still laughing when we got into bed at ten o'clock, but we had drunk two bottles of red wine.

Friday 5ᵗʰ November 2004.

Bonfire night at home but not a sign of it here! My visitor arrived again, and the rain came down from six a.m. until ten like a torrent. We were quite dry as Brian had banked up the gravel and our pitch was quite "shielded" as it was next to the Spanish permanent homes. Others weren't so lucky and we heard a lorry load of gravel being tipped at Bill and Evelyn's as they were almost washed out.

But by twelve the sun was out again so I decided to wash. Brian borrowed some ladders from Les and a saw from Bill and proceeded to cut some of the higher branches off the trees around our pitch.

Whilst Brian was walking the dogs, I got a text from my Dad which said that our new Visa card "chip and PIN" numbers had arrived and our new cards would follow shortly. This puzzled me, as our Visa cards didn't expire until next year. I would ask Mum next time I rang.

I drove to the Ferreteria to replace the gas and tried to buy a new quilt cover for my visitors coming on Sunday. I quickly realised that they don't have such things in Spain – all I could buy were sheets and blankets so Gill and David would have to make do with the bedding we had.

Driving back to the site I noticed the sign for "Farmacia" so I called in. I had with me the empty cartons for Brian's blood pressure tablets and my thyroid tablets. The chemist took them and retreated to the back of the shop, then reappeared with two months supply of each. They were different brands but it didn't matter, and at just over five euros for both I was very pleased.

I could smell the chicken curry as I drove to our pitch and it didn't disappoint.

After tea, we were watching Henk and his wife Ria packing up ready to leave. It was quite sad as they had been here virtually full time for five years and although Henk didn't really want to give it up, Ria was missing her children and grandchildren in Holland so they had agreed to call it a day.

Over the years they had accumulated a boatload of things and they seemed to be throwing most of them in the bins. Henk brought us a lovely big pan, which he had never used and he said he knew Brian enjoyed cooking so he wanted him to have it. They also gave us some plates and a few glasses to supplement our small collection.

We would be sorry to see them leave on Wednesday.

Saturday 6th November 2004.

A cloudy start to the day and it was raining slightly but I still managed to wash the bedding ready for Gill and Dave coming. We had decided it would be best all round if they had the fixed double bed and we slept on the made-up bed at the front with Jack and Jill. Our guests would also be able to use the loo in the night and we could pop across to the shower block without disturbing them.

Henk called to tell us that the supermarket at Playa Honda, not far away, had an offer on cans of Dutch lager, at only 28 cents a can, so "tight arse" Brian had us there in a flash! We did a general shop at the Upper and I bought a tin of biscuits and a nice bottle of wine for Ted. He was having a car boot sale and tombola for charity on Sunday morning, but we would miss it, as we would be at the airport collecting Gill and Dave.

The people who the cats belonged to came to say hello and we asked them what the cats were called. The dogs were used to them now and all four of them spent most afternoons cuddled up together in the dogs' beds in the sun! They told us that both cats were called "Nanny" which we found strange and that they were brothers. We asked various members of the family but got the same answer so we will call them both Nanny!

I didn't fancy the sound of a "fish casserole" but it was very tasty and not a bone to be found. Thanks Brian.

We made the bed up and it seemed strange to be at the front of the caravan in sleeping bags – you soon get used to the luxury of having a fixed bed.

Sunday 7th November 2004.

David and Gill landed on time and we were all back from Murcia airport at half past eleven. We couldn't have wished for a nicer day and we sat in the sun eating pizza and various nibbles, catching up on the gossip and asking how everyone was at home.

Later, Gill and I took the dogs on the beach whilst Dave and Brian had a few beers and disturbed the rest of the street! Although they are cousins, you would think they were brothers. They are both "larger than life" with voices to match! We could hear them miles away as we returned from our walk!

Whilst Brian was cooking a huge paella, Antonio came round with some whisky and some photographs of his sons, daughters and spouses and children to show David and Brian. The three of them were struggling with the language but it didn't seem to matter, they were having a laugh.

After the very authentic paella and more wine, David decided I could cut his hair. He agreed to a number four cut like Brian's and Gill was quite horrified as she saw his lovely locks falling onto the awning ground sheet! David said he liked it but he was three sheets to the wind.

We all became quite giggly and went to bed the worse for drink at ten o'clock!

Monday 8th November 2004.

Brian was off to the gym as soon as it opened at nine thirty, and the rest of us had a leisurely breakfast and got showered and dressed.

After calling at our supermarket, we decided to take a picnic to the beach as it was going to be a sunny day. We had the beach at Calblanque to ourselves although the white horse was still wandering around. At midday, we were all swimming except Gill – I think she was so tired she could barely stay awake to read her book. David and Gill both have jobs in different areas of Lancashire Police and they are both under pressure most of the time.

Back home, we all agreed we would eat at the site restaurant tonight and then go straight into the quiz. The meal was very good but the quiz seemed very hard this week and we only scored forty out of sixty.

Home again for eleven, we had cups of tea and coffee and rewarded our terrible efforts with marzipan sweets and chocolates. The diet may have to take a back seat this week!

Tuesday 9th November 2004.

The radio brought us the sad news that Emlyn Hughes had died at 57.

We took the dogs round to Bill and Evelyn's so that the four of us could go to the market and then we drove to Cabo de Palos and sat outside at the harbour restaurant, the Miramar.

All choosing different dishes we ended up with garlic prawns, prawns in white wine, whitebait, sardines and salad. With a couple of drinks each the bill was 52 euros and was very acceptable.

Calling at the Mercadona on the way back we were able to buy what the four of us wanted for the week and we had a bit of a song and dance at the till after we had agreed to pay half. And then Gill was insisting on paying more than me, 'cos she'd put a bottle of something in the trolley that she liked!

Brian prepared a chicken curry and whilst it was slowly cooking, he took David to have a game of boules. We had bought our own set of eight boules but hadn't played with them until now.

Evelyn said the dogs had been fine and Jack was much more

settled. She had also fed them with some grilled sausages and lots of other treats. Spoilt or what?

After Gill and I washed up, the three of us had a game of Scrabble whilst Brian had a few glasses of wine and sulked for a bit! He doesn't often get moody but when he does I just ignore him, as he soon comes round if nobody pays him any attention. Thanks for that advice Joan, many years ago!

Wednesday 10th November 2004.

The whole street were up and outside in their nightwear at nine o'clock to wave Henk and Ria off. Some concerns were raised about the caravan as it had been parked in that pitch for five years, but the men soon rallied round and found it was in good working order. There were tears from Ria and a lot of the winter residents, who had been close neighbours and friends for years.

Everyone waved them goodbye and wished them a safe journey back to Holland. The end of an era on this street.

Gill walked up to the shop – she's like a hamster in a wheel, always on the go! She brought back some treats for the picnic we were taking on our walk up to the Portman Guns. They both love a good walk and although Brian and I are not in their league as regards walking, we felt they would enjoy this walk and the spectacular view at the top.

The picnic was lovely at the top of the Guns walk, and no one else was there so the dogs could be off the leads and have a great run around. Gill sunbathed for a while and it was then that I remembered why I hate her – she's slim and fit and I'm neither!

Back home, a game of boules between the four of us was over after an hour so Gill and I went to the beach for a coffee. It was very windy on the beach and the few windsurfers that were out were coming in, as the winds were too strong. I looked for Les and Anita as they are both keen windsurfers but they weren't that brave.

As we were getting ready to go out, we received a text from Simon which read "Congratulations! You will be grandparents next summer. We are thrilled to bits". I was so excited I nearly dropped the phone. Brian on the other hand declared that he was pleased for them but it wouldn't change his life. What he meant was he wouldn't reorganise his life around a grandchild. He knows a lot of people who have retired and planned to do all sorts, then stayed at home to look after their grandchildren but this was not for Brian. But, as David said, you don't know until you're a granddad.

The Chinese was fairly quiet when we arrived and we enjoyed many different dishes and a bottle of Mateus Rosé wine. Brian wanted to bring the bottle home to make into a lamp. He does live in the past! David insisted on paying the bill of 80 euros.

On the way home I dropped Brian at the phone box so he could ring Simon and Harry soon to be a great granddad!

Thursday 11th November 2004.

Jack was a bit off colour this morning so I let him stay in bed! It was windy but warm (a bit like Brian!) so whilst Brian went to the gym and I did a bit of washing, David and Gill went for a walk.

They were gone a couple of hours and had walked quite a way down the strip. It seemed a shame to waste such a sunny afternoon so we had a barbecue that appeared to last for ages, washed down with a jug of sangria and some red wine.

I broke off briefly to ring Mum and was pleased to hear they had finally booked their flights. They seemed quite expensive at £140 each return, but at least they were coming.

We were still sat about drinking at eleven o'clock. David and Gill are such easy company I could go anywhere with them, not that they would want Brian tagging along!

Friday 12th November 2004.

It had rained and thundered in the night and didn't look as though it was going to do much else for the rest of the day. Why do we feel responsible for the weather when we have people visiting?

Dave and Brian went to the restaurant and had the English breakfast fry-up, toast and coffee for six and a half euros each. Then we went for a drive along the strip and right to the end of the landmass. We were fortunate to see a flock of flamingos towards the end and then we called at the English bar called "Nobby's" that Margaret had recommended. After nibbles and a few drinks we booked a table for Saturday, David and Gills last night.

Tonight's meal was a whole salmon, which Brian cooked with

vegetables and potatoes, and everyone enjoyed it. Gill tried to make her famous chocolate chip cookie pudding with cream, but we couldn't find any whipping cream in the supermarket and we ended up with a curdled bowl of some other cream so the pudding stayed in the fridge!

As we were having a few drinks, I had a text from Dad, one from Pam to say she was home and they'd had a wonderful holiday, and one from my old work mate Danni.

We were all awake for a while once we got to bed as the thunder and rain sounded so loud.

Saturday 13th November 2004.

We were determined to go on the organised walk as we felt that Gill and David would enjoy this. Gill and I packed a picnic and drinks and we left the car park at ten as usual. It was a lovely picturesque walk over hills and beaches and into the national park. Jack and Jill were having a lovely time, until Jack decided to snarl at Misty and he got a sharp nip back – served him right!

Back at the site after a round trip of about ten miles everyone had a drink in the beach bar, and after about half an hour we left Gill and Dave talking to newfound friends. They came back an hour or so later and both said how much they had enjoyed the day. But it wasn't over yet, we still had Nobby's to come!

I had a text from my friend Noz with a bit of gossip, then we all went to Nobby's and I was driving again! I am so good.

The lads enjoyed a football match that was on the television in the bar and were a bit annoyed that we moved into the restaurant when the meal came, as the view of the telly wasn't as good as in the bar. The food was nice but very English and although I agree with Brian that it's nice to have something that tastes like home occasionally, it's not what we had come to Spain for. Who knows if we will return there?

Sunday 14th November 2004.

Time just flies and I couldn't believe it was time for them to leave. We dropped them at the airport just after nine for their flight at 11.10 a.m.

Typically, the sun was now beating down so we sat in the sun in our new chairs and chilled out. Antonio brought us a branch of a date tree and told us to plant it in the gravel and water it. We didn't know whether he was auditioning Brian for the part of the village idiot or if he was serious, but we planted it never the less.

We walked down to the restaurant for a meal, calling at the phone to ring Pam, Mum and Janet. As we got to the restaurant we bumped into Les and Anita who were also going for the Sunday night special of La Manga Lamb so we had a table for four.

Just getting into bed at ten, we had a text from Dave and Gill to say they were home safe and had really enjoyed themselves.

Monday 15th November 2004.

I had loads of washing to do today so I was up early and setting up my little electric washer and the spin dryer. Bedding, towels and other things kept me busy until lunchtime, whilst Brian was at the gym.

It was cool but sunny so Brian went down to the beach fishing with his friend Helmut. Later on, I walked the dogs along the beach and called at the phone on the way back. I rang Brian's cousin Donald and his wife Kathy back in Blackburn. Don had taken redundancy in July and they were really looking forward to retiring to Spain once their house was sold. They had bought a property near Elche about two year before and Don had been to Spain several times making lots of improvements to the house and gardens. A pool had been installed and as he was very talented at all do-it-yourself tasks, we knew that the place would be beautiful once he had finished working on it.

They were coming for a two-week holiday in December and we were trying to arrange which would be the best date for us to visit. Friday December tenth was agreed and I was pleased to hear from Kathy that they had sold their house and should have the sale completed by early January.

I walked up to reception as there were notices around the site informing everyone that the games room now had three computers with Internet access, but you needed to buy a card which cost five euros for three hours.

Whilst in reception I asked about the phone cards they

explained that the one which now gave the best value was a "Telefonica" card at ten euros for 150 minutes. So I bought one of those.

Corned beef hash with a crust on and mushy peas awaited Brian when he got home but he was looking very pleased with himself and proudly showed me a fish! I was in the midst of congratulating him when he confessed Helmut had given it to him as a present! Never mind, he would catch one soon.

Mum was home when I rang her later and she told me she now had our new Visa cards and the new PINs that we had been issued with. She would post the cards to me and I would ring her when they arrived and get the PINs. It was a good job the mail was going to Mum's, otherwise I wouldn't have known about the new cards- until I came to pay the site fees in March when my card would be declined!

It was a cold evening so instead of going to the quiz; we put the heating on and prepared to overdose on a video of "Coronation Street" that Gill had brought out for us. Dev and Sinita's wedding was brilliant.

Tuesday 16th November 2004.

Keep Fit was a joy as the sun was out and we then went to the Mercadona for some shopping. I called at the vet's and bought the collars, which Margaret had recommended, and some worming tablets. The assistant threw in a few free pigs' ears.

Brian cooked some Dorado fish for tea and I prepared a salad and a dish of potatoes with green beans and almonds.

Barbara called and told us she had been to the quiz last night and wouldn't be going again. She said one of Ted's questions was about a bone in the arm, and when he gave the answer out, some English woman bounced over to him, took the microphone from him and said she was medically qualified and he was talking rubbish! I told Barbara we'd never seen anything like that when we went to the quiz but nothing surprised me any more.

Dad sent me a text with two items of news. My doctors had written to confirm that my smear test was clear. Good news- but not something I really wanted to share with my Dad! And he had won £300 on the premium bonds. He would no doubt spend it on the grandchildren as usual.

Wednesday 17th November 2004.

Whilst Brian was at the gym I sat in the sun and planned our route to Kathy and Don's. I went down to the games room and tried the Internet for an hour. Lots of news from home but nothing very exciting. It was much better having the Internet on site as it saved me driving down the strip.

Gwen called to introduce herself and gave me a note confirming that her caravan was reserved for Mum and Dad in February. Eric took Brian fishing to Cala Reona for the afternoon, which meant I could sit in the sun and read without being disturbed.

The intrepid fishermen were back at five, with the news that Brian had caught a small fish but threw it back, then his line got tangled and he lost a float. Eric concluded that what he really needed was a new rod. He explained that Brian would be much better with a fibreglass telescopic rod for this type of beach fishing. Right, that could be his Christmas present, so Eric agreed to take him to buy a rod on Friday afternoon.

A late barbecue and a few glasses of wine set us up for an early night.

Thursday 18th November 2004

Keep Fit was becoming second nature, but it was quite worrying when I heard some English ladies behind me commenting that they would follow my movements as I always seemed to know what I was doing! ! Not a good idea.

After barbecued beefburgers for lunch Brian was off fishing again, so I sunbathed whilst playing Scrabble and had a few martini and lemonades.

Spaghetti bolognese was accompanied by some of my homemade garlic bread and we walked down to bingo. Ted's bingo calling skills were improving each week, but this was not our lucky night.

We listened to the radio when we got home and heard that it was snowing in Preston and Wakefield.

Friday 19th November 2004.

It was like Christmas Day to Brian. He was so excited about going to get a new rod with Eric.

After doing a small load of washing, I sat in the sun and finished off a book that Gill had left for me. It was Brian's Auntie Evelyn's birthday today and I texted Gill to remind her to give the card I had left to Evelyn and to thank her for a really good read.

A new couple arrived at the back of us on Happy Oldies Avenue. They both looked familiar but it wasn't until later in the day when the wife came round to wash up, that I realised where we knew them from. They were here last year in a different pitch, but I remembered we had jokingly called her "Mrs Bucket" pronounced "Bouquet", as she seemed to be in a cleaning frenzy most of the time. We hardly ever saw her without her red and blue striped apron and yellow rubber gloves. Her husband spoke good English and was a vicar back home in Holland. They were a very nice couple, just obsessively clean!

After lunch Eric arrived and went with Brian to the Ferreteria for a new rod.

They were home an hour later with a real bargain- apparently. Only 60 euros for this very nice telescopic rod, and Eric demonstrated how to extend it. He pointed out that each section had to be gently twisted so that it held together, and he repeatedly told Brian to be careful not to twist it too tightly. I think already, Eric had realised that Brian was a heavy-handed clumsy bugger!

Using Henk's pan, Brian cooked a very tasty prawn stir-fry. We later played a dice game called "Crag", and I received a sad text from my friend Tracy to say she was getting divorced. It was only four years since we had been to Scotland for their wedding, and their little girl was just two years old. How sad.

Saturday 20th November 2004.

We had planned to go on the Saturday morning walk, but Brian's knee had been hurting since last Saturday's walk so we gave it a miss.

Instead, we sat in the sun again, the weather just kept getting better all the time. We had a text from Neville to say they were at

Loosehill in Derbyshire in their camper van and it was cold and snowing. Another text came from our friend Marie who finally seemed to be getting over a broken marriage after meeting someone on the Internet. They were moving into a new house together in Doncaster and she was really happy at last.

I left Brian preparing a pork, apple and cider casserole whilst I walked to reception to see if Mum's parcel had arrived. And it had.

We now had our two new Visa cards and two videotapes of "EastEnders," "Emmerdale" and "Coronation Street." Also included in the parcel was an information sheet from the Blind Society which Mum must have mistaken for something else. A bank statement and some other bits of post made interesting reading.

Our Dutch neighbours had invited us to a night of music and dancing at the function room tonight. This featured Dirk and Okke, two Dutch entertainers playing the keyboards and singing. We felt we should go, as they had been good enough to ask us.

What a great night it was. An excellent atmosphere and very good entertainment. We were joined at our table by two English couples that we had met on last Saturday's walk. In the general conversation, they mentioned that they had been to the quiz. I told them that my friend Barbara had recounted the tale of some mouthy English woman who had taken the microphone off Ted and the lady sat next to me said "Oh yes that was me!" I could have crawled under the table but it was too late. She did find it amusing and admitted that she was out of order. Bet we don't see them again!

The evening finished around half past eleven and as we walked home, Joop invited us back to their awning for a nightcap. There were about a dozen of us there including the singer and his wife, Miep's friend Lineker and her husband also called Joop. We were drinking and singing, and I went to our caravan to let the dogs out for a wee, and returned to Joop's in my pyjamas, allegedly!

Sunday 21ˢᵗ November 2004.

The morning after the night before I will never drink again. It was two o'clock before I could face getting up and showered.

Good old Brian prepared a roast chicken dinner, whilst my biggest achievement of the day was ringing Mum. She gave me our "PINs" and we had a good chat about everything and nothing. They were getting ready to go for a meal with Sheila and Patrick next door, who were treating them as my Dad had done some work for them and wouldn't take anything for doing it.

Isn't it strange how you can be so hungry after a good drinking session? I really enjoyed a huge dinner followed by fresh fruit salad and squirty cream. The washing up was left to Brian and I was in bed even earlier than usual. Goodnight.

Monday 22nd November 2004.

A few clouds were about, but today we decided to take a picnic and all go fishing to Cala Reona with Brian's new rod. He excitedly set up his equipment and I took the dogs and let them have a good run about along the rocky shoreline, as there was no one else in sight. After a couple of hours, it finally happened. Brian caught a fish, and I was ready with the camera to capture the moment. He was thrilled to bits and I was pleased for him. November 22nd last year had also been a great sporting moment, when England won the rugby World Cup!

It was getting a bit cool so I went back to the car with the dogs and said we would wait for him, no rush as I could read the paper and have a drink of coffee from the flask.

An hour later he approached the car, with a face to the floor. His telescopic rod was almost full length. Why hadn't he reduced it to the carrying size? He explained that he didn't know how it had happened because he had been really gentle, as Eric had told him, but somehow the rod was stuck and wouldn't go any smaller. We just managed to get it into the car, and Brian was trying to convince me that the rod must be faulty, as he was sure it wasn't his fault. Keep calm Julie!

Back home, we were trying to loosen the rod when Wim came past. He said he thought it was well and truly stuck but told us about a Spanish man that repaired fishing rods at Cabo de Palos. After explaining which side street this man lived on, Wim wished us good luck and went home.

I know I should have gone with Brian to help him but I was so annoyed at him and so convinced he had broken the rod through his usual carelessness, that I thrust a fifty euro note at him and walked into the caravan.

After half an hour when I'd had a muscatel and calmed down, I was feeling awful as Brian didn't have the Spanish phrase book with him and I just knew he would be struggling to get himself understood.

He finally arrived home and as he walked into the caravan, I could see he was hiding something behind his back. He furtively began, "Please don't be mad with me but this is what's happened. I found the man in the fishing tackle shop and showed him my new rod. He threw his arms in the air, which I took to mean it was beyond repair. He then showed me this other rod and crossed out the ticket price of 52 euros and wrote down 30 euros. I assumed he was making me a deal for a new rod so I paid the 30 euros and was just about to leave, when he said, 'Rod mended by Wednesday you come back.' So I think he is mending my rod but I have now bought another one. Help!"

We both started laughing, it was no good being annoyed. But how many rods did he need, for God's sake?

After the day we'd had, we ate chicken soup that Brian had made and decided we didn't have the energy to go to the quiz. Sorry Ted.

Tuesday 23rd November 2004.

Another nice day and I noticed on my way to Keep Fit that the date tree was actually producing ripe dates. We left Jack and Jill with Evelyn and Bill and we went shopping with Barbara and John to a new shopping centre near San Javier.

Arriving back on site about four o'clock I called into the supermarket for some milk and was tittering as I read a poster at the till. It was printed in four languages, and the English translation read, "Please sow up your bag at the till, if asked."- I assume this should have read, "Please show us your bag".

Jack and Jill had been very good and were cuddled up inside the caravan when we went round to Bill and Evelyn's.

Brian made a quick chilli and I walked down to the Internet café to catch up on home news.

In the evening, wearing his new jogging bottoms that we'd bought that day, Brian sat in the awning making up some fishing bait with pieces of French bread surrounded by barbed hooks.

About nine o'clock, I could hear him shouting "Help" in his most pathetic childlike voice. When I went into the awning I was not surprised to see that he had got one of the hooks caught in his trousers and he couldn't get it out.

It was caught in the crotch area of his trousers so as he sat on a chair, I knelt down to try to release the hook. It did occur to me that people walking past might wonder what we were up to, as they could see straight into the awning, but then as Brian often reminds me I should get down on my knees most days to say thanks for meeting him!

After ten minutes of me kneeling down trying unsuccessfully to loosen the hook, I decided it would be far easier if he wasn't wearing the trousers, so I tugged them to pull them down and unwittingly pulled his underpants down at the same time. So there he was, bare-arsed at the awning window and of course the washing-up area was full!

Eventually I had to cut a small hole in the jogging bottoms to free the hook, and then stitch up the hole. This fishing lark was costing us a small fortune!

Wednesday 24th November 2004.

Happy 30th Birthday Simon. He texted us to say thanks for his present and card that we had left with Lorraine.

Brian went to the gym and on his way back he bumped into Ted. He mentioned to Ted that the equipment at the gym was out of the ark and Ted said he would mention it to the reception staff.

We didn't know what would happen when Brian returned to the fishing shop at Cabo de Palos. Would his rod be repaired? Would he buy another one? He returned with his old rod repaired as good as new for 16 euros. So he now had three rods altogether. And still only caught one fish!

Whilst the meat was marinating for our curry, we took the dogs for a long walk over the fields.

At seven o'clock we had just finished our curry when Evelyn called round to ask if I would go to Brazil with her to visit a woman that lodged with them years before as a foreign student. Pardon? She explained the woman had just rung her and wanted her to go for a holiday to Brazil. Bill wasn't really fit enough to fly so Evelyn thought I might like to go. It was very nice of her to ask but I didn't really think it was what I wanted to do.

In the midst of this discussion, Brian went to the phone and rang Simon and Harry. No snow in Congleton, but quite cold.

Thursday 25th November 2004.

We drove to Los Belones to get some water and bought a light for the awning at the Ferreteria.

Back home, Wendy called round with some tapes of "EastEnders" for us to watch. I went round to Emmy's as she makes handmade cards. I ordered some Christmas cards for family, including two with robins on for Pam and Harry, as Joan always loved robins.

Another recommendation of Margaret's was Watts Frying fish and chip shop. We drove there and ate our fish, chips and mushy peas in the small café. They weren't cheap at 18 euros for the two, but they were the best we'd had in a long time.

On the way down to bingo I rang Janet who told me she had booked their flights but would be landing at Alicante as the flights were a lot cheaper than coming to Murcia. They would be here on February 6th so Mum would be thrilled that she was here for her birthday.

Bingo went really well, and I won 140 euros for a full house. I had spent it in my own head before we got home!

Friday 26th November 2004.

What could that noise be at 7.45? It was like a pounding sound that I couldn't quite put my finger on. I opened the blind in the bedroom and I could see what it was. Mrs Bucket was beating her rugs over a clotheshorse! Oh what joy!

It was a cloudy start and Brian looked up in Pam's phrase book how to say, "What is your name?" before setting off to the gym. His conversations with this "tricky bird" were still very brief but he was trying.

I popped round to Barbara's to get weighed. I knew she had some scales as she told me last year that she weighs herself every Wednesday morning. Eleven stone two pounds, so I had lost ten pounds. I could feel that I had lost some weight but was thrilled that I was almost down to eleven stone. The doctor had warned me that the underactive thyroid condition made dieting harder but at least I was losing some. I had a spring in my step for the rest of the day. Barbara suggested that the four of us had Christmas lunch together, in our awning. John would do the cooking, Brian could make the starter, and we would split the cost. Excellent.

When Brian came back from the gym he said all his illusions had been shattered. Expecting his friend at the gym to be called Maria or Madonna, he was taken aback when she told him her name was Mabel! Not that there's anything wrong with being called Mabel but it didn't quite fit the fantasy.

He also asked if I thought Ted could walk on water then explained that the gym now had all new equipment! There was a rowing machine, a bike that worked, new weights and a host of other brand new state of the art items. I think the new things were probably stored somewhere on the site and as Mabel would tell the management, "There's only one daft old bloke using the gym, so leave the new equipment 'till someone asks for it". Anyway, Brian was thrilled but decided to keep it quiet, as he didn't want other people descending on the gym.

After going shopping and walking the dogs, I had grilled gambas and Brian had sardines, with a dish of pasta and some salad.

Three hours of "EastEnders" made the evening fly by.

Saturday 27th November 2004.

I don't know why I couldn't sleep but I was up at 4 o'clock reading, and couldn't get back to sleep. I woke Brian with a cup of tea at 9.15 and saw an ambulance pull up at the pitch next door. Our Dutch neighbour Martin was taken to Cartagena hospital where he was operated on for appendicitis and an ulcer. What an unlucky pitch that was, the same one where our neighbours last year were both taken ill.

A sunny start to the day, but it soon clouded over and became cool. After a walk on the beach it was shampoo time for Jack and Jill- neither of them liked getting soaped up but they behaved quite well and were soon shaking themselves dry.

I called round to Emmy's to collect my Christmas cards, which were lovely.

Anita and Les had said they would like to have a look at Gwen's caravan in case Les's parents decide to come over next year when they return to La Manga. They had arranged to meet Gwen's husband at the caravan at five o'clock and I went round too just to be nosy, as I couldn't remember what was in it. Mother wanted to know if there was a washing machine, a microwave for her wheatbag and whether there were towels provided. The answer was yes to all three. I texted Dad to let Mum know and I knew she would sleep better for knowing these facts!

Tonight's tea was one of my favourites, spicy duck breasts with pears. After tea we put the radio on and listened to Spectrum as usual. Were we in for a treat! Saturday nights would never be the same as we heard that their DJ Kane McLane was hosting a new show, all night called "Boogie on the Beach". He announced in his most smarmy, cheesy voice, "Tonight, ladies, you will be grabbing your hairbrush and singing along to the sounds of the eighties, so boogie on down". There was no disputing that the music was fabulous stuff that I could remember playing during my years as a DJ from the late seventies until the late eighties. I don't believe this bloke's real name was Kane McLane it was probably Arthur Archibald but that wouldn't really fit the image!

We enjoyed a few drinks and going back down memory lane. Brian recounted some of his recollections of humorous events and we ended up having a good laugh before getting into bed at eleven.

Sunday 28th November 2004.

We woke to a much better day and set off down the beach with the dogs. We walked to Pepe's at Mar Cristal and we enjoyed tapas of garlic potatoes, chicken wings, onion rings, squid, bread, two coffees a beer and a tonic. Eleven Euros was really good value and the food was just enough without making me feel guilty about eating fried things.

Calling at the phone booths we rang Tony and Ann who were adamant that they would be joining us next year when we returned to Spain in October. They were interested to hear about the lifestyle, what was on the site and what we do all day.

Pam was next on the list and she was excited that she had a moving date of December 18th. A bit near Christmas but at least they would be in for the New Year so she was busy packing everything up, in between working full-time, running the house and keeping an eye on Harry. A quick call to Mum, they were fine and looking forward to Christmas as they were going to Janet's for Christmas Day, then Chris was picking his three children up on Boxing Day and they were staying at Mum's for two nights.

Les and Anita came past pushing their bikes. They were cycling down the strip to meet Fran and Geoff in one of the bars. But they were a bit early so they sat down and had a few drinks with us, and didn't resume their ride for two hours!

Lasagne and garlic bread was a quick easy meal and we finished the day with a toast to Joop and Miep who were celebrating their wedding anniversary.

Monday 29th November 2004.

Although I had bought a couple of Christmas cards from Emmy, this year I wanted to send cards to friends back in England. I set up a little "scene" in front of our awning and used the timer on the digital camera to take a couple of shots of me and Brian with Jack and Jill. I used this to design a Christmas themed postcard and was busy printing thirty off, when Ted called to see us.

Brian thanked him for the miracle he'd performed at the gym. Ted told us he only mentioned it at reception, and was surprised and pleased at the influence he appeared to have. Ted told us he now had Internet access on his laptop in his caravan. He explained he had bought a receiver box for 100 euros, then signed up for unlimited access for 25 euros a month. This sounded just up my street.

I was off to reception soon afterwards, and they said someone would call later to install the Internet on my PC. I bought stamps and posted my cards allowing lots of time for them to be received by Christmas.

Back home, a smiling Brian returned from an afternoon's fishing with two fish! They were only small but he filleted them and put them in the freezer, the grand plan being a lovely paella at a later date, when he'd caught loads.

We had just sat down to liver and onions when the Internet man arrived. He installed the Internet and I bought the box and signed up for three months access, which should just take us to the beginning of March when we went home. This could be my Christmas present.

Les and Anita, Fran and Geoff and the two of us had a brave attempt at the quiz. We scored 46 out of 60 and came fourth. Ted asked if I would sell some raffle tickets for his Christmas charity and he gave me a book of white tickets.

What a busy day this had been so I knew I would sleep tonight.

Tuesday 30th November 2004.

I woke up with a slight headache, which could have been the result of the two bottles of rose wine that Fran and I finished off at the quiz. I struggled to Keep Fit and the timing was perfect in that at eleven o'clock as we finished it began to rain. Unfortunately, it rained all day long and my headache just got worse so I went to bed.

Brian did some shopping at the Upper and made a very tasty beef stroganoff. I allowed him to pamper me and I did manage to get up after tea to watch some more "Coronation Street" that Wendy had dropped off for us. By half past eleven I was crawling back under the duvet like a big lazy cow!

Wednesday 1st December 2004.

We had invited Les and Anita and Fran and Geoff round for a curry at two, so I was busy making nan breads and Brian prepared the chicken curry before he went to the gym. I tidied the awning and the caravan ready for my visitors, just like the mad cleaning frenzy women tend to have at home when people are coming round. Mrs Bucket would be proud of me.

Brian made an accompanying dish of spicy potatoes and cauliflower and we were just about ready when I received a text from my friend Julia to say she couldn't come for Christmas but was coming on the 14th for a week.

Anita brought a lovely orange liqueur jelly with real oranges in it and we all thoroughly enjoyed the superb meal. Everyone brought beers and wine and we had a great laugh, even though we had to sit in the awning because of the rain.

By nine o'clock we were all flagging, except Brian who washed up when the others had gone. Isn't he just wonderful?

Thursday 2nd December 2004.

My visitor arrived as I awoke, so Brian decided to go fishing with Wim and let me suffer by myself. I was having great difficulty getting onto the Internet so I rang them and they said they would ring me back. Bill was passing and he came in to ask how my emailing was going and I told him about my problem. Good old Bill knew just what the problem was and sorted it out within two minutes. He is very patient and knowledgeable and he is like my surrogate Dad here in Spain! I know he will always find a solution to a problem, just like my Dad.

I wrote a long letter to Mum and printed it in huge print so she could read it. I posted it with a few bits of information about the site, and a Christmas tree decoration, which Emmy had made for me. It was to hang on the tree and was a bauble that contained a photo of the four of us in Spain. Tacky but personal!

Now that I knew when Julia was coming, I was able to text Kathy to ask if we could visit them on December 10th and she replied that it would be fine, and we must stop the night.

Harry was treated to a phone call from his loving son and he said it was very miserable weather in Congleton, raining and dark. The nurse was coming to see him about his prostrate problem and they would discuss the possibility of a permanent catheter.

I did tea for a change but could only muster up a chicken and walnut dish with Moroccan rice. We indulged in the final hour of "Coronation Street" and then played Hearts on the computer.

Friday 3rd December 2004.

Happy birthday Gary. I had left a card and present with Pam for Gary's birthday and just hoped she could find it in the midst of all the packing she was doing.

I got a call on my mobile from the Internet company, to say that there had been some problems but everything should be OK now. I agreed to try again later, and didn't mention that the original problem had been due to me being gormless. The call to them and their return call had cost me over seven pounds and I knew we needed to think about getting a Spanish sim card before too long.

It was a dark and thundery day not what we had come to Spain for. So I sat in the warmth of the caravan whilst Brian went fishing, and I emailed everyone!

Up to reception at five o'clock, I collected a parcel from Mum. When I got home I opened it to find a Christmas card, a Christmas badge with a flashing battery light, some more videos and two vests for Brian. I had mentioned in passing that we were struggling to find sleeveless vests for him to wear at the gym, so she had bought him two. No wonder he says she's in his top three mother-in-laws!

I rang Mum on the way back home to thank her for the parcel and when I asked her how she was getting on at the slimming club, she pretended it was a bad line so I knew she hadn't been for a few weeks.

An ugly-looking huge fish was Brian's tea and he'd made me a pork chop with a barbecue sauce. Guess what we watched on the video? Yes, more "Coronation Street" and some "Emmerdale."

Saturday 4th December 2004.

When would this weather improve? The thunder woke me up at five o'clock and it rained until two. We then put our waterproof jackets on and walked Jack and Jill so they didn't go stir crazy. Brian gave Ian a ring. He had kept saying he was going to come and see us but didn't know when. Now he thinks he won't come as he's saving up to get his own flat. I was disappointed, as I knew he would enjoy the windsurfing here, weather permitting.

Les and Anita came round at seven and the four of us went to the Chinese as arranged. We had a great meal and each of us ordered a different dish and tried them all. We had a bottle of wine and a few drinks and the bill was 70 euros. Apple schnapps or Chinese wine was offered with the compliments of the house.

Sunday 5th December 2004.

Even though we have retired, I still feel less guilty about having a lie-in on a Sunday than during the week. Today was cloudy so I snuggled back down the bed and didn't get up until half past ten. We walked to Pepe's and had a coffee and then set off back under the grey skies.

It started to rain as we approached the site, and as we got back to our pitch, the heavens opened. We sat in the awning and Brian prepared a chilli for tea, and I made half a dozen scones.

Brian received two text messages. He complains that I get far more text messages than he does, and I've tried to explain it's because I text people whereas Brian can't be bothered! Anyway he got two. One was from David, asking if we would be interested if our annual cricket tour was to France as opposed to Nottingham next June. The cost would be very high as it was proposed to fly there. We replied that we would think about it, depending on the price.

The other text was from Norman and Lynn in Murcia. They had now had all of their plastering done and just wondered if we would like to go to visit them whilst we were here. We texted back that we would love to and that we could sort out some mutually convenient dates later.

Monday 6th December 2004.

Another bank holiday so the gym was closed. Mabel would be having a day off. Most of the night we laid awake listening to the thunderstorm, and the rain never stopped. We were not surprised when we walked into the awning to find the groundsheet was slightly swamped and the rugs were soaking wet.

I took two bags of washing to the launderette, which was open as usual, but she told me she was very busy and my washing wouldn't be ready until Wednesday. No problem, I couldn't get it dried myself in this weather.

A text came from Dad which read, "Parsl as cum yor mamy lyks ur trea fing" roughly translated this meant the parcel had arrived and Mum loved her tree decoration. What's he like?

By lunchtime, the rain had stopped and it was looking brighter. There was a German Craft Fair down the strip so we drove down to have a look. John told us not to have any lunch before we went, as last year there were about thirty different stalls serving hot dogs and really tasty snacks. What a disappointment! There were only six stalls and two of them were people from our site selling cards! Apparently, due to the bad weather, the organisers had decided to cancel the fair, but not everyone got the message.

Back home for two, I took my phone card and return ferry confirmation to ring the Caravan Club to change our return date. Telling Brian I would be back in five minutes, I set off with a new return date in mind of Thursday 10th March 2005.

I got through to the call centre quite quickly and explained what I wanted. The operator put me on hold for five minutes and then I was cut off! I rang again and got through after about ten attempts, as all the lines to England were busy. Another operator apologised and after putting me on hold for a further five minutes told me that it would be no problem to amend the return date, and the nine a.m. crossing would only cost me a further £105 plus £10 for amending the booking. I explained that this was not what I was expecting and that within reason we could travel at any time. She promised to ring me back on Tuesday so I had to switch my mobile on to give her the number – it's far too long to memorise.

I was very disappointed that this procedure had not been as simple as I had imagined, and of course Brian was into the realms of "What if we can't get home and we have to stay here?" Not only does he natter like an old woman; he worries like one too!

The corned beef hotpot was very nice and after watching an hour of "Emmerdale" we played a few games of cards on the laptop.

Tuesday 7th December 2004.

The weather had improved enough for Keep Fit still to be held, and Brian went to the gym at the same time. He came home with a pained look on his face and said he'd torn his pectoral muscle, whatever that is. Anita called round and said Les was busy cleaning their camper van as they were leaving next Sunday. She was going to cycle to the Mercadona and do some shopping. Brian offered to take her in the car as he was going to do the shopping so off they went.

I walked to the phone and rang Mum. We were just having a chat when my mobile phone started ringing. I had to cut Mum off and answer the call, which was from the Caravan Club as promised. They couldn't get the price down at all for the nine o'clock crossing. I explained again that we didn't ask for a nine o'clock crossing, and requested that they tried again to get me a more reasonable supplement. Again they promised to ring me back later.

Brian came home after doing a good shop and Anita was very grateful for the lift as it meant she could get all sorts of heavier things that they needed. As Brian was cooking the fish curry, the Caravan Club rang me again. The supervisor apologised that I had been misinformed when I booked the tickets, and she had managed to get us a crossing at 3.15am for an additional £20 plus £10 for amending the booking. This was a much more acceptable increase but three o'clock in the morning was hardly ideal! Anyway, I accepted this and paid the charge with my new Visa card.

The Internet was connected and I had nine emails, which I enjoyed reading and replying to. One was in response to my letter in the Caravan Club October magazine, and suggested a different route through France which avoided Lyon. We studied our maps, and the alternative journey using the A75 through Clermont-Ferrand looked excellent. So we spent the rest of the evening looking at different campsites in France and deciding which route we would take.

Wednesday 8th December 2004.

Seventeen years today since our first date! We sat in bed with our cups of tea laughing about what we thought of each other on that first night. I'll never forget the horrendous blue-grey cardigan than Brian wore on our date. It had a huge collar and I thought it was so old fashioned.

It was raining again but I walked up to the supermarket with the dogs and an umbrella. I called at Gwen's to give her Mum's deposit.

When I got back, the electricity had just gone off on the whole site. It was two hours before it came back on and Brian was able to get on with the chicken in red wine casserole that he was making in the electric pan. We could always revert to the gas oven but we were hoping the power cut had just been a temporary blip.

I washed up and Brian rang Simon, who wasn't in, then Harry who was in and who reported that it was still cold in Congleton.

We watched "Ocean's 11" on DVD, which we enjoyed.

Thursday 9th December 2004.

We didn't need an alarm as the sound of a spin dryer woke us just before eight o'clock. Good morning Mrs Bucket.

Not many at Keep Fit today. But I met a new friend called Ruth and it was her first time at Keep Fit. We hit it off straight away and I said I would see her next Tuesday if not before. When I got back, Brian was looking really pleased with himself. He had seen someone put a set of Christmas lights by the bins, and knowing that I would like them, he'd tried them and they worked! So I fastened them all along the top of the windbreak and they looked a treat.

Jack and Jill were tethered at the front of the awning as usual and one of our German neighbours came over in between washing up, to chat to them. This lady called Bridget had been in the same pitch last year on Happy Oldies Avenue. She was an obvious dog lover and had called almost every day last year to say hello to Jack and Jill. But Jack always barked at her. This year, he was getting more used to her and she had now started bringing a couple of dog treats which went down really well.

After a cup of tea and some toast we walked to Playa Honda along the beach and back around the top of the site.

I checked for any messages when we got back and found an amusing email from Janet. She said she had decided she must get on a diet, so she got on the scales (without her glasses on in case they weighed a lot) and the scales said "Fatt!" She was quite shocked, until she put her glasses on and realised it said "Batt"-meaning the battery was low!

What a miserable day it was with grey skies and the threat of rain hanging over us. At four o'clock we took Les and Anita with us to a local garden centre. We bought a pot duck as a little house-warming present to take to Kathy and Don's tomorrow. Then we went to Watts Frying and had lovely fish, chips and peas.

On the way back, Brian decided he needed some new trainers so Anita directed us to a big shoe shop. It took Brian an hour to choose a pair but they seemed good value at 48 euros.

We plugged our new lights in and guess what? Bang the plug fused! No wonder they had been thrown out.

An hour of "EastEnders" completed our day and then a text from Kathy to say they were looking forward to seeing us.

Friday 10th December 2004.

We set off in the rain at 11.45 and made our way towards Elche. Kathy had given us directions to a garage, which we found without any problems and Don came to meet us. Their house is in a village called Hondon de las Neives and we were soon sat on their patio enjoying a glass of wine and the lovely views.

They proudly showed us all around their lovely home and the gardens that came with it. We could see the work that Don had been putting into the renovations at every opportunity, and we were excited for them at the prospect of moving here in January. Brian was looking outside at where some plastering would need doing once they moved in, and he offered to do the work for Don. We agreed that I would bring Brian over, leave him with them for a few days so that I had the car and then they would bring him back to La Manga. Don's Mum would be with them in February and of course my Mum and Dad would be with me so we would cart them along for the day out!

We drove to the village and had the menu of the day at a local restaurant. I had kidney soup, then liver and finished off with cheesecake, wine and a coffee for seven euros. A very unusual, but tasty meal and what good value.

Back at their home we had lots to catch up on and some hours later after consuming much local wine, we all went to bed!

Saturday 11th December 2004.

A much brighter morning so we sat on the patio where Don served us with a full English breakfast. We then went to Romana market and Brian bought a padded jerkin for eight euros, which he said he needed for fishing. I had to steer him away from several shoe stalls and Jack and Jill were mesmerised by the live rabbits and chickens that were running around in cages. How cruel.

We had a coffee and brandy at the market bar and on the way back to the car, Donald rang his Mum Alice. Brian's late Mum Joan and her sister Alice were very close and Brian and Don had spent a lot of time together when they were growing up, as they were the same age. Don's lovely Dad Tom died only a few months before Joan and now Harry and Alice ring each other every Saturday at ten o'clock. She passed on the news that Harry now had a permanent catheter fitted and that Pam's house sale had fallen through. Within half an hour, I received a text from Pam telling me the same news. She was devastated about the house as they were due to move in a week's time and everything was packed up and ready to go.

Back at Kathy and Don's we had a lovely chicken salad lunch and we set off back across the mountains at half past three. As we were getting into the car, Donald asked if we had Brian's driving licence with us. I told him it was back at "home" in the caravan at La Manga. He explained that all drivers must now carry their passport, driving licence, insurance certificate and vehicle registration at all times as the police can ask to see them during a spot check. He proceeded to recount some very worrying stories of English drivers who didn't have their documents with them when stopped by the authorities. We would transfer all the required documents to Brian's wallet as soon as we could. Of course, all the way home Brian was in a sweat, in case we were pulled over by the police. Thanks for that Don!

When we got home, I rang Pam and we had a long chat, which didn't really cheer her up, as she was still very upset. I gave Mum and Janet a quick ring before heading home for an early night.

I found Brian looking around the awning and in the cupboards in his usual tidy fashion. He couldn't find his brown shoes. Guess what? He'd left them at Don's! Serves him right for needing more than one pair of shoes when you're only going somewhere for 24 hours. I texted Kathy to tell her Brian's shoes were under the bed and he would pick them up in February.

Sunday 12ᵗʰ December 2004.

Drizzly rain welcomed this Sunday morning, so I decided to give the inside of the caravan a bit of a spring clean. The day got better and by eleven o'clock I was washing and Brian sat in the sun.

We walked up to the supermarket for a Sunday paper and when we got back we settled down with a few beers and enjoyed the warmth of a pleasant December day.

Anita and Les called round, as it was their last day. They were all packed up and ready for the off, first thing Monday morning and wondered if we would like to join them at the site restaurant for their last evening meal.

Our next-door-but-one neighbour Diego called, and he brought two bottles of champagne and two champagne glasses for me, and two bottles of red wine for Brian. Although he didn't speak any English, he managed to convey that this was a gift for us to say thank you for looking after the cats! We only hope this is not to say, "Thanks for taking them back to England when you go next March!"

We had a lovely meal at the restaurant as Sunday night's menu was invariably La Manga Lamb which was tasty and very tender. Exchanging email and home addresses with Les and Anita, we promised to stay in touch.

Monday 13th December 2004.

Our new alarm call woke us up at eight o'clock. Mrs Bucket was washing again! I think this shaped (or do I mean shamed?) me into action and I had the bedding stripped, washed and hung out before you could say "Room for a pony!"

Brian set off to the gym at 9. 20 so he'd be there when Mabel opened the doors at 9.30. He was back home for quarter to ten and explained that some bloody German women had started having a Keep Fit session in the gym on Mondays and Fridays from 9.30 until 10.30. How dare they use Brian's gym?

We went to the Mercadona for some shopping and on the way back we called at our supermarket for the milk we had forgotten. Whilst walking round, Brian saw a paella ring on a stand and thought 30 Euros was exceptional value so we bought it.

Later in the afternoon, Brian returned to the gym and about an hour and a half later I walked up with the dogs to meet him. I saw Margaret walking with Misty and she told me that Norman had been in hospital in Cartagena to have a hernia removed. He was now back at the motor home and was recovering slowly.

I then called round to Ruth's pitch to ask if they wanted to come to the quiz, but her husband said he was watching football on Sky as he's a Manchester United Fan! It may not be a good idea to go out with them after all, as Brian hates Manchester United!

Whilst Brian cooked some pork steaks with a cream and brandy sauce I went on the Internet which was really slow. But I had an email from my friend Marie. She was almost ready to move into a new house with her boyfriend Rod, but they had fallen out and she had left him. She was back at her Mum and Dad's, feeling a bit fed up. So I replied that she could come here for a few days if she wanted cheering up. She's always found Brian hilarious for some reason!

Later on we rummaged through the videos and found an episode of "The Bill" to watch. Too many glasses of muscatel and I was sent to bed at nine o'clock for being silly!

Tuesday 14th December 2004.

Although it was cloudy, Keep Fit was well attended and the

temperature reached 62 degrees before lunchtime.

I cut Brian's hair with the usual number four blade, and he looked much better. Julia was arriving later so we busied ourselves tidying up and cleaning the awning and cutting the trees back. I walked up to the shop to buy a small hand rake so we could clear out under the hedges around the pitch. We were sure that Mrs Bucket would approve.

During the afternoon, I walked round to a few pitches selling raffle tickets for Ted, and I was quite pleased with the response. I bought the first two strips as no one ever wants to buy the opening numbers ie. one.

Our next door neighbour Martin and his wife were taken to the airport by Jean-Pierre as they were going home for Christmas.

We met Julia at Murcia airport and her flight was on time so we were back home for half past seven. Our meal at the restaurant was very nice and is so much easier than making something when visitors arrive in the evening. Lots of news and gossip to catch up on and we sat up until eleven o'clock having a few drinks.

Jack and Jill were very excited when they realised that Julia was sleeping in the made-up double bed at the front of the caravan and they could sleep with her! We had offered her our bedroom but we agreed that this way round would be better as Julia was always up early, so she could get up when she wanted and could go into the awning for a cigarette if she liked. And we all slept well.

Wednesday 15th December 2004.

Dad's birthday today, so I texted him to say Mum had got his present and card hidden somewhere and I hoped he liked them.

I was disappointed that it was cloudy but we all got dressed and went to the Mercadona to do some shopping. Brian was busy planning this week's meals checking which foods Julia liked and asking if she had any special requests. He's very good when it comes to food, as he loves it!

Julia and I had a walk down to the restaurant as there was a German Craft Fair advertised. There were however only a couple of stalls and they were selling very boring dolls clothes and over-priced cards. Here on the site, one of the popular hobbies is crocheting carrier bags together to make plant pot holders! It takes all sorts to make a world.

On the way back we noticed the function room above the restaurant was open so we wandered in. The lady there told us this was a one-day course to teach you to paint the Bob Ross way, and the cost was 59 euros. She assured us that if we signed up for the next one in January, after the six-hour course we would take away our own masterpiece! I made a mental note that I might like to have a go.

We walked up to reception to collect the four Christmas cards that had come in the post, and on the way back we stopped to ring my Dad. Yes, he'd had a lovely day. Mum had taken him breakfast in bed but this happened every day, not just on his birthday! He liked his card and present and had to read out to me the card that the next door neighbour Sheila had sent him as it was hilarious. We share the same sense of humour and I agreed it was very funny. If I have room at the end of this book, I will share it with you!

Our meal of steak, salad and potatoes was very nice and whilst Julia and I washed up, Brian went to ring Harry and Simon. Harry was doing very well with the catheter and it had been a dry and crisp day in Congleton! Simon and Lorraine were very well and looking forward to breaking up from school for Christmas.

The three of us sat in the awning with the fan heater on and chatted about all sorts. Another late night and we were ages getting to sleep as Brian had a few too many brandies and was making different animal shadows on the wall when we got into bed! He was making rabbits and elephants (so he said) but they just looked like him wriggling his fingers to me!

Thursday 16th December 2004.

I did invite Julia to join me at Keep Fit but she declined the invitation. Lazy cow! The day was much nicer and temperatures were soon up to 65 degrees. We drove into Los Belones, as Brian now needed another new pan for the paella ring he had bought. The new bodega had some lovely muscatel and red wine and we called for some water from the mountain tap before heading home.

After a bit of lunch and a few hours in the sun, we agreed to go to the first "Line Dancing for Beginners" with Bob! We arrived at the patio area at three o'clock and there were around fifty people there. Brian does not have a great sense of rhythm but had always wanted to learn to dance better, so we thought line dancing would be a good start. Julia had been to line dancing classes a few years before with Danny from work so she would be miles ahead.

Everything started off quite slowly, but within five minutes as the whole group performed the first routine, it was apparent that Brian had two left feet. He was facing the wrong way every few bars and his ankles seemed to have gone into spasm! The second dance was even more complicated and half way through that one Brian went to the bar for a pint! Julia thought this was very advanced for a beginner's class, and looking round, I don't think there were more than four of us who had never done line dancing before.

Back home Brian made a very tasty stir-fry and opened a nice bottle of wine. Julia and I couldn't wash up, as we had to get ready for bingo. We called for Evelyn and when we got to the bingo, I had time to go round selling some more raffle tickets. I told Ted I would bring the folded stubs and the money round on Saturday morning. The first game of bingo started at eight and by ten past, I had won the first full house! Two hundred euros! That would be lovely to take shopping tomorrow. I bought a double round of drinks and couldn't wait to tell Brian when we got back at eleven.

Friday 17th December 2004.

We didn't need Mrs Bucket to get us up today as we were looking forward to going shopping. It was a sunny day and we were at the Dos Mares shopping centre, about half an hour's drive away, for eleven o'clock. I was determined to buy myself something new to wear at Christmas with my winnings.

I soon realised that most of the trousers I was trying on were hipsters not an ideal style when you've already got hips like an elephant. Anyway, I did buy some brown trousers with an orange pinstripe and a nice orange jumper.

We had lunch in the food hall and chose a Chinese stall, which was very good value. Two courses and any drink for a total of 15 euros for the two of us.

I bought a nice champagne glass and a small bottle of champagne for Evelyn for her 69th birthday on Christmas Day. Then some home made chocolates for our guests on Christmas Day and a very cheap-looking but colourful table decoration! There was no price on it in the shop but Julia agreed it would probably only be a euro as it was quite tacky and was the last one. When we got to the till, the assistant rang everything else through then we had to wait about ten minutes for someone to get the price of the hideous table piece. In the meantime, Julia popped out for a cigarette, and when eventually the price was confirmed at nine Euros I didn't have the guts to say I didn't want it!

Our big mistake was going into the kitchenware shop as I was drawn towards a bargain twenty-piece dinner service. China, white with three pansies on each item and half price at 30 Euros! I couldn't resist it for Christmas Day so I bought it. We have always had our melamine plates and things in the caravan, but as we now seem to be living in the caravan more than at home, I didn't see why we shouldn't have proper plates and dishes!

Arriving back at half past four, we emptied the car before sitting Brian down to explain about the dinner service as I knew he would go mad about the weight of it. But as I put it, at such a bargain price, and considering I bought it with my prize money, we could always throw it away when we went home if it was too heavy to carry. He didn't see much point in arguing and served up spaghetti bolognese instead.

Julia and I played a few games of Scrabble and had a laugh in the awning whilst Brian kept us supplied with drinks and cheese and biscuits. Midnight saw us climbing into bed after a busy shopping day!

Saturday 18th December 2004.

A sunny but windy day and we were showered and dressed in no time well, by eleven o'clock at least.

Julia walked round to Ted's with me about ten minutes' walk away. I had folded the stubs and put them in a bag. The money, 168 euros, was sealed in an envelope. I also took the remaining tickets still in the book and a Christmas card for Ted. When we got there, he was not at home, but we noticed that the bedroom window was slightly open. The curtains were closed but when I peeped in, I could see the bedspread so I put everything on the bed and closed the window. Ted was drawing the raffle at Monday's quiz so he needed everything in before then.

We called to see Eva who is a beauty therapist and we booked for a luxury pedicure for both of us on Tuesday afternoon. This was my treat for both of us from my winnings!

185

Brian made tasty barbecued beefburgers for lunch and we all then went to the beach at Calblanque. Jack and Jill were soon swimming in the sea and although it was still windy it was quite warm.

We called at the Upper supermarket for a few things and back home the wind had gone completely. We only have the sun on our pitch until four o'clock but the washing up area opposite is sunny for a further hour, so we took our chairs and a small table to the sinks. Before long we were engrossed in another game of Scrabble and had to ask Brian to fetch us a long cool drink, which he did.

About six o'clock, we walked up to reception to see if there was any post and I had a parcel from Janet! Although we had agreed not to exchange Christmas presents, Janet had sent us just a bit of something to open! I put these under the little tree together with a surprise gift that Julia had brought with her from Danny.

The Chinese meal we had later was superb and we were back home for eleven o'clock.

Sunday 19th December 2004.

A very sunny day so we didn't want to spend too long at the market. We bought some broad beans and two lighters for Julia to take home- one for Danny and one for Trudy whom I used to work with.

Back home, we set up our comfy sun loungers and settled down for a sunbathing session. In between, I was preparing and cooking a roast pork dinner so that Brian could have a rest.

Mid-afternoon, Brian drew our attention to Mrs Bucket who appeared to be pulling up weeds, washing them in a bowl of bleach then putting them in a pile. What was all that about?

John brought round a video of the day's Test cricket and after our lovely tea we all watched the match except Julia and me! We carried on gossiping and yes, you've guessed it, we had another game of Scrabble!

Monday 20th December 2004.

Another shopping day was on the agenda, as soon as Evelyn had told me about "El Corte Ingles" in Cartagena apparently the

Spanish equivalent of Harrods! Brian stayed at home to look after the dogs and make a curry and we were off!

We found the store no problem, seven floors of everything. In the pet store I found the cutest leather boots for dogs and at just eight euros for a set of four I had to have them for Jill! Jack got a Christmas stocking and Julia bought some toys for the two cats that she has already fallen for.

It was a lovely shop, though we agreed it was more like John Lewis's than Harrods. Julia bought some perfume and I bought Brian a new toilet bag for the showers as he'd broken the zip on his other one, and some aftershave for Christmas.

In the lingerie department I asked if they had any bras in my size, which is 34H. Both assistants looked at me as though I was making it up and shook their heads! I did buy some black and white checked tights and some orange knickers for Janet. I had them gift wrapped and Julia said she would post them when she got home so Janet would have a little gift from me on Christmas day. We had coffee and a huge cake before setting off back home.

Brian's curry was as good as ever and we escaped washing up again, as we had to get ready to go to the quiz.

Before the quiz started, Ted announced that he would draw the winning tickets for the raffle. The first three numbers drawn were pink tickets, then two blue followed by another pink and more blues! When all eighteen prizes had been announced and not one white ticket had won, I stood up to go and speak to Ted. Two people approached me waving their white tickets and asking why the tickets I had sold didn't appear to have been in the draw. As I was explaining that I was just going to see Ted, he announced, "If anyone bought white tickets, I don't know who you bought them from but it's nothing to do with this raffle!" I could have died of embarrassment.

When I finally reached the front I told Ted that I had sold all white tickets and I had put them through his bedroom window on Saturday morning with the money and his Christmas card! He told me he doesn't use that bedroom and hadn't been in there since September!! It never occurred to me that it was a two-bedroomed caravan and he might not use one of them. He immediately announced that he had made a cock-up and that the white tickets would be drawn on their own on Wednesday night at the bingo. Talk about shown up! Anyway, people seemed to understand it was a genuine mistake and had now calmed down. Roll on Wednesday.

Julia and I were terrible at the quiz and were surprised when we scored only 23 out of 60 but didn't win the booby prize!

Tuesday 21st December 2004.

Cooler but sunny, and Julia and I went to Los Belones for a look round the market. We had a coffee and a cake and Julia bought her cigarettes in the tobacconists to take home. Twenty five euros for 200, much cheaoper than in England, but it made me realise how soon I had forgotten how much I wasted on them.

Julia went round to Eva's first, whilst I walked the dogs with Brian. Then it was my turn for ninety minutes of pure luxury pampering. A wonderful dish called Normandy chicken, which Brian had copied from one of John's cookery books, was Julia's final meal with us. As she was packing, she gave me a wrapped gift which she said was a surprise from Brian and also a present each which were from her for giving her a great holiday. The presents under the tree were building up!

We dropped Julia at the airport at half past five and came home to settle down to a quiet night. We both enjoyed watching "Muriel's Wedding" on video and had been asleep for two hours when the rain started at midnight.

Wednesday 22nd December 2004.

A text from Julia let us know she had arrived home safely and on time after an exciting time in the airport which she promised to email me about. It was raining, and looked as if it could be in for the day. I hadn't done any washing whilst Julia was here so I decided to treat myself and take all the washing to the launderette. Bedding, towels, everything was put into four bags and Brian helped me carry it round. I handed over the 24 euros for four loads, washing and drying and she told me it would be Friday before it was ready. I think everyone had the same idea today as she was snowed under with dirty washing.

Back home we had a coffee and cereals and Miep came to the awning asking for Brian. I couldn't hear what they were saying as I was sat inside the caravan, but Brian was standing on one leg! He didn't seem to be grasping whatever it was that Miep wanted and after a few minutes he came in laughing. Apparently she had asked if he had "balance." Brian stood on one leg to show her he could balance but what she was asking for was a pair of "scales" to weigh their suitcases on! She must have found someone else who had some and she brought them round to show Brian that they said "balance" on them!

Joop and Miep were going back to Holland for Christmas and New Year and came to say goodbye before they left. They would be back on January 13th. At least Corrie and Jean-Pierre would still be here as Corrie's Mum and brother were due to arrive today on the same flight that Joop and Miep were leaving on.

Our last "big" shop for Christmas and we bought quite a few treats and an electric kettle. We had always used a gas one as Brian worried that an electric kettle would overload the system, but we bought a low wattage one and didn't realise until we got back that it matched the toaster that Dad had bought the year before.

I also managed to sneak into the trolley a set of posh cutlery to go with my new dinner service! This cheap Christmas dinner was becoming more expensive every day.

Liver made a cheap tea with plenty left over for the dogs. I then walked to bingo with Barbara, Angie and Jill, as Evelyn didn't feel up to going. Of course Ted was ready with the white raffle tickets and half a dozen prizes, but I was again quite embarrassed when the first ticket drawn was number seven and it was mine! The rest of the evening was uneventful and none of us were anywhere near winning anything.

Thursday 23rd December 2004.

The sun had returned and we were going into Cartagena today so Jack and Jill went round to Evelyn's and we set off at half past eleven after I had been to Keep Fit.

A pleasant drive and although we didn't have a clue where we were, we ended up in an underground car park near the harbour which was an ideal place to be. We walked around the city and towards the shops, and called at a little pavement café for meatballs, chips, bread and two white coffees. Only ten euros and very tasty and we then walked around the many shops, including designer ones. I bought some festive clips for place cards on our Christmas table. Brian said if I bought much more for the bloody table, we wouldn't get the food on!

We had a coffee in the historic harbour before we set off back and we'd had a lovely day. Neither of us could believe how quiet the streets and shops were the day before Christmas Eve.

Jack and Jill had been spoiled as usual and whilst I walked up for the post, Brian cooked a large steak each in a creamy mushroom sauce.

Mum was in when I rang her but she was a bit upset. She had opened one of our letters, which was from the T.V. Licensing Authority and it said that if we didn't get a licence within 14 days we could be fined up to £1000. She had rung them and explained that we were abroad but told them she knew I wouldn't have not bought a licence and asked if they could hold any action until I came home in March. They said they would make a note on their files, but confirmed they had no records of any licence! I was furious that I had made proper arrangements and even had a refund from them in October, and now they were worrying Mum because of their incompetence. I explained what I had done to Mum, but told her to just send the red letter to me and I would write to them.

We were both quite tired after going shopping and we were asleep by ten o'clock.

Friday 24th December 2004.

After collecting my four bags of washing, I busied myself with cleaning the awning and the caravan whilst Brian was at the gym. For the first time since we arrived I plugged the iron in, just to iron one of Brian's shirts. Most clothes that we wear are easy care fabrics that don't need ironing so this was quite novel for me to actually iron a few things.

The day was soon very hot and the temperature was 72 degrees. I quickly made some mince pies but when they came out of the bun tins I could "hear" that they were like rock cakes! Never mind, we shouldn't be eating them anyway.

A lovely afternoon to sunbathe, whilst Brian made a belly pork and black pudding casserole with lentils and beans.

In the evening we settled down to watch a DVD which Simon had lent to us, and after half an hour of "Me Myself and Irene," there was a power cut. Two hours later the electricity came back on so it was a film in two parts and we didn't go to bed until after midnight. Would Santa still come?

Saturday 25th December 2004.

He's been! Merry Christmas. I made us both a cup of tea and we each took our daily tablets so we could then get on with opening presents. Jill wasn't very impressed with her little boots but Jack enjoyed opening the doggie stocking and they shared its contents.

Brian got a nice leather wallet from Julia, the aftershave from me and some very warm-looking pyjamas from Janet. I also got fluffy pyjamas from Janet, some jewellery from Julia and the present she had bought me from Brian was a gorgeous handbag that we'd seen at the shopping centre. She must have bought the presents whilst she was pretending to go off for a cigarette. Danny's gift was a selection of miniature bottles of port, which I love.

We eventually got dressed and I set the table for lunch. It must have been two hours before Brian noticed the new blue cutlery and I had to confess that we had bought it at the supermarket! The extortionate table decoration looked surprisingly nice and the four crackers that Janet had given me in September were soon taking pride of place.

I walked round to give Evelyn her gift and to wish her a happy birthday, and then we walked to the phone booths to ring home.

They were all busy but we eventually managed to get through to Pam, Harry, Simon, Ian, Janet and Mum. Everyone was having a lovely time, especially as they all had a white Christmas. Brian went round to John's to help bring some food round to put in the steamer and the electric pan to keep warm.

At half past one we had nibbles and champagne and Brian's prawn cocktails were served at two. I had melon but that's my problem!

We then went back into the sun and had a few more drinks until three o'clock when John served up a chicken, bacon and pork roll, garlic mash, sprouts with chestnuts, leeks, mushrooms, carrots, stuffing and gravy. It was delicious and we opened some of the red wine that Diego had given us.

The dinner was followed with John's homemade Christmas pudding and cream, mince pies (far superior to mine which were now in the bin), and Christmas cake.

I made coffee and handed out the handmade chocolates. After eights, cheese and biscuits, brandy and port. By six o'clock John was shattered and excused himself for a lie down back home. He had been working all morning preparing everything. Barbara managed to stay until seven and after the power cut at half past seven, we were both tucked up in bed by nine. We had no idea when the power would be back on and neither had anyone else on the site.

Sunday 26th December 2004.

We realised the electric was back on when we woke up at eight to the sound of Mrs Bucket's spin dryer, honest. A very windy and much cooler day and by mid morning it was decided that the usual Boxing Day charity swim would have to be postponed until New Year's Day.

Walking up to the supermarket for a newspaper we both felt much colder than recent days. As we approached the shop we were surprised to find it closed. Reception informed us that the electricity was still off at the top end of the site so the shop hadn't opened today.

By one o'clock, our electric was off again so we put the gas fire on and played dice. I then taught Brian how to play crib although I was a bit rusty as it had been years since I had played with Gran.

After yesterday's food we hadn't even thought about a meal for today, until Evelyn called round. She has brought four boxes from the Chinese where they had been for Christmas day with Wim and Emmy. There was so much food she explained, that they hadn't touched a couple of the dishes, and she knew the dogs would enjoy them. Two hours later, when the power came back on, we warmed them through and ate them for our tea! Don't tell Evelyn or Jack and Jill.

Barbara brought another tape of England's Test Match for Brian to watch. I put the radio on and heard the news that a tidal wave disaster had killed an estimated 6,000 people. How awful.

Monday 27th December 2004.

Today could almost be described as bitterly cold but the sun was peeping through so I did some washing. My "visitor" arrived, as I was finishing hanging the washing out so I went inside, put the heating on and had a cup of tea.

Brian was still at the gym when Geoff called to ask if he could borrow the secateurs to cut some branches down at his pitch.

I tried to log onto the Internet without success so I rang the company from my mobile and after speaking to a man for a few minutes that didn't speak English, he asked me to call back later. That call cost me six pounds.

After walking the dogs along the beach and whilst Brian went shopping, I rang Pam to wish her a happy fiftieth birthday! She loved the presents and card I had left with her in September and was having a lovely day. She sounded much more cheerful and it was nice to hear her laughing again.

Later she was expecting to go for a drink with Gary and Hannah. Unknown to her, a stretch limo would pick her up and Gary had arranged a little surprise party for her. I then tried ringing Mum and David and Gill, but they were not in. On the way back from the phone I noticed my friend Kay was selling some videos for a couple of euros, so I chose "Road to Perdition" with Tom Hanks and thought we could save it for a cuddly night in again!

Another one of John's recipes was Mexicano chicken with rice and it was very moreish.

Brian watched cricket after tea but not before I listened to the radio briefly and heard that the tidal wave was now being described as a tsunami and that latest reports said that up to 10,000 could have died.

Tuesday 28th December 2004.

I again rang the Internet company who assured me that someone would come out today, but I wasn't holding my breath.

It felt cold again so I wrapped up well, put the heating on and felt sorry for myself as I had tummy ache.

Brian took the dogs for their walk and then he made perch for tea. I was too mardy to argue about not wanting fish, and when he served the meal I was pleased I'd kept my mouth shut as it was really nice. After tea we noticed our neighbour Diego taking some kitchen cupboards and placing them at the side of the bins. We went to see what they were like and before you could say, "Pass me a J-cloth," two of them were in our awning! White and blue, they matched perfectly and I soon had them wiped over and positioned at the side of the wine rack table.

Before long, Brian had filled them with spices, pans, plate's things he used in the awning whilst cooking, and as he said, even if we threw the cupboards away when we left, they would be handy for the next few weeks.

Latest figures on the six o'clock radio news said 25,000 people were now feared missing or dead and it named India amongst the places affected. I sent a text to Janice and Malcolm asking if they were OK in Goa. Luckily, Janice replied almost immediately that they were fine as the tsunami hadn't hit their side of India, but she said the sea looked decidedly strange and somehow menacing.

Wednesday 29th December 2004.

Thankfully it was a warmer day and I had stopped wallowing in self-pity. The Internet man came at half past eleven and explained that the problems had been caused by all the power cuts. He had my system up and running within ten minutes, but just as he was leaving, Wim called round u

and asked him to go and see him next, as he was far from happy with his Internet performance. Oh dear, trouble at mill!

Brian went to the gym and I was back on the Internet with a vengeance. My mate Gill emailed me to say she had lost almost two stones at the slimming club but she couldn't report on Mother's progress, as she hadn't been for ages. Wait until I ring her next. I was catching up with lots of news, including Julia's airport saga. After we had left her at Murcia airport, she had been to the toilets and left her handbag! She was then tannoyed to go to the information desk and when she'd retrieved her handbag, the airline realised they had put her luggage on the flight to Manchester instead of Leeds Bradford! They did manage to get them on the right plane in time but not what you would call a straightforward check-in.

I walked up to the supermarket and whilst in there I saw the new trendy hairdresser that was here on the site. Christine said she could come and cut my hair tomorrow at two so that was that.

As the sun came out I thought I would let Brian have an easier day so I made tea, a very exciting spaghetti bolognese.

Our neighbour Antonio called with a bottle of Chivas whisky and I brought two glasses and the Spanish/English dictionary outside and the two men had a drink and a few laughs for a good hour!

Bingo was on again and I was really pleased when Angie won 115 euros. She treated the four of us to a gin and tonic. We were talking about the tsunami disaster and the others were saying the number of dead had now risen to 60,000. They said that the pictures on the television were very upsetting and I was pleased in a way that we hadn't seen the pictures and I could only imagine how terrible the scenes must be.

Back home, Brian watched cricket until half past one. How's that?

Thursday 30th December 2004.

I woke with a headache and it didn't help when I saw the dark clouds outside. However, the sun soon made an appearance and at half past ten Brian drove to Cala Reona to do a spot of fishing.

Walking up to the supermarket to buy some nail varnish remover, I was laughing to myself about something that had happened years ago, on our first holiday together. We had been in Majorca a few days when Brian was in the bathroom getting ready to go out for the evening. I was drying my hair at the dressing table in the bedroom when I heard him scream. He came into the bedroom clutching his face in his hands and when I saw what he was holding I knew what had happened. He was looking down at a small plastic container, the label of which read "Body Shop Moisturiser". I had washed this empty bottle out before we came, and filled it with nail varnish remover! Stupid Brian had covered his newly shaven face with my nail varnish remover and apparently it was my fault? Since then, I have been very careful to label things correctly as things don't always "do just what it says on the tin".

Christine arrived at two and gave me a very trendy cut and dry, and at eight euros she was just too cheap! I then dyed my hair to cover the grey and by the time Brian arrived home at half past four I was like a new woman!

There was a power cut at five o'clock and we were pleased

that we had decided to go out for an Indian meal in Los Belones.

It was my turn to drive again but who's counting? We went into TJ's English bar for a few drinks before our meal. I had my first alcopop since September and Brian enjoyed a couple of pints of draught Murphy's beer. Sky News was playing on the television at the end of the bar and these were the first pictures we had seen of the tsunami disaster. They were now reporting the death toll at approximately 125, 000, which was almost incomprehensible.

The Indian restaurant was quite busy and we were seated at a nice table. We shared a mixed starter for two, then each chose a dish, and I had a peshwari nan, Brian had his usual three chapatis and we ordered a side dish of Bombay potatoes. Two beers and a coke brought the bill to 46 euros and the food was faultless. Not huge portions but superb quality and taste and the service was good too. We would be back.

Home for nine o'clock and after a coffee, Brian was fast asleep by half past. He's not used to Murphy's!

Friday 31st December 2004.

Getting out of bed at four a.m. to go to the loo, I tried unsuccessfully not to wake Brian. He also got up for a wee and then we were awake. I made tea and Jack and Jill came to snuggle down the bed with us. We talked about lots of rubbish and were still awake at eight o'clock when daylight started to come through the roof light.

It's amazing what you can get done when you get up early and I was doing the washing before Brian set off to the gym. There was a notice up in the toilet block to say there would be no electricity on our block from 10. 30 until 12. 30. As it turned out, the power was off from 12. 30 until four o'clock.

After the gym, Brian went fishing and I went to ring Mum. They were fine though my Dad had a bad knee, which was keeping him awake. I rang Janet and she had some bad news – Jake had been mugged. At fourteen he is a tall lad and the previous night he had walked through a local park with his friend about nine o'clock. Two older lads and their girlfriends had attacked them and taken Jake's mobile phone and new gloves and his mate's new gold chain. The police had been excellent and had said the lads might have to attend a "video identification" in a week or two. Luckily, neither of them was physically injured, just shaken up. Janet confided in me that it may be a blessing in disguise for Jake as he's at that age when he won't listen to anything Janet or Jimmy say–he knows best. Janet has repeatedly told him not to walk through the park after dark but he had always been sure that nobody would come near him and he'd be safe, and Janet was just a nattering old fart.

On a lighter note, Janet said that Mum was going to book a cottage in Blackpool for July, so that Mum and Dad, Janet, Jimmy and the boys, Chris and his children could all have a week's holiday together. Mum likes to be very organised and is quite obsessed with food but Janet thought it was a bit premature when Mother asked her if she thought they should have a shepherd's pie one day!

Back home I texted Dad- "About this shepherd's pie in Blackpool–ask Mum if she's putting grated cheese on it".

Brian returned at half past four, empty-handed. I was cooking a stuffed veal roll for tea and some fresh vegetables and roast potatoes, but just before I was going to serve it, Diego came round and insisted that we went round for a drink to celebrate the new year. I switched everything off, put the dogs in the caravan and off we went. We were made very welcome and introduced to all the family, sons and wives, daughters and fiancés and a total of four Yorkshire terriers including Diego's dog Rocky. Benito the parrot was in fine voice. Our other Spanish neighbour Antonio was there and also the very friendly builder who had been working on the improvements that Diego had been having done. They were having paella later, probably about midnight, and Diego's wife and the girls in the family were preparing the meal in the kitchen.

After a few gin and tonics the electricity went off again, and candles were quickly found and lit. We left an hour later and had a late reheated tea and the remaining bottle of red wine that Diego had given us before Christmas. We had a few more drinks whilst sending text messages to friends and we received a message from Pam to say her and Gary were on their way to the Lake District for New Year. We also had a text from David and Gill to say they had been to the Lakes for a few days but were now home so that's why they weren't in on Monday.

Who knows what time we got to sleep, does it matter? The fireworks were very loud at midnight but didn't seem to bother the dogs. We watched the colourful display through the roof lights and wished each other a Happy New Year with a big sloppy kiss and then I took my teeth out! What a romantic thought to end 2004.

Saturday 1st January 2005.

Happy New Year. A sunny day to start off 2005 and whilst Brian took the dogs on a very long walk, I gave the caravan a good clean.

We showered and got dressed later as we had been invited round to Evelyn and Bill's for the afternoon. Of course the dogs were invited too and we arrived on time with a bottle of bubbly to see in the New Year. Evelyn had made a lovely buffet of ham, salad and some interesting nibbles and we enjoyed good conversation and some nice wine. Bill showed us photographs of their new apartment near Edinburgh on the computer.

We came home around six and were going to watch a video, but when we turned the television on, we were receiving BBC1 perfect picture but no sound. Up until now we could only get Spanish television programmes and we were so engrossed with English telly that we watched an episode of "Casualty" without any sound! How sad is that?

The news followed and the death toll for the tsunami was now 150,000. Of course, Brian had to stay awake for hours so he could watch "Match of the Day."

A late text from Dad read "Api Nu Yeer. Ad gud nite hat Sheylas an plaied kards till free ow clok!". Brian hadn't got a clue what Dad was talking about, but I was pleased they had enjoyed themselves.

Sunday 2nd January 2005.

It felt like a Sunday morning somehow and Brian suggested that we went down to the restaurant for the full English breakfast. I was starving so we enjoyed bacon, eggs, tomatoes, mushrooms, sausages, toast, orange juice and coffee.

The sunshine seemed to put a smile on everyone's face and I walked up to the supermarket to get a Sunday paper. Several texts came whilst we sunbathed; Pam had enjoyed the Lakes but Harry was furious with her for going, as Hannah had asked him to pick her and a male friend up in Macclesfield ten miles away. It takes him half an hour to get the car out of the garage and at eighty-one he shouldn't be expected to be used like a taxi service, so I could empathise with him.

Bridget called round as usual to bring the dogs a biscuit and she also brought us a plate of German cookies that she had made herself. I took a photo of her with the dogs, and she seemed quite astonished when, ten minutes later, I took a postcard to her of the photograph.

After the huge late breakfast, we both settled for a sandwich and crisps and nuts for tea, then we settled down to watch the video "Road To Perdition," which we thoroughly enjoyed.

Monday 3rd January 2005.

Twenty to eight was showing on Brian's watch when Mrs Bucket commenced her Monday morning washing ritual! Today was dull and much cooler but she would probably still get her washing dry. It would be hung out early enough!

We drove to the Ferreteria to get some fluid for the caravan cassette toilet. There doesn't seem to be the same choice as in England and although we managed to get some, it was more expensive than back home and didn't seem as good. Something we would put on our list for next time to bring with us.

Calling in the mountains for some fresh water, we drove on to the Upper for a big shop and were tempted by a hand-mixer and grinder. We had brought ours from home as Brian uses it a lot for making curries so we bought one to keep in the caravan permanently. At 30 euros we didn't think that was bad value and when we got back, Brian fixed the "wall bracket" to our kitchen cupboard in the awning. Almost a show kitchen!

I walked up to reception to reserve our pitch for October by making a credit card payment of 360 euros. We could have waited until the end of January, but of course Brian wanted to be sure we could have the same pitch and said he would feel happier once it was booked. Is he short of something to worry about?

I went to ring Pam whilst Brian made a shepherd's pie, and when I got back Antonio came round with an empty rice packet in his hands. We eventually realised he was asking if he could borrow some rice! I gave him a full bag from the cupboard and I really feel like a proper neighbour now.

After tea we washed up together and then played crib. Brian was enjoying playing this new game but was extremely childish and giggled when he was awarded "One for his Nob".

Tuesday 4th January 2005.

The fierce beating of rugs by Mrs Bucket woke us just after half past seven so we had an early start to the day. On my way back from Keep Fit I called to see Jill who comes to bingo with us. She is a keen gardener and has trays of cuttings which she grows and then sells to people on the site. I bought a couple of Busy Lizzies and some other plants as I thought a small display on the corner of our pitch would look nice.

By the time Brian got back from the gym my little garden was complete and although he thought I was mad, he agreed it looked homely.

Returning from our beach walk later in the day, I rang Mum who told me she had posted a parcel today. A couple of videos and a small present for Brian were enclosed along with a few letters she thought I might want to see.

I sat in the sun whilst good old Brian went shopping, and he returned with a Dorado fish which he steamed. Served with stir-fry vegetables it was very nice and I didn't get one bone.

The Internet access was like lightning for a change so I contacted Auntie Jen and Uncle Harry in Norfolk, Janet, Gill and Dave, Anita and Les and Julia. Marie had emailed us to say she would be landing at Murcia on the evening of Tuesday 18th January and staying until Saturday, so I replied that would be great. This kept me occupied most of the evening and Brian was engrossed in his book "Stalin- The Court Of The Red Tsar", which his Dad had bought him for his birthday. I do like a bit of light reading!

Wednesday 5th January 2005.

After breakfast the sun came out and we got ready for a walk along the beach. At twelve o'clock as we walked along the sand we were silent for three minutes, in memory of the tsunami victims.

It was too nice a day to waste so Brian was soon ready and back down on the beach fishing with his mate Helmut. Another afternoon relaxing in the sun for me and I made sweet and sour spare ribs with Chinese fried rice for tea.

Did Brian catch any fish? You're getting as bad as all the neighbours, asking such silly questions, every time he comes home with his rod! No, he didn't.

Barbara wasn't coming to bingo tonight so I called round for Jill and Angie, and discovered that Angie's German next door neighbour Troodle had asked if she could come with us! She didn't speak much English, but eagerly bought five books to play so we assumed she knew what she was doing. We asked her if she had brought a pen, and it was at this stage she told us she didn't know how to play and asked why she needed a pen! This was going to be a fun night.

Luckily, Ted realised that she was struggling a little with the numbers so he kept repeating them in German for her. The three of us were trying to watch our own cards and keep an eye on Troodle and at a very tense moment when Troodle only wanted two for a full house, Angie's mobile phone rang, and she ended up almost under the table trying to tell her daughter she would ring her back later! !

When I got home with the news that none of us had won, Brian told me he had rung his Dad whilst I was out. We have been telling Harry for months that we could smell gas in his kitchen. He was having none of it, we were imagining it. But the district nurse had been and she had rung the gas board who confirmed he had three gas leaks and disconnected his cooker! Now would he believe us?

Thursday 6th January 2005.

It's that bank holiday again. After Keep Fit we agreed to have a go at tennis but I warned Brian I hadn't played since I was fourteen. I did used to play for the school but I'm sure I was only chosen because I would always turn up on a Saturday. I doubt my ability had any bearing on my selection.

We were surprised how much we enjoyed an hour's knock about and said we would start playing more often.

After a welcome shower it was time to sunbathe again. We were both relaxing in the sun when Antonio called round with a bottle of champagne. I think it was a bank holiday celebration of some kind so I fetched three glasses and the Spanish dictionary and we talked about family and children.

We had an early tea of liver and onions and had just finished when Fran appeared on her bike. She almost fell off as she reached us and when I invited her in she said she would love a glass of red

201

wine. She rambled on for an hour or so and we realised she had come straight from an afternoon session in the bar. I walked her and the bike home about seven o'clock and Geoff was just about to serve up their teas!

A tabletop sale and tombola had been organised in the pool-bar so we made our way up there. All proceeds were for the tsunami fund and Angie had also been round the site most of the day collecting donations. I bought some kitchen scales for a euro and we had a few drinks at the bar with Diego and his wife who were also supporting the event. Brian insisted on buying Diego a pint of Tetley Smooth, and he drank it, saying it was very different but nice.

Barbara had left a video of England's Test cricket efforts which Brian watched, whilst I set the computer up and watched two girlie DVD's that Fran had lent me.

Friday 7th January 2005.

The washing basket was almost overflowing so I needed to get on with it. Whilst Brian was at the gym, I did all the washing and had some tea, toast and fruit for breakfast.

Cala Reone was calling for Brian to go fishing, and he went off with his fishing box and rod, a sandwich and a beer. He posted a card to my Auntie Joyce on his way out of the site, as she would be 76 next week. I walked the dogs along the beach and rang Mum on the way back.

The washing soon dried in the breezy sunny conditions and I sat in the sun chatting to various people that came past during the afternoon.

I prepared the tea and Brian didn't get home until nearly six o'clock but guess what? He'd caught three fish. Two escaped but he brought one home, which he filleted and put in the freezer. It was smaller than a fish finger when he'd finished, but he thought if he caught a few more over the next few weeks he might eventually have enough for a meal.

A huge steak each with chunky potato wedges and vegetables meant there was plenty left for Jack and Jill to enjoy.

Saturday 8th January 2005.

It was quite cool at ten o'clock as we walked along the beach but by lunchtime the sun was trying to get through. Dad texted me to say there were gales in England but they weren't expecting to get too much of the bad weather in Yorkshire.

Fishing again (!), so I made some nan breads and let the dough rise in the heat of the afternoon. I was talking for over an hour to a chap called Brian who was here with his wife and she had broken her arm in Denia on their way here. Angie also came round and told me the site had risen over 4,000 euros altogether, which was excellent.

An empty-handed but not altogether disgruntled Brian returned home and made a creamy but spicy prawn and pineapple curry and a side dish of curried chickpeas. After mopping us the last bits with my scrummy nan breads we settled down to watch the DVD of "The Two Towers" from "Lord of the Rings," which Simon had lent us. I fell asleep at nine o'clock but Brian watched it until midnight and said it was brilliant.

Sunday 9th January 2005.

Right, I was determined to go round to Barbara's today and get weighed. Hooray 11 stone exactly, so I had lost twelve pounds since we arrived. I was feeling much better but was slightly disappointed that I hadn't managed to get below the eleven stone barrier. Women, we're never satisfied.

A brisk walk to Mar Cristal where we stopped for coffee and Tapas. Barbara and John were at the same bar with Marie and Richard and they were having plates of chips with their coffees. I asked Barbara how they managed to get their coffees served in glasses instead of cups. She said you just ask for "en vaso". So we did and that's just what we got. The tapas consisted of prawns, squid, garlic potatoes, cold pork with tomatoes, potato and onion tortilla and a mashed up fish thing that I let Brian eat! Our bill of eight euros was very acceptable.

Back at the site we walked up to the shop for a newspaper, milk, sausages and eggs. It was cloudy but warm so we sat out reading the paper and having a beer when we got home.

Who should turn up but Derek and Ann! We were thrilled to see them and they told us they had only arrived on Friday and were right at the top end of the site. The reason they had only just arrived was because Ann had decided she wanted a Christmas at home, as simple as that. It was great to see them and we would be seeing them again now we knew they were here.

Rod and Wendy called with Wendy's Mum Beryl and we wished them a happy new year as they had just got back after spending Christmas in England.

Tonight we were going to go to the pool bar as there was another Dutch dance night on, but Brian didn't feel too good, so we had lasagne and garlic bread and stayed in just for a change! I did go to the phones to ring Mum, Janet and Gill who were all at home so that passed an hour on!

Monday 10ᵗʰ January 2005.

Me and Mrs Bucket were almost washing in unison, but not quite. A warm sunny day so after walking the dogs Brian returned to our beach to do some fishing and I treated myself to a new paperback book. Believe it or not I had never read any Jeffrey Archer so when I saw "A Quiver Full of Arrows" and "A Twist in the Tale" in one book priced at only four euros I bought it. I had looked in the free library but there was nothing that appealed to me that was in English.

There was great merriment amongst the neighbours when Brian returned triumphantly at five o'clock with two big fish. Some of them joked that he must have been to the Mercadona for such a catch, but he carried on filleting and freezing them as planned.

Plain old sausage and mash for tea and then I got a text from my Dad. He'd been to the doctors and he has arthritis in his knee for which he's been prescribed some tablets. He also said that Mum had lost her collapsible white stick and thinks she may have folded it and put it in the parcel she'd posted to us! I replied that I would let him know when the parcel arrived!

Several games of crib later, when I had beaten Brian five games to two, he gave up and went on the Internet instead. What a bad loser!

Tuesday 11th January 2005.

John called as I was setting off to Keep Fit to see if he could go to Los Belones market with Brian to get some mangoes, as he was going to make some mango chutney.

Whilst they were out, John had explained to Brian that if we had a television that we bought in Spain, we could now receive BBC1 free from the aerial that had been fitted at the bottom of the site.

By the time they got back, Barbara and I were hurriedly loaded into the car and we were on our way to the Carrefour Supermarket at Cartagena where the sales were still on. We bought a portable telly for 99 euros and I also bought a pair of bathroom scales.

Once back home, Brian couldn't wait to unpack the box and John was fashioning an aerial for us from some wire, a broom handle and some string. By four o'clock we were tuned into BBC1, CNN, and an English speaking German sports channel. I packed up the old TV/video and stored it under the bed for now.

Whilst Brian made a spaghetti bolognese I walked to reception and Mum's parcel had arrived. She had sent us two tapes of various programmes, two sports vests for Brian which he was pleased with, a watch strap for me as I had been unable to buy a Swatch strap in Spain, and several letters. But no white stick!

I rang Mum to let her know the parcel had arrived and she told me she had found her white stick in her handbag. Whilst walking back home, I bumped into Derek and Ann who invited us to their pitch on Friday afternoon to play cards.

After tea, we watched "EastEnders" and lots of rubbish that was on afterwards.

Wednesday 12th January 2005.

A cool morning and I noticed that the electricity had tripped out in the caravan. We had been leaving the electric heating on during the night, on its lowest setting, just to take the chill off. I reset the trip switch and everything was OK but we couldn't understand why it had tripped out.

Mum had sent me the red letter from the T.V. Licensing Authority so I composed and printed a letter of complaint to them. I had also had a lengthy letter from my friend Jean who I had worked with some years ago when I was the bar manager at a hotel. You remember the canteen lady from "Frost" on the 'telly! I knew she enjoyed getting my annual newsletter so that took me a while to incorporate all my news. Next I typed a letter to Mum – she enjoyed getting a letter especially as I would print it in huge letters so she could read it. She had paid a couple of our bills and I would be paying her rent for the month so I listed everything we owed each other and in the end, she owed me just £100. I enclosed a paying in slip and an envelope addressed to my bank so she could post a cheque.

I wrote two birthday cards that I had bought from Emmy, one to Danny and one to Jill from the cricket club. Their birthdays were both on January 24th so I thought I would post them early. Jill and Colin's daughter Emma was getting married in August so I had chosen a card for Jill of a gorgeous woman in a huge picture hat and suggested Jill could model herself on it as mother of the bride.

During my busy day, Brian went fishing again but didn't catch anything. Corned beef hash with a nice light crust and mushy peas accompanied by a bottle of red wine and then we settled down to watch one of Mum's tapes. We enjoyed six episodes of "Coronation Street" and the new Christmas "Vicar of Dibley".

Thursday 13th January 2005.

This morning's Keep Fit was the busiest I have attended. There were fifty-seven people today and it was probably due to the lovely blue skies and warm weather.

The phones on the site were all out of order and Bill said this was due to the system being updated to support the Internet lines.

Barbara and John came with us to Lidl's where we stocked up on drinks and things and then we called at another supermarket called "Plus". As we were walking into the store, my sandal broke and I had to buy some slippers to wear, as I couldn't keep my sandals on! I was getting some funny looks with my black cut-off trousers and orange slippers.

We had toasted sandwiches and coffees before setting off on the return journey. We called at the village of Los Nietos to see the house that John and Barbara would be renting in October, as they have decided to sell their camper van when they get home in March.

Joop and Miep returned to a big welcome from everyone. They brought us a packet of twelve "Stroopwafels" which were like biscuits with caramel in the middle. Very low calorie I'm sure, but how kind.

Two steaks that we had bought earlier were cooked to perfection and then I swapped the televisions over, as Brian wanted to watch another video of the cricket that Barbara had taped. It would be ideal to have one telly in the awning but we didn't have a table to stand it on, so for now we would keep swapping them in the caravan.

An uneventful night at bingo with Barbara and Angie as Jill had gone back to England for a couple of weeks and Troodle hadn't asked to come this week!

Friday 14th January 2005.

Once again, the electricity had tripped out in the night, so I put the trip switch on to restore the supply. Bill called round so I asked him if he knew what could be causing it and he suggested we try to eliminate various appliances to see which one was overloading the system.

Whilst Brian was at the gym I did the washing, and in between the different loads I was unplugging and plugging in various things but nothing seemed to affect the electric.

We had a text from Norman and Lynn asking if we would like to visit them this weekend. I replied that Sunday would be a good day so they texted some directions and asked us to ring them when we got to a certain car park.

I had an email from my mate Gill telling me how pleased she was to have lost nearly two stone. Also Noreen emailed telling me she'd had a great time working in Malta at the new call centre.

At two o'clock we walked up to Derek and Ann's armed with a bottle of bubbly and a pack of cards. Derek had said they only had an old pack, but we had a few with us so they could keep this pack. Both of their dogs were sitting in the sun and didn't really notice we were there. We had drinks and a good chat for an hour or so catching up on one another's news and we told Derek we had taken his advice and had a mover fitted on the caravan. He still wanted to play bridge again so I told him he should have an afternoon with Mum when she arrived and then maybe he could go to bridge with her.

Ann was hilarious playing cards and I told her she reminded me of my Aunt Edith who was always making us laugh when we played cards. She asked what Aunt Edith was like and when I told her she had died several years ago, Ann replied, "Well that's really nice, saying I remind you of someone that's died!" But she knew what I had meant. Despite saying she didn't know what she was doing throughout the game, Ann ended up winning just like Aunt Edith used to do! At five o'clock we set off walking back and thanked them for a fun afternoon.

A late tea of beef curry, rice and nan breads and I washed up, as Brian wanted to watch more cricket! I must remind Barbara that she can accidentally forget to set the tape sometimes.

Saturday 15th January 2005.

A disappointing cool and misty morning which was overcast and foggy, so we were quite annoyed when we realised that the electricity had tripped out yet again. Neither of us knew anything about electrics–where was my Dad when I needed him?

We looked through the most recent editions of the free local newspapers. Round Town News and The Costa Calida Informer were available from reception and in most supermarkets every week and made for some good reading and local news and events. There were a couple of adverts for electricians but not specific to caravans.

As we discussed the dilemma in the awning, I saw an English chap called Mark whom I'd spoken to a few times, putting something in the dustbin. I knew he lived on the site permanently but didn't know what he did for a job. I asked him if he was an electrician by any chance. "No," he replied, "but my brother is!" He rang his brother James who was working on a job in Cartagena, and within an hour James was here, had diagnosed a faulty trip switch, driven into Los Belones to get a new switch and fitted it! We were so grateful, I could have kissed him, but instead, when he told me the total bill including the new switch was fifteen euros, I gave him twenty. How lucky was that?

We were pleased that it had been a minor thing as Brian had convinced himself that the whole caravan would have to be scrapped! The heating was now back on full to warm the caravan, and Brian decided he would go on the Internet to look for a holiday for us.

In June, we would celebrate our fifteenth wedding anniversary, which was quite an achievement for both of us. As Brian also pointed out, he would have thirty years of marriage in by June if he added up all three wives! How cheeky is that? So he happily spent most of the day looking at holidays in Italy, Cuba, Greece and all sorts of places that took his fancy. For the last few years we have been on a cricket tour for four days in June and whilst the lads play cricket, the few women that go just drink a lot, laugh a lot and generally have a ball! Last year we went to Cambridge but no one seems prepared to organise another one so it looks like this year's tour is off!

I made a pork apple and cider casserole after which we walked up to the pool bar for a Dutch dance evening. We had a great time and our neighbours insisted that we sat with them. .Thankfully they spoke English most of the night, though Joop did confess that although he could understand me, when Brian spoke he usually didn't have a clue what he was saying as he speaks too quickly!

In bed for midnight ready for a drive up to Murcia to see Norman and Lynn tomorrow.

Sunday 16th January 2005.

We were looking forward to seeing Lynn and Norman, as we hadn't seen them since Brian's retirement do in July 2003. Sixty-two miles to the car park near Mula and we rang Norman who came to lead us to their house. The village was like stepping back in timema unspoilt and quiet and when we reached their property we loved what we saw. A beautiful detached house with a large pool and orchards to the side and the front. Lynn served drinks in the sun as we caught up on their lives since they moved to Spain a year ago. They had done lots of work in the house and it looked lovely. Inside, every room had been fitted and furnished to a high standard and they had bought the best of everything. Norman explained they still had a lot of work to do outside but they had all the time in the world to get the alterations and improvements done.

Sam was their very old black Labrador and he was too fussy for our dogs so we made them take it in turns to have a run around whilst the other dogs stayed in the cars. Jill had a paddle in the pool whilst attempting to retrieve a ball that was floating.

Their friends Jane and Derek arrived about two o'clock and we all got acquainted and were soon sitting down to an excellent lunch of steak, salad, new potatoes and stuffed peppers. Pudding was a lemon pie that Jane had made and it was very tangy and tasty. Apparently this is a Spanish tradition; to take the sweet if you are invited somewhere for a meal. I shall have to rustle up a trifle if we are invited again!

The local red wine and the conversation were flowing but I only had one glass as I was driving. We have always had a rule that if we are going somewhere and one of us has to drive, whichever one of us is closer to the people we are visiting gets a free ride. I seem to be doing my share of driving, don't you think?

Lynn's Mum would be staying for the month of February and we aranged that they would bring her to see us for the day sometime whilst my Mum and Dad were with us.

After cheese and biscuits, coffee, After eight's and some hilarious tales of old fashioned policing, we finally left around seven o'clock. We had had a really good day and Jane and Derek felt like old mates, as they were such easy company.

Monday 17th January 2005.

Brian took some time coming round and after several cups of tea and coffee in bed he finally emerged around eleven o'clock. Serves him right for drinking Norman's best brandy. Although there were bright blue skies I wasn't convinced that it would turn out such a warm day, so I took two loads of washing including the towels to be washed at the launderette.

On our way back from a walk along the beach I rang Mum, who had received my letter today and she said Dad's knee was much better since he'd been taking the miracle painkillers that the doctor prescribed. I asked if I should put his name down for the line dancing but I didn't get a reply!

I went shopping later and Brian had recovered enough to go fishing after lunch but moaned that he was hungry but we had run out of bread. What a shame. Back from the supermarket, I made bacon sandwiches, wrapped them in foil to keep them warm and walked down to the beach. Am I a gorgeous wife or what?

It was a stroke of luck that I had bought some fresh fish to barbecue for tea, as Brian's story of the one that got away was becoming quite repetitive!

Cricket was compulsive viewing for a change as England had a fantastic win.

Tuesday 18th January 2005.

A windy morning and I had to tidy up and spring clean ready for Marie coming whilst Brian went to the gym. When he came home, he had that furtive look on his face with a childish grin and something behind his back. Yes, another bloody fishing rod! This one, it turned out, was just too good a bargain to miss, and Helmut had sold it to him for just ten euros. This seemed a far cry from when we arrived in October and Brian had just one rod and now he had four! Of course this new one was longer than the one he brought with him and the extra length and the flexibility of this rod would almost guarantee more fish.

In reality, it was a small price for a hobby that kept him occupied every other day but then he suggested we could go to the Ferreteria now as he needed to buy a reel for this rod! That was another fifteen euros but it kept him happy.

The day seemed to fly by as usual and we set off to the airport just after six o'clock. The flight had landed half an hour early so Marie was waiting for us when we got there. It was lovely to see her and I had a stiff neck when we got home from turning round and talking to her.

We walked down to the site restaurant and whilst Brian and I had the menu of the day, she just had a spaghetti bolognese. Plenty of cups of tea and other beverages before we settled into bed around midnight. Jack and Jill were delighted that they could sleep on the made-up bed at the front of the caravan again.

Wednesday 19th January 2005.

As Marie was only here for three days, I really hoped she would get some nice weather and this morning did not disappoint. Blue skies with a few clouds that were clearing steadily so we drove to Los Belones after we all took the dogs along the beach. We went into the pound shop and I think Brian regretted showing me a solar garden light that looked like a gnome design, but on closer inspection was actually one of the seven dwarfs! He was pointing out what a hideous thing it was but realised too late that I actually loved it, and had to have it for my little garden!

Calling for a coffee Marie and I decided to have a hot chocolate instead, and it was like drinking a melted bar of dairy milk. I steered her to the tobacconists and explained that unlike in England, supermarkets do not sell cigarettes and if she wanted any duty frees she should buy then here, which she did.

We called at the bodega on the way home and replenished our stock of red wine and muscatel. The owner also convinced us we couldn't live without a three litre container of local Baileys Irish Cream for 12 euros, and a bottle of the local vodka.

Back home, the sun loungers were positioned and we were soon reclining, drink in hand, in the midday sun. It reached 72 degrees and Brian waited on us, as he prepared and cooked delicious paella. After tea, still clad in our swimwear, Marie and I were having a game of Scrabble when Jean-Pierre came past. He looked at us relaxing, laughing and drinking and said, "Julie, what a lovely body you have". Pardon? I laughed and said thank you but I did think it was rather forward for Jean-Pierre! Two minutes later when he was returning from the toilets, he approached us, red-faced. "I am very sorry Julie, I get my words mixed up in French. I meant to say you have a lovely 'life,' not 'body'!" All three of us were laughing at his mistake I must tell Corrie that her husband has his eye on me!

The rest of the evening flew by as Brian watched some football match and we were still talking nineteen to the dozen when we fell asleep at half past ten.

Thursday 20th January 2005.

A morning shopping was on the agenda, so we were showered and dressed and there for ten o'clock. Whilst we were emerging from the shower cubicles, the man that fills up the hand towels and toilet paper dispenser was just leaving the shower block and I think I nearly had his eye out! He normally shouts to let us know he's in there, but he appeared to have lost his voice today allegedly! I saw Corrie in the shower block and was recounting yesterday's incident. She said she thought Jean-Pierre had got it right the first time, as she explained in her best English, "He like the big tit that you have because I have none!"

I had a text from Dad on the way to say I had won £100 on the premium bonds, so when I saw a pair of brown leather boots, half price at only 48 euros, I couldn't resist. Marie bought a new handbag and purse and after a slice of pizza and a coffee each, we made our way home.

We were back for half past twelve as we didn't want to miss this gorgeous sunshine, and whilst we'd been away, Brian had prepared the curry for tonight's tea.

He set off for the beach with his new rod and said he would be back about half past four.

When he hadn't returned at five I wondered if he'd caught so many fish he was struggling to carry them home. He finally came home at twenty to six, and when we asked if he'd caught anything he told us to bugger off! Why was he in a bad mood with himself? He sat down and confessed he'd been walking round the site for ages, as he'd got lost!! I know it's a big site but we've lived here for nearly six months altogether and I thought he would know his way about by now. After a beer we had a good laugh about it, and we got showered and ready to go to bingo whilst Brian dished up his usual special curry.

Bingo was very busy and we had a laugh but didn't come back with any winnings. I was talking to Ted and he told me he was flying back to England in the next week or so to go for a check-up at the hospital. He was diagnosed with lung cancer some years ago and it was in remission. But he'd had the flu bug that had been going round the site at Christmas and he couldn't seem to shift it off his chest. So he was just going for his own peace of mind, or so he said.

Friday 21st January 2005.

Another scorching hot day for Marie to put the final touches to her tan. Corrie and Jean-Pierre came to say goodbye as they were going back to Holland for two weeks to see their daughter Valerie. Corrie said her friend Magda would be taking the Keep Fit in her absence.

As Marie fancied getting some boots or shoes whilst she was here, we all went down the strip in the car and in the second shoe shop she spotted a lovely pair of denim high heeled sandals at only 12 euros.

Back home we barbecued some sausages and had butties and coffee before setting our stall out again for more sun bathing. Brian wanted his hair cut again so I brought the extension lead out and gave him a number four in the sun.

A few drinks and more Scrabble and gossip before it was time to shower and get dressed ready to go to the Chinese. Before we set off, we had time to print off some photos for Marie to take home with her.

The meal was really nice again and although Marie doesn't normally drink gin and tonics I persuaded her that we should have at least one each. This led to another one each and Marie agreed she'd never seen drinks this big! We split the bill of 48 Euros between us and Brian took us home, as it was his turn to drive.

Saturday 22 January 2005.

Marie couldn't believe it was time to go home. We got her to the airport in plenty of time for her flight, which was leaving at 11.10 a.m. She thanked us for a great little holiday and for looking after her. She said she hadn't laughed so much for ages.

Back home we had bacon, sausage and egg before Brian went fishing and I prepared for another day lazing about. Derek came by on his bike with John and Barbara not far behind. He asked if I had seen Ann, as they were all going off on a bike ride, but somehow they had misplaced Ann! I told him I hadn't seen her and hoped she would turn up somewhere. She's as bad as Brian. At half past two I received a text from Marie to say her Dad had just picked her up from the airport and she thanked us again for having her.

As I read my book and took another sip of martini and lemonade, I saw Diego taking something to the side of the bins. I was up in a flash and delighted when I found it was a small mahogany table with two drawers, which he was throwing out. I found the perfect position for it and was soon bringing the TV/video into the awning and it looked as though it was meant to be there. So now Brian could watch his cricket videos in the awning whilst I watched BBC1 inside the caravan.

Brian came home with two big fish and praise for his new rod. I had made a tuna pasta dish and some garlic and tomato bread and for a treat an apple crumble for pudding.

One of our neighbours, Pete called round to warn us that some "polar" winds were due to reach us early next week so we could be in for a cold spell. It was hard to imagine cold weather after the fabulous week we'd just had.

Getting himself comfy in the awning with this newly discovered viewing position, Brian grabbed a beer and watched today's Test Match. I think I had worn myself out talking whilst Marie was here and I was in bed for nine o'clock.

Sunday 23rd January 2005.

Right on time "my visitor" arrived. I was thankful it didn't spoil my fun whilst Marie was here. The cloudy start didn't deter us from a Sunday morning walk along the beach to Mar Cristal. Pepes was still closed for the "Christmas" break so we sat at the café next door and had coffees and Spanish tortilla.

I walked up for a paper later and rang Mum, Janet and Pam. I tried to ring Gill as she had texted me to say she was off work with a bad back and neck but she wasn't at home. Maybe David had taken her to her Mum's for some pampering.

The afternoon was warm and I read the paper whilst Brian prepared tea. Today he was making a simple shepherd's pie, so he cooked the potatoes in the pressure cooker as usual. After the allotted time, he turned the pan off and was supposed to be releasing the pressure but was busy talking and not concentrating as usual. Bang. The valve blew out, the lid came off and there was hot potato everywhere, and I mean everywhere! It was all over the cooker, on the ceiling, on the carpet, all over the bathroom mirror and vanity unit, splattered across the grill of the extractor fan you name it, it was covered!

Almost an hour later my tongue was sore as I was still biting it, whilst I cleaned up the mess. But the shepherds pie was good and I was ready for something to eat after all that hard work.

When John came round with today's cricket tape, he said that play had been interrupted a few times with thunderstorms so he had filled the tape with a couple of episodes of "It Ain't Half Hot Mum." One of Brian's favourites, so we watched the cricket and then I tried to read my book whilst Brian was laughing his head off.

Monday 24th January 2005.

Busy day for birthdays today and I had a text from Jill, an email from Danny and an email from Norman all saying thanks for the card!

The washing seemed to have piled up so I took three loads to the laundrette to be washed. I picked them up at 11. 30 and hung them out, as it was warm and breezy. After some fruit for lunch it was hot again so I put my tankini on (don't try and picture this, you'll never eat your dinner!) and I lay back, hidden by the windbreak. Brian went shopping and walked the dogs when he got back as I still had tummy ache.

A bottle of our favourite cheap white wine was the perfect choice for a prawn stir-fry with Chinese rice.

Brian rang Ian and when he came back he said Ian had told him that Lorraine had been in hospital quite poorly with "sweets in her blood" or something. But she was now back home and everything was fine. I assumed he meant "sugar in her water" but I texted Simon to find out and ask if she was all right.

Whilst Brian watched cricket I decided to get the map books out and confirm our proposed journey home. I knew that once Mum and Dad arrived in a week's time I would have very little time for this sort of thing. I emailed two sites in France to advise them when we would be arriving, but the third one didn't have an email address. I think we will just risk that one as I'm sure they will have room at this time of year. Don't tell Brian otherwise he won't sleep for worrying!

I printed the route and the map and put stickers on the appropriate pages of the Caravan Club Europe book for easy reference. Get a life!

Tuesday 25th January 2005.

We both woke in the night, as it was very windy and raining. This didn't deter Brian from going to the gym, but it was just the excuse I was looking for so I didn't go to Keep Fit, even though I knew deep down that it would still be on.

Brian returned about two hours later and said Mabel had taken him into her office today. I couldn't wait to hear what was coming next! She had been quite upset at having to explain that the site owner, Maria, had now decided that everyone must pay to use the gym, as they do for the swimming pool. Brian told her not to worry, as he knew it wasn't her decision and he would buy a membership card before his next visit to the gym. But he was quite put out really and said if he was going to be paying for the facilities he hoped "Maria" would invest in another music tape other than bloody Demis Roussos that's on every day! He also thought that the sauna, which was currently like a shed with an electric fire in it, should be improved. I went to reception and got him a card, which entitled him to 30 sessions including swimming, for 65 euros. It was apparently valid forever so we could continue to use it in October.

I rang Christine and made an appointment for a trim at one o'clock tomorrow, and I rang Mum to see how excited she was about coming next week.

A pork and cider casserole was simmering when Wendy and her Mum Beryl called. We had invited them to join us at Mum's birthday bash but they were going to give it a miss. Wendy had attended the Keep Fit and said a lot of people had left half way through the session as Magda was doing completely different exercises to Corrie. I was glad I was such a lazy cow this morning.

After tea it was cricket again (!) so I played Scrabble on my own. Come back Marie or Julia. Whilst watching cricket, Brian was again scouring the Internet searching for a holiday for us in June to replace the cricket tour.

Wednesday 26th January 2005.

We had left the heating on all night as it was turning really cold. It was windy and cold again so we stayed in bed with cups of tea, which I had to keep making, and watched breakfast television. How lazy and retired is that?

By eleven o'clock Brian said he felt guilty being in bed so he got up, got dressed and took Jack and Jill along the beach. I didn't feel a bit guilty and was still in my pyjamas when he came back.

I had an email from Janet which was actually from Connor. He told me what he was up to at school, and how he was looking forward to coming to La Manga and sleeping in our caravan, to help me look after Jack and Jill and the two cats!

Christine made a lovely job of my hair again and I said I would

217

need her in February before we went home. From one o'clock until eight o'clock Brian was engrossed by the Internet and was scribbling lots of notes with different Greek islands and prices. I made kidneys in sherry and cream and boiled rice, which Brian managed to eat in ten minutes flat so he could go back to his holiday search.

The gas ran out at half past ten. It's sod's law that it will run out when it's dark and cold or raining, or all three. After a couple of hours of telly we were snuggled in bed for midnight.

Thursday 27th January 2005.

When we woke up it felt very cold, and the wind had dropped completely. As I climbed over Brian to get out of bed and make the tea, he said, "It's so quiet, it feels as though it's snowed!" I was waiting for the punch line as when we were growing up my Dad regularly came into mine and Janet's bedroom and announced it was snowing. We would jump out of bed and rush to the window, and he would then say… "In Greenland".

I switched the kettle on and opened the blind as usual, but as I looked out of the awning my mouth gaped open for at least a minute. Gobsmacked! It was white over with at least an inch of snow and big flakes were still falling. I was like a kid on Christmas Day and opened all the blinds to show Brian that, for once, he was right!

Neither of us ever expected to see snow in Spain, and we went outside in our dressing gowns with the camera. I've never seen the site so busy, so early. Everyone was outside taking photographs of this extraordinary scene and even Jack and Jill looked quite taken aback.

I texted my Dad and told him to pack Mum's thermals, and I emailed one of the photos to several people as I knew they wouldn't believe me otherwise.

Brian still went along to the gym, taking his membership card to show to Mabel. I walked the dogs up to the gym later to meet him and I enjoyed chatting to everyone who was still outside, taking in this wintry scene. Apparently it had been over fifty years since there had been any snow at La Manga, and someone was quoting 1933 as the last known year to see snow, but I don't know how accurate that was.

A walk along the beach was very cold but enjoyable, as there were no other dogs out walking! We must be mad.

As the snow slowly melted we ate hunter's chicken for tea, another recipe from Pam's book.

Bingo had soon come round and Angie's neighbour Troodle was with us again, as were Jill and Barbara. I must have drawn the short straw and ended up sitting next to Troodle having to check all her numbers, as well as my own. By the third game we were getting a bit complacent until I realised that Troodle only needed one number for a line and it came up so I had to shout for her, as she didn't have a clue what was going on! She won 65 euros and was still looking a bit confused. The next game was slow starting, but I soon realised that she was only one number off the full house and there it was. House! ! ! Another 150 euros and of course, everyone thought it was me that kept winning. We explained to Troodle that the English tradition is to buy a round of drinks, so it was five gin and tonics please.

We had a good laugh, but of course Troodle then announced that she would now come every week without fail and her husband might want to come too! I think I will go to bridge with Mum next Thursday just to watch!

Arriving home about eleven, Brian was dying to show me the holiday of his dreams to Paxos, in a private cottage right on the beach, and it looked gorgeous. We agreed we would have a good look at it in the morning and book it over the Internet.

Friday 28th January 2005.

Cold but sunny, and no sign of any snow today. We logged onto the Internet about ten o'clock and I noticed I'd got four emails. The first one was from Gill and David. Guess what? The cricket tour was back on, 19th June, going to Pershore, and they had reserved us a double room. After an hour's discussion, we agreed that trying to do both holidays would be too expensive and the only reason we were going to go to Paxos was to replace the tour, so we were just being greedy trying to do both. Poor Brian, days of searching for this holiday and now we're not going. Never mind.

I had replies from Danny and Noreen and Gill from my old work – they thought it was highly amusing that we were having snow.

Wrapped up in my fleece and wearing Brian's gloves, I walked

219

to the top of the site and took Gwen Mum's balance for the caravan. She usually goes to bingo but hadn't gone last night as it was too cold. She would bring me the keys on Monday, which meant I would have a day to make it homely and get the heating on.

I thought I had better ring Mum and let her know the snow had gone, which she was quite relieved about. She was glad I'd rung, as she wanted to ask if she could buy All Bran in Spain or should she bring some with her? I told her I had seen it on sale in the supermarket and I would buy some for when she gets here. What's she like?

We ate a very hot chilli, which Brian denied spicing up, but even Jill was drinking water every half an hour during the evening so I know he'd put loads of extra chilli in it. He said we needed something hot in this weather. Not a bad night on BBC1 and we had a few glasses of wine before getting into bed at eleven.

Saturday 29th January 2005.

My nephew Joshua would be two today and I'd left his present with Chris, as he would be going to Peterborough to see him.

Blue skies were back–hooray! It was still cool but it was definitely warmer and Brian was telling everyone that this was because the wind had changed direction. How long has he been a weather presenter? Whilst he went to the gym, I went to the big Upper and Brian requested pork spare ribs for tea. The ones we had the other week were very tasty and a cheap meal.

At the Upper, I went to the butcher's counter as most of the meat is served to order. Very few meat products are pre-packed. I pointed to a rack of ribs, which consisted of about ten or twelve and the butcher asked if I wanted them chopping into individual ribs, which I did. He then weighed them and wrapped them, placed them in a carrier and stapled the receipt to the bag. As I continued shopping, I looked to see how much they were. Twenty-two euros. Pardon? It dawned on me that they must be lamb, which is outrageously expensive over here, though it's not cheap back in England. A quick calculation of 22 times 7 worked out at about £16 for a few ribs! How could I have been so stupid and what would Brian say? I was wondering how I could explain them away, when it suddenly dawned on me. I didn't have to buy them if I didn't want to, so I discreetly placed the carrier bag in the next fridge I passed! I know I should have taken them back, explained my mistake and got the proper pork ribs but I was too embarrassed. Sorry. I hurriedly picked up a pack of chicken thighs and a few other bits and got through the checkout as soon as I could.

Within the same building, I noticed a new beauty salon had opened, and I picked up an "English" leaflet. It read:

Dear Lady and Dear Sir,

We are sure that you were pleased with our services like or has before happened with other compatriots yours and that now or they are clients and friends. I ask for pardon by not knowing how to speak its language but with good will and a good service we have gotten to surpass that disadvantage.

Who was I to find amusement in this sincere attempt at English, after my pathetic effort to buy a few ribs?

Back home, there was washing to be done and whilst I got on with that, Brian helped Martin next door to cut back a few of the trees that separated our pitches, so that they could get some more light. It would mean less protection from the wind for us, but we had our windbreaks so it didn't matter.

I gently broke the news to Brian about the ribs. I did consider lying and saying they didn't have any, but he can always tell when I'm not telling the truth. To try and make up for his disappointment I made chicken kdra with chickpeas and almonds, fresh broad beans and jacket potatoes. It was lovely, but it wasn't spare ribs!

Diego called round and showed us a key on a key fob. He explained in gestures that his six-berth boat was now in the harbour at Mar Cristal and he indicated that he would take Brian fishing in it. I wondered if this trip would happen before we went home?

Brian watched Manchester United beat Middlesborough 3-0 and then we settled down to watch a film on BBC1. "The Rock", staring Sean Connery had been on for an hour when I realised that I had seen it before. What a relief. I went to bed, as I was tired, even though I couldn't remember how it ended. Who cares? Goodnight.

Sunday 30th January 2005

What's happened to the weather? The rain woke us at three a.m. so we had a cup of tea and fell back asleep. It continued to rain until about eleven so our usual Sunday walk was cancelled. The fields would be like a bog.

I watched two films that John had taped for us from Sky. One was about Jackie Onnassis and the other was about Benji the dog. Brian was feeling a bit homesick. I'm sure he has that S. A. D. syndrome. He's always fed up when the sun goes in.

I threw together a sausage and belly pork casserole which was very filling and the dogs and cats enjoyed the left overs.

Brian rang Simon who apologised for not replying to my text messages or emails. He is just so busy! Lorraine had spent a couple of days in hospital with some sort of virus but she was now back at work and baby was fine. Brian was a bit dismayed when he informed me that Simon had mentioned that it was Lorraine's birthday tomorrow. I explained it was all in hand I had posted a card to her and had asked Mum to order some flowers to be delivered to school tomorrow.

We rang David and Gill, as Gill was due to go to a police convalescent home on Monday as she had been off work with a bad back and neck. David's daughter Sarah told us they had both gone today as it was in Scotland so I told her I would text Gill next week to make sure she was OK.

On the 'telly was "Superstars" which was filmed at La Manga. I texted Dad and asked him to ring Janet to tell the lads to watch "Superstars" and see what La Manga was like.

John had taped the first of the one-day cricket matches so Brian had a couple of brandy and Baileys whilst watching the cricket.

Monday 31st January 2005.

The first thing I noticed this morning was that the German chap who had been here since before we arrived had gone. He had become part of the landscape and it seemed strange to have an empty pitch almost opposite. The other strange sight was the ice on the car windscreen – was this really Spain? It was obviously very cold but as the morning progressed the sun came out and it became warmer.

At ten o'clock John and Barbara came round as arranged and we drove to Los Nietos to buy some cheap potatoes! Yes, John bought a huge sack because they were cheaper than any others he had seen. God knows how long it will take the two of them to eat half a hundredweight.

We called at Los Belones and bought some red wine and a bottle of Limoncello from the bodega. Then on to the village of La Union, where we discovered some fantastic cheap shops. Barbara and I both bought a stretch denim skirt for eight euros- about six pounds! The shoe shop was like a jumble sale and all the shoes and boots were either three or five euros- if you could find a matching pair!

Back home for half past one, we unpacked the shopping and had some lunch then took Jack and Jill for a really long walk on the beach. It was cool by the sea but there wasn't a cloud in the bright blue sky.

Gwen's husband Ken came round with the keys to Mum's caravan and he showed us how all the appliances and the heating worked. We switched the heating on so that it would be nice and warm when Mum arrived tomorrow.

Brian made a spaghetti bolognese whilst I rang Mum to tell her we were warming the caravan up for her. She was looking forward to coming and I said we would see them at the airport about seven o'clock tomorrow night.

We settled down to another episode of "EastEnders" and a few glasses of Limoncello. Three glasses later I could see two Pauline Fowlers! Bedtime.

I had just climbed into bed when I received a text. It was from Jill to say that Colin was in intensive care after suffering a heart attack. I put my fleece jacket over my pyjamas and dressing gown, grabbed the torch and phone card and went to ring her. The fact that I didn't have any teeth in didn't strike me until I was half way there, but who cares. Their daughter Emma answered the phone and Jill explained that Colin had not been well in recent weeks but had a heart attack on Saturday night and he was in Leeds General Infirmary. They were going to operate tomorrow but didn't know what they would be doing until they opened him up. Trying to squeeze a cuddle for a mate down the phone is difficult but I tried. I promised to keep in touch and asked her to tell Colin we were both thinking about him. Poor Jill and Emma, what a worrying time for them.

Tuesday 1st February 2005.

Another icy morning gave me the perfect excuse not to go to Keep Fit, and I was also going to be busy cleaning up ready for Mum coming. With Brian at the gym out of the way, I had soon done a load of washing in Mum's machine, and managed to clean through the caravan and awning like a whirlwind. I went to our supermarket to get Mum a "welcome pack" which included absolute essentials like some marzipan sweets, crisps, cashew nuts, chocolate bread and a bottle of bubbly! I know I should be encouraging Mum to cut down but she'll be on her holidays, and I haven't seen her since September.

Brian went fishing in the afternoon, and as he arrived back home (yes empty-handed), Wim called round. He told us that if we wanted to hire a pallet to store our heavy things here during the summer, we should go to reception as soon as possible. This was a facility that Wim and Bill had suggested to Maria the owner a couple of years ago, and it would certainly be a great help to us, as we had accumulated so much useful furniture that we couldn't carry back to England. I went to reception and paid to secure a pallet, which was ten euros a month.

Mum and Dad landed half an hour early but we were there as they came through the arrival door with their luggage. It was lovely to see them both and we soon had Mum warmed up in the car. Dad sent a text to Chris saying they had arrived OK. Their caravan was lovely and warm, as we'd left the heating on all day, and as I helped them to unpack and settle in, Brian helped himself to Mum's cashew nuts and sat on a seat in their kitchen and broke it! I can't take him anywhere although Dad said it had been broken previously and he would mend it.

Fortunately Mum and Dad are used to Brian breaking things as he once stayed at their house for five days whilst they were in Benidorm and I was at Janet's. During his stay, the kitchen light broke, the central heating stopped working, he pulled the shower switch so hard it's now permanently turned on, he ran over a plastic croaking frog that Dad had in the garden and then he sat on Mum's rocking chair and fell through the bottom of it! He's like a very butch Frank Spencer.

Our meal down at the restaurant was very good, and the waiter Pepe asked me if my daughter had gone back to England. I thought he was confusing me with someone else until he pointed to the table we had sat at two weeks ago with Marie! I know she's only 35, but surely I don't look old enough to be her mother, even if Brian is actually older than her Dad. How rude!

We were all tired so we all went home and I felt sure Mum was much happier than last year as I knew that she wouldn't be cold. She might even sleep in just her nightie – that would be a treat for Dad.

Wednesday 2nd February 2005.

I replied to an email from Janet telling her that Mum and Dad had arrived safely. She said she'd had her hair cut short and didn't know if she liked it. Connor had told her it made her look like me, and the naughtiest girl in Janet's school had asked her if she'd cut it herself! Can't wait to see it on Sunday.

Round at Mum's, they thought they had a gas leak but it turned out that the grill had been on but not lit! What is it about old people and gas? No, that's not what I meant!

After showers I did Mum's hair and we went to the Mercadona for some shopping. On our return, we were surprised that the pitch that had been vacated on Monday was now retaken. I took Mum round to Emmy's and she bought a few birthday cards. She wrote one to her friend Jackie and we walked to reception to post it. On the way, we called to see Ann and Derek, and Mum gave him some bridge books. We arranged that they would come round on Saturday afternoon so Mum and Derek could discuss whether they would be a winning couple to go to bridge.

We also took the broken seat top to Gwen's and her husband Ken made a replacement within minutes. Dad was sitting in the sun doing his puzzle book, which had always been called "Tsunami". In light of the recent disaster, the books had been renamed "Hanjie".

Brian made a delicious dish of poached salmon fillets with sliced lemon potatoes and vegetables, followed by a fresh fruit salad. Dad and I washed up and we all played cards until half past ten. The fresh air and sunshine seems to have made us all sleepy. I think we're all in for a good night's sleep?

Thursday 3rd February 2005.

It was ten o'clock before Mum and Dad woke up! Although Dad was finding the bed much shorter than his king size at home, Mum said she'd slept like a top.

It was again warmer weather and whilst Mum and I were getting dressed in the shower block, we said good morning to a lady who was dressed as a clown! Mum thought it was her failing eyesight playing tricks on her, but someone later told us it was German "Crazy Lady Day", and all the women get dressed up and have a day doing just what they want! Sounds like a good idea to me.

By the time we were ready to go shopping at twelve, Brian had been to the gym for two hours and come home again. Barbara called to say she had a sore throat so wouldn't be going to bingo, but Angie, Jill and Troodle were the advance party and would save Mum and me two seats.

Dos Mares shopping centre was very quiet again, but we enjoyed looking round all the shops and Mum and I managed to get some lovely presents for Janet's birthday on February 23rd. She could take them home with her as we would both still be in Spain. Dad bought himself some shoes and was pleasantly surprised at the low prices. He was even more surprised that most of the shop assistants didn't speak English. He was used to Benidorm where English was a first language.

Another nice meal was on the go when we arrived home. Chicken and mushrooms in a white wine sauce. Dad and I washed up again but he was quite upset when he broke two of my new dinner plates. I think he's trying to get out of drying up next time! Brian rang Harry who reported a dry sunny day in Congleton.

Mum and I went to bingo, and although Mum couldn't see the numbers very well, she enjoyed the company and we had a laugh. I won the last full house and shared with another lady. My winnings of 95 euros was split with Mum so we felt we'd had a very successful evening.

When we got back to Mum's caravan, Dad was watching Italian football and said he'd left Brian watching the one-day cricket that John had taped for him.

Friday 4th February 2005.

Broken cloud prevented it from being a sunny day, but we were sat outside, when Norman, Lynn and her Mum Maureen arrived at one o'clock. A large bag of oranges and lemons and some almonds was gratefully accepted. They were amazed at the size of the campsite and we went for a little walk around to show them some of the facilities.

After a few drinks and nibbles, we made our way down to the restaurant and enjoyed the menu of the day followed by coffees out on the terrace, watching the calm waters of the Mar Menor.

More drinks back at our pitch and then we walked up to reception where they had left their car. We really enjoyed their company and it was nice for Mum and Dad to have somebody different to talk to.

After Brian rang Ian, we reported round to Mum and Dad's and played cards until almost midnight. We had taken Jack and Jill with us, and the cats had followed us and were still sitting on Mum's step when we left!

Saturday 5th February 2005.

What a miserable day. It rained on and off all day long, so whilst Brian went to the gym I took Mum and Dad to the Mercadona to get some provisions for Janet's gang arriving.

At two o'clock, Derek and Ann arrived as arranged but it was too wet to sit out so we went round to Mum and Dad's warm caravan. Brian stayed at home lazing about and watching sport on the telly. Derek and Mum sat talking about and playing a few hands of bridge, whilst Ann, Dad and I played a card game called "Phase 10".

We ate so many nibbles at Mum's that when Ann and Derek had left, none of us were hungry. I returned home to find Brian starving so I threw together a quick prawn stir-fry and he ate it whilst watching Wales beat England at rugby.

Sunday 6th February 2005.

I was disappointed to see a cloudy day when I woke up, and

Brian set off to Alicante at 9.45 to pick Janet up.

Jake sent me a text to say Brian had met them OK, but they had got lost in the car park trying to find the parking pay machine. However, they were now on their way and should be with us in an hour.

An hour and a half later I texted Jake for an update. He replied that they were lost and thought they were near Madrid next to some orange groves! This turned out to be a complete exaggeration but they had been around Murcia by mistake but would be with us soon. Finally, at half past one I was relieved to see them all in one piece. Apparently they had been taken for a very interesting mystery tour courtesy of Brian, but the sun was trying to get out and they were all excited about being here. It was great to see everyone and we got them all settled into Mum's caravan and then had some lunch.

We all went for a walk around the site in the afternoon and then went to the restaurant for the Sunday special La Manga lamb, which was very nice. A couple of nightcaps and then it was off to bed for everyone.

Monday 7ᵗʰ February 2005.

Round at Mum's, I asked how they had all slept. Mum had slept "like a top" and Jimmy said he'd slept "like a spinning top"! The mattresses on the two single beds were wafer thin and the double bed in the lounge was very narrow so the lads didn't get much sleep either. Connor decided he would be sleeping in our caravan tonight with Jack and Jill.

After breakfast, we walked up to the supermarket. It was cloudy and windy but we glimpsed the odd bit of blue sky. Dad and Jake played table tennis and Jimmy bought some sessions for the gym and swimming pool.

I took Mum and Dad, Janet and Connor to Los Belones but we were very disappointed to find the pound shop closed for a week's holiday. Dad treated us to a hot chocolate and we distracted Mum whilst he went to buy her some chocolates for her birthday.

Although it was a bit chilly, we sat out in the afternoon and Brian made paella for all eight of us, which was gorgeous. We had it with salad and crispy bread rolls and a jug of sangria.

The lads took the dogs along the beach and it was soon time to get ready as we were all going to the quiz.

We set off at seven and as we approached the road to walk up to the pool bar, we noticed a small crowd and then we saw the water. The road was flooded and there was a torrent of water, which had risen above the kerb and was now starting to flow onto the pitches that were at the side of the road. An unprecedented storm had hit Murcia earlier in the day and rumour had it that the rain from that storm had made the reservoir here burst, and this was the resulting chaos. The quiz was not going ahead as it was impossible to cross the road, so we all went back to Mum's and played cards.

Connor came home with us and was soon snuggled into bed with Jack and Jill – what a treat!

Tuesday 8th February 2005.

My plan was that Janet and Mum would accompany me to Keep Fit, but the road was a mass of mud and still impossible to get across without wellies on, so they got out of that nicely.

A very cloudy day so Jimmy, Brian and the lads went to the gym for the morning and the rest of us went for a drive along the strip, calling at a couple of shoe shops on the way, and fetching some water from the mountains on the way back. Mum bought a couple of newspapers for Brian and Jimmy and the headlines were congratulating Ellen McArthur on her solo round the world sailing record.

A few games of table tennis and half an hour on the Internet kept the lads amused in the afternoon and Dad was very grateful when John and Barbara called round as John managed to tune in BBC1 on their television.

The site was being cleaned up as quickly as it could be, but the roads were still thick with mud. It would have helped if the sun had been around to dry things up, but the weather was showing no signs of improving.

At least we had Mum's "party" to look forward to. We got taxis to the Chinese and we thoroughly enjoyed the set banquet and the atmosphere for Chinese New Year. It was a different entertainer this year, who was a bit of an Elvis impersonator. The Chinese seem to like that sort of thing. But even the lads got up for a dance with me and Janet and they enjoyed the fireworks at midnight. Mum was presented with a birthday cake and was given a very nice card and seemed to enjoy herself.

Arriving back on site at half past midnight meant we had to walk back to our respective caravans from reception, but we were soon home and in bed. Checking my mobile I was pleased to hear from Jill that Colin was home and doing well. Mum also had a message from two of her sisters wishing her a happy birthday.

Wednesday 9th February 2005.

Happy 70th birthday Mum. After the heavy rain and hailstones during the night, I knew I would need to put more than my slippers on to go round to Mum's.

We had bucks fizz whilst Mum opened her presents and cards, and Chris sent a text message saying happy birthday. But what an awful day it was weather-wise. It rained all day long and the site near the roads was like a bog. I felt sorry for the people with pitches at the side of the roads as their groundsheets and awnings were covered in mud and sludge.

Jimmy took the lads to the gym and for a swim, and I took Mum and Janet to a hobby exhibition above the restaurant. We managed to get there without getting too muddy and we each bought a few homemade cards. There were quite a few stalls selling a range of things like marmalade, sketches, paintings, jewellery, embroidery, and we saw further examples of the fascinating craft of crocheting strips of plastic carrier bags together to make plant pot holders! Of course Mum had to buy one of these for her Auntie Joyce.

Meanwhile, back at the ranch, Brian prepared a chicken curry and some Moroccan potatoes for tea. I made some nan breads and we all enjoyed a creamy but spicy meal. A bread and butter pudding, which I had concocted, was soon wolfed down together with ice cream and cream.

The "men" watched football and then we played cards and Scrabble. It had been decided that it was Jake's turn to sleep with Jack and Jill so that's what happened at eleven o'clock, and I prayed for some better weather!

Thursday 10th February 2005.

At last the sun was here. Janet and I drove to Los Nietos to buy some strawberries and get some general shopping and when we got back, Brian took Jimmy, Jake and Connor fishing to Cala Reone.

Mum and Janet made themselves comfortable in the warm sunshine and I brought them both a cocktail – they asked what was in them but I told them I couldn't reveal my secret recipes. In truth, I was using up all the odd bits of spirit and liqueurs to get rid of them, but they needn't know that.

I insisted that they had a relaxing day and I busied myself preparing tonight's meal. So whilst I waited on them, I made a chilli con carne, a lasagne, some garlic bread and some cheese bread and a great big dish of chunky potato and sweet potato chips. Dad kept popping round with his puzzle book but was quite happy to sit at home in the sun.

It was five o'clock before the intrepid fishermen returned with their catch of the day, four for Brian and one for Jake. At least they'd caught something.

They were all ready for this tasty tea which was soon eaten, but we all had room for some fresh fruit salad afterwards.

Derek arrived to collect Mum for bridge and off they went. Janet and I got ready to go to bingo and the lads thought they might watch some films that John had kindly taped for them.

Another fun night at bingo, with Troodle winning again. Janet had never played bingo before but had to admit to getting quite excited when she only wanted two numbers for a full house. All right, maybe not "excited" exactly but a bit giddy!

Back home, Dad was waiting for Mum and Jake and Connor had decided they would both sleep in our caravan with the dogs. Connor asked if the cats could sleep inside too, but I told him they would be quite happy in the awning. Mum was home at eleven and spent twenty minutes telling us what a good night they'd had and how she was looking forward to going again on Tuesday. She had enjoyed seeing everyone from last year and lots of them came to talk to her, including Corrie's husband Jean-Pierre. He told Mum he thought she was "very beautiful". I think he was meaning she was "good for her age" but we'll let her dream on!

Brian had rung his Dad and it seemed the weather in Congleton had been pretty much the same as we had experienced earlier in the week cold and wet. Pam had broken a bone in her arm but wasn't off work as they were short staffed! Simon was looking forward to coming on Sunday and Brian was pleased that they were coming to Murcia airport and not Alicante!

Friday 11th February 2005.

Clear blue skies and the prospect of another hot day. Dad was treating us all to tonight's meal down at the restaurant so we planned a lazy day.

Jake and Connor were finding it hard to get out of bed as they were in fits of hysterics at Brian's jokes. He then told them a saying of his which goes "No bloody wonder, you fart like thunder eating Parker's bread!" Well, this had them crying with laughter and the more I reprimanded Brian for telling them rude sayings, the funnier they found it. Janet would have to sit them down when they got home and try and erase all Brian's quips from their minds. Good luck with that, Jan!

The lads and Jimmy went to the gym again and then they joined Brian down on the beach to do some fishing. Mum decided she would like to stand in the sun and do some ironing – we must get her some treatment! Janet and I walked along the beach with Jack and Jill to Pepe's. We ordered two large coffees and Janet asked if we could have a Tia Maria in them. The waiter brought the coffees and placed the bottle of Tia Maria on the table for us to help ourselves. He also brought us a taste of an apple flan.

The bill of 2.40 euros seemed very cheap, and we enjoyed sitting in the sun watching the world go by.

Afternoon activities included playing boules with Dad and Connor, who had soon become bored with the fishing. Brian only caught one, which was so small he threw it back.

We had a late shower and I did Janet's hair for her and then did her nails. What a treat. Connor was persuaded to let me cut his hair as Janet said he would not go to the barber's at home. So we were all spruced up when we went down to the restaurant for our meal. Friday night is "fish and chip" night so Jimmy, Brian and Connor had fish, chips and mushy peas and the rest of us ordered different things. The lads finished off with a Knickerbocker glory each and Dad was pleased with the bill of 93 euros. Very good value.

Back in our awning we sat having a few drinks and talking and Jake decided he would sleep in our caravan again. Let's hope for a sunny day tomorrow for their last day.

Saturday 12ᵗʰ February 2005.

The wind threatened to spoil an otherwise perfect day. Brian and Jimmy went to the gym and I took Janet and Connor to the Mercadona for some shopping. On the way back I decided to book a table for six for the St Valentine's Dinner Dance on Monday evening at the site restaurant. Simon and Lorraine and Mum and Dad would enjoy the meal and a night out with us.

The wind dropped and Brian took Jake fishing whilst the rest of us walked down the beach to Pepes at Mar Cristal. Janet and Jimmy wanted to treat us all to a final meal and Mum wanted to try tapas, as she'd never had it. We had a lovely meal in the sunshine and finished off with waffles covered in cream and chocolate. No idea when I would be brave enough to get weighed again! We finished off the jug of sangria whilst Jimmy settled the bill of 62 euros.

Brian was ready for the drive to Alicante and familiarised himself with the route before setting off at six. We waved them off and Mum and Dad came to our caravan and anxiously waited for Brian whilst I made a spaghetti bolognese. At eight thirty we were delighted to see Brian parking the car with a smile on his face – no problem this time.

We enjoyed supper and all agreed that Janet, Jimmy and the boys had enjoyed their holiday. Just time to catch my breath before Simon and Lorraine landed tomorrow morning.

Sunday 13ᵗʰ February 2005.

A loud bleep woke me up at seven o'clock. A text from Simon to say they were boarding at Leeds Bradford airport, and I'd also had a text from Jimmy around midnight to say they had arrived home safely and it was freezing in Manchester.

When Brian arrived back from Murcia airport at half past eleven it was 84 degrees! The hottest day we'd had for weeks and Simon and Lorraine were soon relaxing in the sun with a drink. They were both tired and Lorraine needed a sleep in the afternoon, whilst Simon said he needed a drink with his Dad down at the beach bar, so off they went.

I busied myself making a curry, spicy potatoes and some

homemade nan breads. By six o'clock Mum and Dad had come round and we all sat down to enjoy my chicken and cashew curry and a jug of sangria. By nine o'clock we were all tired and a little worse for a few drinks so we all got our pyjamas on and had an early night.

Monday 14th February 2005.

Happy Valentine's Day. Simon and Lorraine had brought cards to give each other and Simon had received one from some pupils at school. Lorraine couldn't believe he'd actually brought it to Spain but Simon's lame excuse was it just happened to be in the pocket of the coat he'd travelled in. All three cards were soon on display in the awning. How romantic!

Despite the winds during the night, the sun was out and a lovely calm day awaited us.

After a leisurely breakfast and shower, we went to the Mercadona and brought back lots of food. Brian decided he would barbecue sardines and mackerel and I prepared a salad to have with them.

Later in the day Lorraine and Simon walked up to the gym and had a swim, and then they had a walk on the beach.

I had an email from Janet thanking us for a wonderful holiday. She said Connor's favourite bit was doing the washing up and Jake's was fishing with Brian. They both still couldn't stop laughing at Uncle Brian's jokes and she thanked me again for his unwelcome influence!

Tonight's meal would be mine and Brian's treat, and all six of us scrubbed up well. We were greeted with a champagne cocktail on arrival and were seated in the restaurant, which had been made to look very romantic. Prawn cocktail was followed by mushroom soup, then La Manga lamb with potatoes and vegetables, and to finish a heart shaped sorbet with ice cream and chocolate. Coffee was also included in the price of 15 euros each, and Dad insisted on paying for the wine and drinks we'd had. The music started around ten o'clock but we were too full to dance and eventually sauntered home around eleven. An excellent meal and good company!

Tuesday 15th February 2005.

Although it was sunny again, it was quite breezy but after making all the excuses under the sun, I felt Mum and I should make the effort and go to Keep Fit today. So we did. Brian and Lorraine walked up to the gym as Lorraine was fancying another swim. Dad and Simon took the dogs for a walk along the beach and tried not to laugh when they came past the Keep Fit class. Mum did really well and managed most of the exercises.

We took Simon and Lorraine into Los Belones to see the Bodega and the market and after showing them round a few shops we went for a coffee and a cake.

Back home, we were soon relaxing in the sun and Brian prepared his paella. Mum and Dad joined us for tea and then I did Mum's hair, ready for her to go to bridge. Her partner Derek was running late and they didn't get there until five to seven, by which time all the tables had been taken so they couldn't play. They were very disappointed when they came back home so Brian and I went round to Mum and Dad's to play cards with them. We also thought Lorraine and Simon might appreciate an evening on their own looking at their Valentine's cards!

Wednesday 16th February 2005.

The day started off quite cool so we drove up to La Manga golf resort to see how the other half live. After driving through the security gate, we took in the sights of luxury villas with their own pools and room for a pony. The resort was much bigger than I had imagined and was like a town with lots of restaurants and bars. We stopped at the Last Drop Inn for lunch. The sun had come out so we sat outside and ordered steak baguettes with salad and Brian had steak pie chips and vegetables, even though he'd said his stomach was a bit "off"! With coffees and drinks the bill was 33 euros, which was good.

On the way back, we drove to Calblanque beach to give the dogs a run. As soon as Jill was out of the car, she raced towards the sea and was swimming along the shore before we had reached the beach. They were soon tired out running in the sand and fetching sticks from the sea so we dried them off and headed home.

Brian was not feeling well so he went to bed, but the rest of us caught the days last few rays of sun. We had planned to go to Los Belones for an Indian meal but with Brian in bed, we decided to go down to the site restaurant with Mum and Dad. We all had menu of the day except Simon who had calamares to start, then a fish platter which was enormous. He ate everything that was put in front of him. He is his father's son! The total bill for the five of us with drinks was 70 euros and Simon paid before we had a chance to argue. Brian would be furious he'd missed out on a free meal.

Thursday 17th February 2005.

Brian was feeling a bit better but still not fully recovered so when Simon and Lorraine said they would like to spend the morning at the gym and swimming, I decided to take Mum, Dad and Barbara to La Union for a look round the shops. Mum bought some casual shoes for eight euros, and a nice jumper for Janet. She also bought a "Baby's First Cutlery Set" for Simon and Lorraine, ready for the baby, which was due in July.

Dad bought us coffee and cakes, and we were given four free cakes, which tasted like trifle sponges! As I drove to our pitch, I noticed that Joop and Meip were taking their windbreaks down. This seemed very premature, as they weren't due to leave until the end of March.

Another afternoon soaking up the sun, though Simon had come out in a heat rash so spent most of the day in the caravan reading. Brian was feeling much better and insisted that the four of us got a taxi to Los Belones tonight for a few drinks at the English bar and an Indian meal.

The meal was very nice though the portions were small and the bill of 102 euros seemed quite steep. But we had enjoyed the evening and couldn't believe it was their last evening with us.

We had a text message from Neville and Margaret to say that they were looking forward to seeing us in March and catching up, and as Nev was off work due to ill health, he could go for a drink any time! Brian was looking forward to a few hand-pulled beers in an English pub with his mate.

236

Friday 18ᵗʰ February 2005.

Simon and Lorraine woke to their final day of sunshine and had both had another brilliant night's sleep. I think they were both so tired when they arrived that they just enjoyed relaxing and not doing too much, and we had tried to give them both a nice rest. They both looked much better then when they had arrived and had really enjoyed themselves or so they said!

We took them to the bodega, as they wanted some drinks to take home. They insisted on buying us a present each so I chose some muscatel in a fancy jug, which I could keep for future use, and Brian chose a bloody expensive bottle of brandy. Sometimes I could kill him!

At the Ferreteria Simon asked if we could carry a paella pan for twelve people home for him! Brian argued that he would probably never invite twelve people round but we agreed it was no problem for us to take it in the caravan.

Today's meal was served mid-afternoon and Brian made steamed fish and a prawn stir-fry with Chinese rice. I made a chocolate sponge for a sweet as my Dad didn't seem to have had a nice pudding for ages. Just after five Brian took Simon and Lorraine to the airport and I washed up ready for an early night. Whilst washing up I saw Meip and asked her why they had taken the windbreak down. She told me that her son-in-law, who was 40, had just found out he had cancer of the lymph glands and they were going home on Sunday to be with the family. I was so sorry for her and gave her a cuddle. She was very tearful and said she just needed to be with her daughter and her four-year-old grandson. Life can be so cruel.

When Brian returned I told him the sad news and we sat down and had a few drinks and talked about how lucky we are to be in good health.

Tonight's "EastEnders" was not to be missed. Den was being killed off so we got ready to watch the one-hour special at nine o'clock. Very exciting, until twenty to ten when the television reception failed right at the crucial moment! How annoying is that? We must catch up with the Omnibus on Sunday.

Saturday 19th February 2005.

My "visitor" arrived as I was reading a text from Simon. They were home safe and it was very cold in England. He said they had both had a great holiday and felt much better and were ready to face another term at school.

A warm day and whilst Brian went to the gym I took Mum and Dad to the Mercadona as they needed some shopping ready for Chris arriving tomorrow morning. Is there no peace? We called at the Pharmacia on the way back as Mum had brought with her some medicine, which was a form of laxative, but was very expensive in England. I showed the chemist the box and he explained that he could give us something with the same ingredients but not in a "medicine" form. The Spanish equivalent was only three euros and he told Mum to take ten drops each evening.

On my return, I explained to Brian what the chemist had given Mum and that she had to have ten drops each night. Mum nearly went into hysterics when I told her that Brian had asked if she had to bend over for my Dad to insert the drops!! He didn't realise they were to be taken orally. God help me if I'm ever ill and Brian is looking after me.

I was quite exhausted and when Brian went fishing I sat in the sun reading the free newspaper. Mum's bridge partner Derek was coming to their caravan for some bridge tuition at three o'clock. Brian had requested a meat and potato pie with a crust on for tea, so when I had prepared it, I walked the dogs down to the beach to see him fishing. At least he'd caught one, even if it was only small. Whilst talking to him I said, "That bloke on that bike over there just looks like my Dad" and it was! Ann had come round with Derek on their bikes and suggested her and my Dad had a ride to Mar Cristal for a coffee. I had never seen him on a bike and could see by his face that he was not finding it that easy.

Our six o'clock meal was lovely and then Brian and Dad watched some football. Dad sat on a cushion for most of the match. Mum and I watched a film that John had taped called "The First of May" with Mickey Rooney and we really enjoyed it.

Sunday 20th February 2005.

The whole street was out at eight thirty to wave Joop and Miep off. Most of us were in our night wear but we didn't want to miss them. They said they would not be coming again as this was their last year at La Manga. It would seem very strange in October not to see them.

When Chris landed it was quite sunny and he said it was snowing at Leeds Bradford airport when he'd left. Mum and Dad showed Chris around the site and went for a drink at the beach bar. I sat in the sun with Brian, and Evelyn called and had a few drinks with us. It was quite busy on our street, as there was a sort of "bridge drive" in progress. Corrie explained that people were playing bridge but they were having a hand at one caravan, and then moving on to someone else's to play the next hand, and this would go on for most of the day. Mum had mentioned it but she felt it would be too much walking for her and too much excitement!

I walked to the phones and rang Janet. Our cousin Melanie was staying with her for a few days but otherwise, nothing thrilling to report.

Mum and Dad took Chris to the restaurant for the Sunday special La Manga lamb, and Brian barbecued two lovely steaks for us as we sat outside in the sun and drank plenty of fluids! He also managed to wash his car in the empty pitch opposite, before we retired inside the caravan for an evening of BBC1.

Monday 21st February 2005.

Typical! Whenever Brian washes his car, it rains- and guess what? It was pouring with rain this morning. We set off to Kathy and Donald's, as Brian was staying with them for a couple of days to do some plastering on their house near Elche. Chris decided he would prefer to stay at Mum's caravan and maybe explore the local area.

Arriving about twelve, the rain had stopped but it was quite cold. Donald's Mum Auntie Alice was staying with them for a couple of weeks and after having a look round the house, we all went into the village and had the menu of the day at one of the local restaurants. Seven euros was about the going rate for villages and the food was nice but not exceptional.

We set off back at four and I told Mum and Dad we would go home through the mountains, as it was much more scenic. What a stupid idea! Within five minutes mother was asleep in the back, and when I asked Dad to help with the map reading, he said he couldn't read it and he hadn't brought his reading glasses! Anyway, we found our way home no problem and I enjoyed the drive.

Chris had walked along the beach to the strip and the heavens had opened. He had bought an umbrella and then got a taxi back, wet through.

Later when I went round to play cards, Chris had gone down to the restaurant for a steak. I returned home at ten with a slightly sore throat and had a couple of glasses of muscatel to ease it of course!

Tuesday 22nd February 2005.

I didn't sleep well due to my sore throat and missing Brian. It was a cold and windy day so as soon as I had taken Jack and Jill round to Bill and Evelyn's as arranged, we set off to Dos Mares shopping centre.

Chris bought himself a jacket and a jumper and he got two lovely dressing gowns for Katie and India and a reversible coat for Joshua. Mum bought some jewellery for her friend Kathy and then decided she would like a new dinner service with square plates! I said this would be no problem for us to bring in the caravan but I didn't think it would be a good idea to mention it to Brian. He would just worry unnecessarily about the weight of it.

We had Chinese for lunch, which Chris bought for us, and it was very filling and tasty. Diet? What diet?

On our return, Mum was quite excited, as it was bridge again with her "student" Derek. I decided to have a night on my own well, with the dogs just doing those things we girls need to do on our own like tidying my handbag and sorting my knicker drawer out. Brian sent me a text to say he was missing me and he'd worked very hard all day. He would be home on Thursday and I couldn't wait.tc I don't know if it's because we're away from "home" but I really missed him. How sad is that?

Wednesday 23ʳᵈ February 2005.

Happy Birthday Jan! Although it was the last thing on my mind when I woke up at seven o'clock with the worst stomach pains I've ever known. I was almost crawling round the caravan getting some water and some painkillers and I was quite frightened to think that if I passed out I was on my own. When it hadn't passed half an hour later, I went round to Mum's and banged on the door until she let me in. I had taken the E111s out of my file just in case and was trying to drink a cup of warm tea. An hour later, the pain had completely gone and I was fine. I have no idea what caused it but I thought I was dying. Luckily I wasn't and I hope I never have it again, whatever it was.

I could see that Mum was very relieved that I was all right and she then told me that last night's bridge had been really good as she and Derek had come 6ᵗʰ out of twenty and were the talk of the bridge club. It was only the second time Derek had played and they were hailing him as some new God! Omar Sharif eat your heart out!

A much warmer day as we set off to the transport museum not far away. I knew Chris would be interested as he's a bus driver and is quite fanatical about his job (don't knock it!). Dad also thought he would enjoy it as the leaflet said there were motorbikes from years ago on display. What a disappointment to find the museum closed. Another attraction that only seems to be open during the summer months.

We drove to La Manga golf club to see the beautiful villas there and the wonderful views and then we parked up in Los Belones. Dad bought us hot chocolate and a cake and Chris had the coffee "solo" which he likes. Far too strong for me. A quick trip round the bodega and the tobacconist's and Chris had everything he needed to take home on Saturday.

Back home, Dad and Chris walked the dogs whilst I made a curry for tea. Later Mum and I went to ring Janet and she'd had a lovely birthday and was just getting ready to go for an Italian meal with Jimmy and the lads.

The evening was rounded off with yet more cards at Mum's and I did persuade her to play one game of Phase Ten which I enjoyed. Briafn texted me as I was getting into bed – home tomorrow. Hooray!

Thursday 24ᵗʰ February 2005.

A gorgeous sunny day and I tidied up whilst Dad took the dogs for a walk. Chris said he wanted to walk to Los Belones and would join us for lunch if he was back. Brian arrived home at half past twelve after getting lost through the mountain roads. Donald was driving and Kathy confirmed that she was almost hysterical in the back seat because they were slightly lost. Auntie Alice remained calm and let it all go over her head – she's used to it by now!

It was lovely to see them all and we had sangria when they arrived as it was brilliant sunshine. We all went down to the restaurant for our menu of the day and Chris arrived just as we were about to sit down. He explained that he'd had a terrible morning as he'd walked to Los Belones then decided to get a bus back to the site. He had waited an hour and a half and when a bus finally arrived, the driver explained that Chris was waiting on the wrong side of the road! Even bus drivers can get confused.

Now, Kathy and Don have been going to night school for about a year to learn Spanish ready for moving out here, and they are both quite proficient though still learning. The meal went smoothly the macaroni starter was superb, and the main course of fish or lamb was excellent. As usual, the sweet choice was fruit or ice cream. Four of us ordered ice cream and the others wondered what the fruit was. Kathy indicated that she would take over from here in her rather loud "Spanish" accent. She pointed to a display of various fruits and said "Fresco por favor". That was that. We were all getting strawberries. Or were we? Our waiter Pepe returned with four apples balancing on four plates! "No," said Kathy quite indignantly, "fresco". He shrugged his shoulders and retreated into the kitchen with the apples. A few minutes later he was back – with four bananas! I was too embarrassed to pursue the matter and three of us settled for a banana. I thought if this goes on much longer we'll have had a whole bloody fruit salad! But Kathy was again pointing at the display cabinet repeating her order for "Fresco". Pepe went away again and then returned with a bowl of strawberries and cream. At last! He explained that the word for strawberries is "Fresa" not "Fresco", which means "Fresh".

After coffees of four different varieties we paid the bill and walked back home. Kathy, Don and Auntie Alice were off around four and they had enjoyed their day with us.

Brian and I watched a BBC one-off drama called "Dad" which

was good and then we hit the sack. I felt sure I would sleep better now he was home. And I did.

Friday 25th February 2005.

A disappointing day as it was cloudy and raining from first light. Christine the hairdresser came at ten to give Mum and me a trim and I wished her a safe journey as she was going back to England tomorrow. She told us she'd heard that Ted was OK. His cancer was still in remission and he would be back in Spain in another two weeks.

Today seemed a good day to go shopping to El Corte Ingles so off we went. Mum bought some perfume and we all just enjoyed having a browse around. I saw several gorgeous outfits in case Simon and Lorraine decided to get married. Who knows?

Our evening meal was fish and chips at Watts down the strip and Chris paid the bill to thank us for picking him up from the airport and looking after him.

At half past eight the rain started to get heavier and we lost the reception for the television. Were we in Spain or England?

Saturday 26th February 2005.

I had to clear the ice from the windscreen before I could drive Chris to the airport. He'd had a great week and enjoyed himself and Dad and I waved him off at nine o'clock. The rain had stopped and the sun was threatening to get out.

Although we weren't leaving until next Thursday, there was a lot to pack up so we started by taking the curtains down in the awning and gently packing a few things away. By mid afternoon when Brian decided to wash the caravan, I thought it was time to dye Mum's hair and mine. So there we sat, both covered in hair dye having a cocktail waiting to be transformed.

We were both less grey when we'd finished and Brian made a spaghetti for tea, whilst I made an apple pie. Then cards round at Mum's before we all fell asleep at eleven. What a busy day.

Sunday 27th February 2005.

Happy 82nd Birthday Harry. It was our last Sunday and Mum wanted to have a look round the huge Sunday market so we went with Dad to search for some bargains. Mum bought two handbags, a nightshirt almost as sexy as last year's- and a jumper. I bought three pairs of knickers, which were exceptional value as he gave me too much change and I ended up with the pants for nothing and two euros! Having said that, the pants were useless and far too small so I didn't gain much.

We did a bit of shopping on the way home and I called at reception to settle our bill. It was 1391. 54 euros for the 153 nights stay. She also said that because we had been here a long time, we would only be charged for one dog, not two. That was a saving of 153 euros so I was very pleased with that. A much better bargain than my knickers. I picked up a leaflet and a price list to take home for Tony and Ann in case they are still coming with us in October.

Brian had tried to ring his Dad but there was no reply. He would no doubt be at Pam's having a meal so Brian would ring him again tomorrow.

Dad took us down to the restaurant for our last Sunday night meal, which was as good as ever. Mum had a sore throat and a bit of a cold so we let them get an early night.

Monday 28th February 2005.

Action stations! Dad came round to help Brian take the car full of things up to reception to be stored on the pallet. Luckily it stayed dry whilst they were loading the things in and the rain held off until about one o'clock.

Brian rang his Dad and was quite upset when he came back as Harry's friend Geoff had died suddenly. He was about ten years younger than Harry, and Geoff and his wife Avelyn were neighbours and friends of Harry and Joan's from years ago. The funeral was next Friday and hopefully Gary would be taking him to Carnforth for the service.

Mum was busy packing and tidying her caravan so I sorted some cupboards out and made a roast chicken dinner in between. They came round at four for an early meal and it seemed strange eating off the melamine plates now that my best crockery was in storage.

A final night at Mum's playing cards, as they would be going home tomorrow, so we had lots of chocolates and sweets to eat up! I must get back on the diet. No; I daren't get weighed so don't even ask!

Tuesday 1st March 2005.

Brian's cousin David would be 49 today and I hoped he'd received the card that Simon had posted for me.

What a night. Rain and winds had kept us both awake for what seemed like most of the night. We took Mum and Dad to the Mercadona and we stocked up on things for the journey home like coffee, crisps and cakes. The four of us went to the Chinese for their "Menu of the day" which at 5. 95 Euros was very good value. This would be our treat. A Mother's Day present for next Sunday.

It finally stopped raining when we got back at two, so Dad looked after the dogs and did some last minute packing, whilst we did some packing up of our own.

We took Mum and Dad to Murcia airport ready for their evening flight and on the way back we called at the bodega in Los Belones for some wine. We bought a bottle of champagne for when the baby's born, and Brian got two five-litre containers of red wine-one for Simon and one for Neville.

After very little sleep and such a hard day (?) we were glad of an early night after watching a bit of television.

Wednesday 2nd March 2005.

It seemed very strange this morning not having Mum round the corner. I had a text message from Dad to say they had arrived safely in a flurry of snow and had enjoyed their holiday.

It rained on and off for most of the morning and we were starting to panic about taking the awning down, as it needed to be dry, ready to put away. However, by one o'clock the sun came out and the afternoon flew by as we dismantled the awning, washed and folded the ground sheet and tidied yet more cupboards. Jack and Jill seemed to know we were packing up ready to leave and the cats were having a "final" play on the dogs' beds.

As promised I rang Mum at six but there were no big cheques in the post, just the usual boring things. Pam wasn't in when I rang her but I had a chat with Gary who told me it was snowing in Congleton. Why is it that men discuss the weather on the phone?

Our final meal at the restaurant was very good and we fell into bed at ten, checking that we had everything ready for an early start in the morning.

Thursday 3rd March 2005.

The whole street was up to see us off at nine o'clock and we knew we would be seeing most of them again in October. I had a last cuddle with Nanny and Nanny and told them we would be back. Diego had promised me he would look after them until we returned. After all, they were his cats!

We couldn't have wished for a better day. No wind, just lovely sunshine and we were soon filling up with diesel at Valencia. As we pulled into the parking area to let the dogs out, a strange looking bloke suddenly started washing the windscreen with something in a spray bottle. I immediately locked the doors from the inside and grabbed my handbag – I think I watch too much telly! Brian thought he was just a friendly chap trying to earn a bit of money and he gave him two euros for his trouble. You see–he has got a heart!

Arriving at L'Ametlla we were surprised to see how busy the site was and were even more shocked to see the German couple who had helped us with our puncture in 2003 were staying here again. They had been here since the end of October and we had a chat with them and the English couple on the next pitch.

Brian made a chicken curry whilst I did two loads of washing and drank some wine. A text from Simon- it's a boy! Lorraine is one of three girls and her two sisters have five girls between them, so I think secretly they were hoping for a boy, as this would be a first grandson for her parents. They had been for the scan today and appeared to be thrilled to bits with the news and also that everything was fine with little "Harry Jack Wilson". I can't wait!

Friday 4th March 2005.

The wind, which seemed relentless during the night, had died down and although it was sunny, it was bitterly cold. I could hardly feel my finger tips as I put my washing line up, but after a hot shower and a big fry-up I was feeling much better.

We both got wrapped up and set off to the beach, with Jack and Jill excitedly pulling all the way. The beach had been cleared of rubbish and was very picturesque. It must have taken us two hours to walk along the beach and through the woods and back again, with several swims for Jill and a few paddles for Jack.

A coffee and a doughnut when we got back, and Brian was packing a few things to return to the beach to do a couple of hours fishing. The day had warmed up, so I sat in the sun with the dogs and read a few chapters of my latest book.

I made spaghetti and some garlic bread for tea, as I was not hopeful of Brian returning with any fish for tea. He predictably came home empty-handed but had enjoyed himself.

No television for a week now, so we played crib until Brian finally won a hand.

Saturday 5th March 2005.

More strong winds in the night were the talk of the site as we got ready to leave. This would be the shortest distance for a day's drive, as we would be travelling slightly over 200 miles to Salses Le Chateau, just past Perpignan.

It was still quite windy when we set off but Brian soon had the cruise control on and we were enjoying the scenery. As we approached Barcelona, I heard a really loud bang and thought we had been shot. I looked at Brian who appeared shocked but still in control. He said he had seen a metal bolt of some kind, which seemed to have come from the lorry in front of us. It had bounced off the road and into the middle of our windscreen, and Brian's automatic reaction had been to duck, as he assumed the windscreen would shatter. Remarkably, there wasn't even a mark on the screen where we had been hit and we were thankful that we had been so lucky.

As usual, we got lost in the village, which we shouldn't have been in at all! The streets were very narrow, there were roadworks in every direction, and a great big coach was parked up. Finding ourselves at the tiny village square and heading towards a narrow cul de sac, I was very pleased that Brian stayed calm and mustered up his best manoeuvring skills to reverse the car and caravan so that we could escape. Back onto the main N9 road, which we shouldn't have come off in the first place, and we were at the correct destination within minutes. Seventeen euros for the night and we parked up on a deserted site, and checked out the showers and toilets which were adequate.

It was very cold outside but we soon had the gas fire on and a sweet and sour pork dish in the oven. Before the night was out, another six caravans and camper vans were on the site so we didn't feel so lonely.

I sent a text to Jill and she reported back that Colin would be off work until April but he was resting and doing well. We would go and see them both when we got home. I also sent a text to Kathy and Don as they were back in England having a "bon voyage" party before they finally came to Spain permanently. Pam and Gary would be taking Harry and we would have liked to be there, but we couldn't be in Blackburn and France at the same time.

Sunday 6ᵗʰ March 2005.

Mother's Day seems to get earlier every year. I thought of Joan today and I knew that Pam would be taking some flowers to her Mum's grave. I had a text from Dad to say Mum was pleased with her card and soap which I had hidden in Dad's flight bag before they returned home. Enough of this, we had over three hundred miles to do today and leaving at eight thirty was just the start we needed.

Everything was going well until we skirted around Beziers but ended up on the motorway instead of the N road. We soon found our way back onto the planned route and heading towards Clermont-Ferrand.

We had heard a few rumours that this route was very high up and not advisable in bad weather. What we hadn't heard was that snow was falling heavily and had been for a few days. The recently opened bridge was spectacular and Brian thought he'd read somewhere that this was now the world's highest bridge. As we continued to climb into higher altitudes, the snow was getting heavier and Brian was becoming visibly more apprehensive.

By lunchtime, we had stopped at some services and the dogs had a great play in the deep snow. We were now 1,100 metres above sea level and the outside temperature was minus four degrees. Brian suggested we parked at the services for the rest of the day and night but I felt we should get a bloody move on! So we did.

Admittedly I was a little worried at times but we took it steady and arrived at Chatel de Neuvre just after four o'clock. A long wooden shack ran along the entrance and I found a bell, which I rang for attention. A very tall Frenchman emerged wearing a trilby, and announced "Good Moaning" in a ludicrous "send-up" of the French policeman in "Allo Allo". He was very friendly and invited me into the reception shack to complete the booking form and for him to check the dog's rabies papers. At 13 euros for the night we weren't expecting much but the site was quite boggy due to the rain and snow they'd had so he suggested we park on the "road" so we didn't get stuck in the mud.

Only one other caravan on this site and after getting warmed up and checking out the "facilities" I took the dogs for a walk through the wood and onto the side of a lovely river setting. Snow was starting to fall again quite heavily so when I got back to the warmed up caravan, we reviewed our plans for this evening. We had planned to drive to the village for a meal, but decided to get a shower and stay in the warmth of our winter home and have a tuna pasta dish. This would save us unhooking the caravan so we could get a really early start for tomorrow's marathon drive of five hundred miles to Calais.

A late text was from Simon wishing me a happy Mother's Day. Bless him.

Monday 7th March 2005.

We both woke up at six o'clock and found that the site was "white over" with snow. The gas bottle had frozen, as had the water pump, so we sorted these problems out and soon had the kettle boiling for a cup of tea. Oh the joys of winter caravanning!

I went along to the toilet and was pleased to find that the owner had put a large paraffin heater in there, which was keeping the frostbite at bay. The owner came to see us around seven and he suggested we didn't set off so early as the roads wouldn't be cleared of snow for another hour or so. He also recommended a slightly different route to the one we had planned and we took his advice on which would be the best roads to use. What a friendly and helpful man.

It was still snowing when we set off at 8.40 but we were onto the main N road within a few minutes. Brian soon realised, however, that his windscreen washers were either frozen or empty or both, but there were no stopping areas on this stretch of road. So he asked for a bottle of water. We always carry at least six litre bottles in the car. He wound his window down and tried to throw water onto the screen. The result? No water on the windscreen, but Brian's sweatshirt wet through. These attempts went on for a while until he managed to find somewhere to stop and he filled the washer bottle. But this wasn't working as the washers were frozen, as we suspected. The outside temperature was now five degrees below freezing so we shouldn't have been surprised.

Once we joined the motorway, we stopped at the first services and bought five litres of screen wash, which did the trick. Hooray, he could see where he was going.

We both felt a bit easier once we were on the motorway and although it would be a long day, we were looking forward to getting near Calais ready for the ferry on Thursday.

I decided to text Bill and Evelyn and tell them where we were. They had left the site on Saturday but I wasn't sure how many stops they were making or where they were catching the ferry. Not five minutes after I had sent the text, Brian asked me what Bill's registration was. Sure enough, they were directly in front of us. How spooky is that? We overtook them and waved but decided not to stop at the next services as it was still snowing and we would both want to be making progress, but what a coincidence. About an hour later at some services near Troyes, we had parked up and were just going for a coffee when they pulled into the same services! We were destined to have a final coffee together, so we did. Evelyn said someone was on our pitch not half an hour after we had left on Thursday and I asked how the cats were. She said they had been walking around the hedges crying at our pitch. Roll on October.

After our final goodbyes, we were back on the road and were relieved that the snow seemed to be turning to rain as we got further north. It was half past six when we arrived at Bal Parc in Ardres and the new owner came and introduced himself to us. We could see immediately that the site had been revamped and looked much more inviting except for the mud! He said the snow had melted and everywhere was like a bog so we parked on the "hard" ground but somehow this was all muddy too. There was no escape. We unpacked as best we could whilst it was still light and good old Brian managed to find an old thick plastic table cloth next to the bins which he laid on the ground outside the caravan door. See, he does come in handy! A text arrived from Ian asking when we would be arriving home and wishing me a happy Mother's Day. Better late than never.

We were treating ourselves to a meal in the adjoining hotel and were just about to go when Brian's mobile phone rang. It was Margaret asking when we would be home as Neville was ill. He'd just found out he had cancer of the lungs and liver and possibly the bones. Margaret said he was on morphine in hospital but had been asking where Brian was, and she said he had deteriorated in the last week or so. Poor Margaret, having to tell us this awful news. No doubt her daughter Joanne would be with her but Brian tried to say how sorry we both were and told Margaret he would ring her on Saturday when we got home.

Neither of us knew what to say for a few minutes and then we had a cuddle and went to the hotel for our meal as planned. We had only been talking about them today on the journey. Brian was wondering if I thought they might join us at La Manga in their motor home one winter. It seemed unlikely now.

Our meal was very nice and the bottle of Cotes de Rhone seemed expensive at 16 euros but what the hell. Brian had scallops then steak; I had pate followed by roast duck in a red berry sauce. The manageress prepared the bill of 48 euros for the meal and 60 euros for the three-night stay. The place may have been tidied up, but the overnight rate had doubled!

We had a coffee back at the caravan and I went to bed to read whilst Brian had a few brandies, no doubt thinking about his mate.

Tuesday 8th March 2005.

A dry drizzly day made it feel like we were back in England. I rang the vet's and made an appointment for four o'clock today. We had breakfast then drove to the Champion supermarket that we had been to last year. Top of my list were tea bags as I had used the last

251

one this morning. I should have bought some in Spain as I now realised that the French have every brand of coffee you could imagine, but they're not too keen on tea. Hence, I had a choice of about twenty herbal or fruity teas but just spotted a pack of twenty Tetley's Breakfast teabags, which were 2 euros.

Several bottles of wine later, we paid for our trolley load of milk, meat, bacon, eggs, dog food, lager and water. We filled up with diesel for the final time in France and at 1.07 euros a litre we knew England couldn't compete.

Lunch was French onion soup, fresh crusty bread and pâté. Why does French food taste better when you're eating it in France? I'm sure we could buy virtually the same food at the Asda but it wouldn't taste as delicious as this.

We played a few hands of crib to pass the afternoon until it was time to go to the vet's. It was a much easier process this year as the vet just needed their Pet Passports and not reams of complicated paperwork. I had taken my own Frontline drops but was pleasantly surprised when the bill came to just 42 euros. Much cheaper than last year. Although Jack had jumped when she was injecting him and he had bled for a few minutes so maybe she felt guilty about hurting him and knocked a bit of discount off? No, Brian said I was talking rubbish too!

I was trying to keep tea simple so that I didn't have to get lots of pans out and I managed to make roast duck legs in a Madeira sauce, with new potatoes, peas and broad beans, with a minimum of fuss or washing up. Let's hope we get a good night's sleep, as tomorrow we would be lucky to get any sleep with catching the ferry at three the next morning. A bottle of wine each seemed a better nightcap than Horlicks.

Wednesday 9th March 2005.

We both slept well and woke to another grey day. Brian cheered us up by making a full English breakfast, including "bacon" that turned out to be more like belly pork. Today was going to be a long day and we just seemed to be "hanging about" for the dogs' treatment to fall within the acceptable departure rules of more than 24 hours but less than 48 hours.

After showering, I did a bit of tidying and Brian gave the car a quick wipe over and cleaned inside it. I decided to watch a couple of films on DVD whilst Brian had a sleep in the afternoon. "Penny Serenade" with Cary Grant had me in tears and then I watched a spy thriller starring Edward G. Robinson. Don't I watch some rubbish?

We hitched the car to the caravan about five o'clock as we wanted to leave with as little noise as possible at half past one in the morning, out of consideration for the other four caravanners who were here at Bal Parc.

At half past five, one of the other campers came across to tell us that he'd heard on the radio that the port of Calais was going on strike. Before long, all the others were gathered round and we were discussing the options if this report was true. One of the men said he would go into reception and try and ring Calais to get some more information. Twenty minutes later he emerged with the news that the strike would commence at nine that evening and continue for twenty-four hours. He had been told that the last passenger ferry had left at five o'clock and the remaining departures would be for commercial vehicles only.

Our main problem, apart from the fact that we just wanted to get home, was that if we waited until after the strike, as well as the backlog of traffic, the dogs would have to go back to the vet's as their treatment would be invalidated. I tried to ring the Caravan Club but couldn't get through, so I then rang the number for P&O Ferries on the tickets. This got me through to a recorded information message, which informed me that ferries coming into Calais might be disrupted due to a dispute with the Calais Chamber of Commerce. After about ten minutes of this drivel another telephone number was given for further information. But when I rang it, I was told that "the number you have dialled does not exist"! After much discussion we made the decision to drive to the Euro Tunnel and see if we could get home tonight.

I don't think we've ever packed up so quickly, and we were at the Euro Tunnel entrance at seven o'clock. Luckily, one of the campers at Bal Parc had advised us to look for the "paw" signs when we arrived as there is a designated area to get the dogs checked in before you board.

We then drove to the ticket desk and asked if we could get on the next crossing. No problem, the next one was leaving at six minutes past eight, and that would be 432 euros please! I didn't imagine it was going to be so expensive but the trusty Visa card was out again and we were on board within ten minutes.

It was quite an experience as we sat in the car for the duration of the half-hour crossing, and I calculated that this "experience" was costing us ten pounds a minute! Whilst sitting there I received a text from Dad telling me that there was a strike at Calais. Thanks Dad.

Folkestone was dry and dark but we were pleased to be back in England and we continued our drive to the Ferry Meadows site at Peterborough. It was half past ten British time when we parked up in the late arrivals area, and we were both starving, as we hadn't had anything to eat since breakfast. So we had soup and more crusty bread and pâté before getting into bed. Another eventful day.

Thursday 10th March 2005.

I was disappointed to hear the rain when I woke up, but needn't have worried as the day soon dried up and became glorious. Maybe we'd brought a bit of sunshine from Spain.

We checked in at nine o'clock and were soon established on a hard standing pitch near the laundry room. I was busy doing all seven loads of washing and Brian made breakfast. It was such a lovely sunny morning that he unpacked the barbecue, and cooked the "funny bacon" and eggs outside.

I rang Mum later and Brian gave his Dad a ring to let him know we were safely back in England. Listening to Radio Two I smiled when I heard the first traffic report announce "Delays at the Thelwall Viaduct." No change there, then.

The day seemed to fly as we cleaned and "sorted", and we were both surprised when a new arrival that parked next to us turned out to be the chap from Bal Parc who told us about the strike. He said he had driven to the port, knowing there was a strike, to see what P&O advised, and they gave him a complimentary ticket for the Euro Tunnel! Oh the joy of hindsight.

I made a call to the Caravan Club to see if they could reimburse us or offer some form of compensation, and they advised me to write in. I had the letter typed and printed within half an hour, so we'll see what comes of that, if anything.

Meatballs for tea after we'd both used the faultless shower facilities and then we made a few phone calls. I spoke to Janet and Brian had calls from Ian and David. He sent a text to his mate Tony to see if he and Ann were still coming with us in October. Tony replied "Yes" and told us they were round at Jill and Colin's having a drink so Brian rang them both there. Colin was not back at work but was feeling better after his heart operation. We enjoyed catching up on the local gossip and it felt like we were "home" almost.

Friday 11th March 2005.

I was pleased that we weren't travelling today as it was very windy and cold. Lots of cleaning and packing still to do so I agreed that it was a good idea when Brian suggested he went to the nearest supermarket to do the shopping so that he wasn't in my way. Reception had given us some simple directions to the nearest Tesco's, which was just five minutes drive away.

Three hours later, Brian was back with several Sainsbury's carriers. Apparently he'd got lost and ended up miles away but found a Sainsbury's store. He had bought food for when we got home and an Indian takeaway to pop in the oven for tea so that we didn't have to unpack the pans and things which had been carefully stacked in the lower cupboards. The Indian meal looked good. He'd bought one for "four" instead of "two". We would look like onion bhajis tomorrow!

I rang British Telecom to reconnect the phone at home and once Brian had emptied the car, we began to pack it ready for the final journey. We needed to pack everything that was coming home in the car so that when we arrived at Derrick's we didn't have to open the caravan again. Brian asked exactly which things needed to go on the back seat of the car bearing in mind we can't use the "boot" as this is where Jack and Jill travel. I braced myself as I pointed to a large heavy box. "What's that?" he asked. I flippantly told him it was Mum's dinner service and I was surprised when he calmly said, "OK, that's fine". But there followed another box containing the matching cups and saucers, another box of matching cutlery and stand, a litre bottle of brandy and a large roll of table covering that Dad had bought! Simons huge paella pan and glass oil jug were well wrapped and packed into the car, together with four boxes of food and toiletries, the laptop, videos and DVDs, books, maps, our new efficient torch, camera and printer, a case of beer, a case of wine and two five-litre containers of wine! You should know Brian well enough by now to imagine the sort of comments he was coming out with.

Anyway, it all went in somehow and when it started to rain at five, we sat down and ate twelve onion bhajis. The next course we ate at half past six and the final two curries weren't served until eight o'clock. Who will be first on the scales tomorrow?

As we ate our feast and played a final game of crib, we were amazed at the continuous arrival of new campers and the site must have been virtually full when we went to bed at eleven.

In the words of the comedian Dave Allen who died today, "Goodnight, and may your god go with you".

Saturday 12th March 2005.

Crisp, cold and clear with no wind – that's the weather, not Brian! We were both now looking forward to finally being home later today and we were packed up and on the road just after half past eight.

Other than a slight detour due to road works we had a good run and arrived at Derrick's about four hours later. After parking the caravan we drove home to a few pieces of recent post, and the sight of daffodils almost in flower.

After putting the central heating and the kettle on, we both got weighed. As I feared, I had gained some weight since Christmas, but at 11stone 6 pounds I was still six pounds lighter than when we set off. I must make more of an effort next time and I may even start going to Mabel's gym? We'll see. Brian weighed in at 16 stone 12 pounds so he'd lost half a stone. How gorgeous.

Although we were pleased to be home, we had really enjoyed our second winter in Spain, and were already looking forward to planning our next trip later this year. Fancy coming?

Oh, I almost forgot. Sheila's birthday card to my Dad went as follows:

Quasimodo had died and the Bishop of Notre Dame was auditioning for a new bellringer. He'd heard dozens of people but no one was good enough, then one day a man with no arms approached him for the job. "But how can you do it without arms?" asked the Bishop. "Observe" said the man and he began to strike the bell with his face, making the most beautiful music. Just as he finished he tripped and plunged headlong out of an open window to the courtyard, hundreds of feet below. The Bishop hurried down the stairs to find a large crowd surrounding the now dead man. "What was his name?" asked an onlooker. "I don't know… " said the Bishop, "But his face rang a bell!"